THE RETURN OF THE MASTER **CHAPTER ONE**

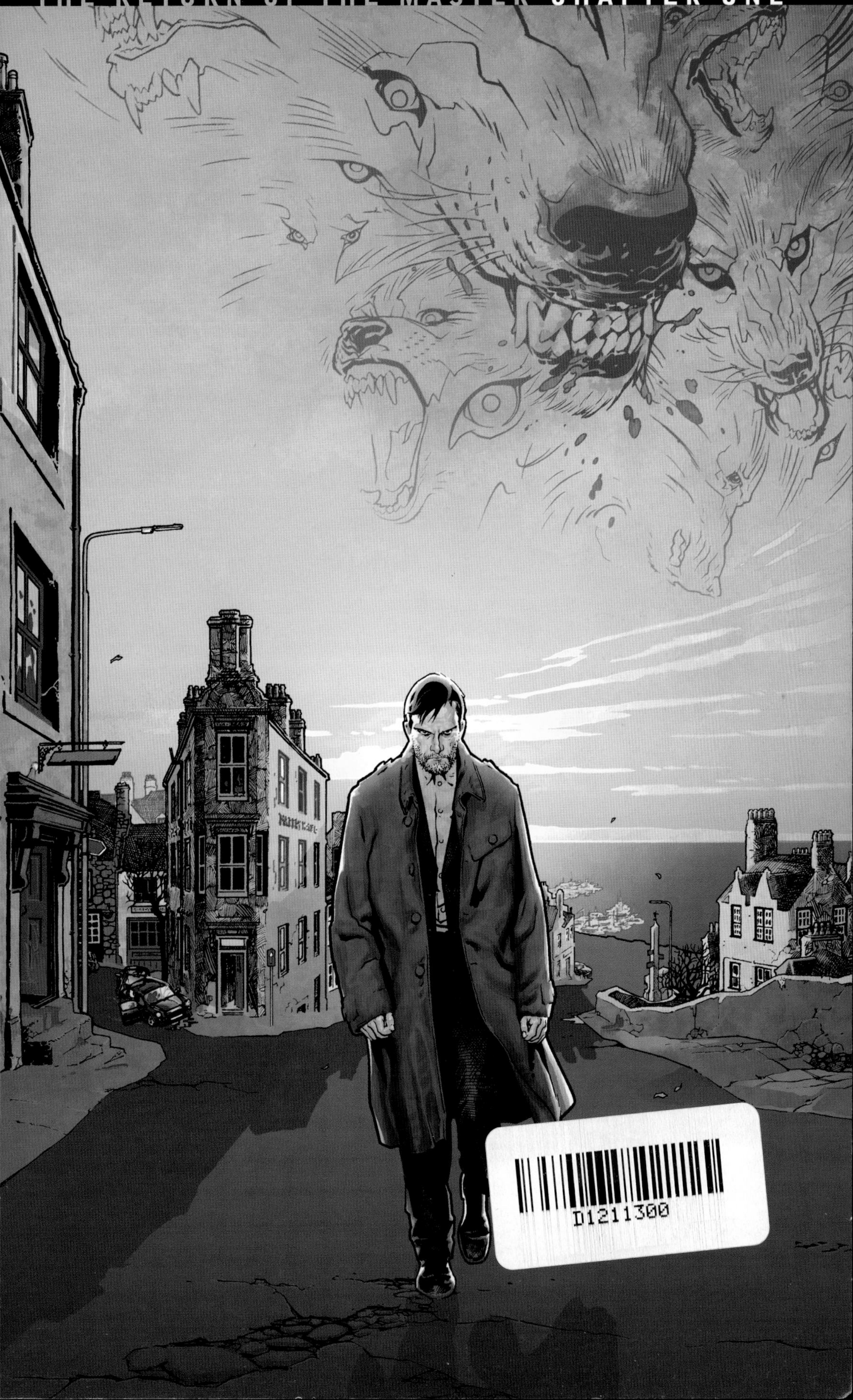

BUREAU FOR PARANORMAL · RESEARCH AND DEFENSE ·

# B.P.R.D. HELL ON EARTH:
# THE RETURN OF THE MASTER

created by MIKE MIGNOLA

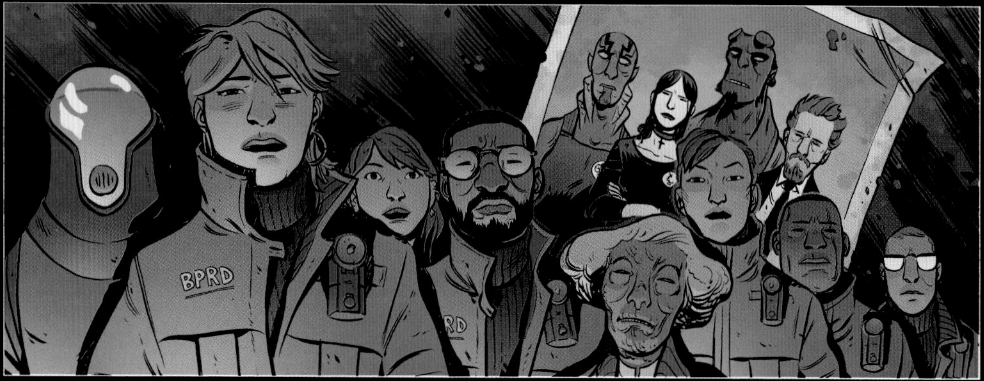
BPRD

Since Liz Sherman destroyed the frog army and the Black Flame in Agartha, the Bureau for Paranormal Research and Defense has seen their charter expanded to oversee international threats, leading to collaborations with Russia's occult bureau. With Liz missing and Abe Sapien on the verge of death, the spotlight is on Johann and more conventional agents. Unknown to the Bureau, Zinco Corporation has recruited a pair of Nazi scientists, long thought dead, for a plan that threatens to end the human race.

MIKE MIGNOLA'S

# B.P.R.D.™
# HELL ON
# EARTH
## THE RETURN
## OF THE
## MASTER

story by **MIKE MIGNOLA** and **JOHN ARCUDI**

art by **TYLER CROOK**

colors by **DAVE STEWART**

letters by **CLEM ROBINS**

cover art by **MIKE MIGNOLA** with **DAVE STEWART**

chapter break art by **RYAN SOOK**

editor **SCOTT ALLIE**

assistant editor **DANIEL CHABON**   collection designer **AMY ARENDTS**

publisher **MIKE RICHARDSON**

DARK HORSE BOOKS

Mike Richardson PRESIDENT AND PUBLISHER · Neil Hankerson EXECUTIVE VICE PRESIDENT
Tom Weddle CHIEF FINANCIAL OFFICER · Randy Stradley VICE PRESIDENT OF PUBLISHING
Michael Martens VICE PRESIDENT OF BOOK TRADE SALES · Anita Nelson VICE PRESIDENT
OF BUSINESS AFFAIRS · Scott Allie EDITOR IN CHIEF · Matt Parkinson VICE PRESIDENT OF
MARKETING · David Scroggy VICE PRESIDENT OF PRODUCT DEVELOPMENT · Dale LaFountain
VICE PRESIDENT OF INFORMATION TECHNOLOGY · Darlene Vogel SENIOR DIRECTOR OF
PRINT, DESIGN, AND PRODUCTION · Ken Lizzi GENERAL COUNSEL · Davey Estrada EDITORIAL
DIRECTOR · Chris Warner SENIOR BOOKS EDITOR · Diana Schutz EXECUTIVE EDITOR · Cary
Grazzini DIRECTOR OF PRINT AND DEVELOPMENT · Lia Ribacchi ART DIRECTOR · Cara Niece
DIRECTOR OF SCHEDULING · Tim Wiesch DIRECTOR OF INTERNATIONAL LICENSING · Mark
Bernardi DIRECTOR OF DIGITAL PUBLISHING

DarkHorse.com    Hellboy.com

This book collects the comic-book series B.P.R.D. Hell on Earth: The Return of the Master #1–#5,
originally published by Dark Horse Comics.

Published by Dark Horse Books
A division of Dark Horse Comics, Inc.
10956 SE Main Street
Milwaukie, OR 97222

International licensing: (503) 905-2377

First edition: August 2013
ISBN 978-1-61655-193-3

10 9 8 7 6 5 4 3 2 1
Printed in China

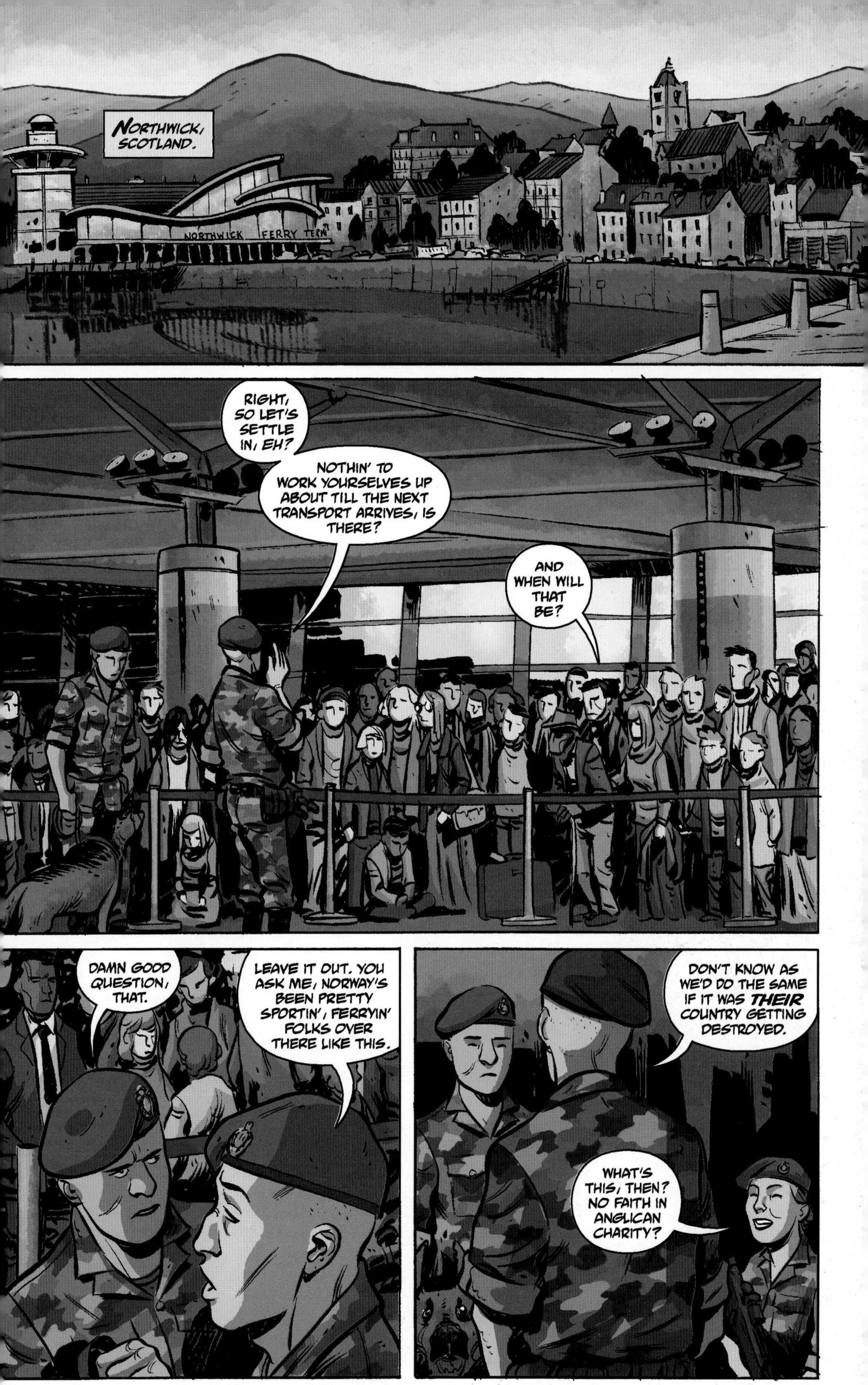
NORTHWICK, SCOTLAND.
NORTHWICK FERRY TERM
RIGHT, SO LET'S SETTLE IN, EH?
NOTHIN' TO WORK YOURSELVES UP ABOUT TILL THE NEXT TRANSPORT ARRIVES, IS THERE?
AND WHEN WILL THAT BE?
DAMN GOOD QUESTION, THAT.
LEAVE IT OUT. YOU ASK ME, NORWAY'S BEEN PRETTY SPORTIN', FERRYIN' FOLKS OVER THERE LIKE THIS.
DON'T KNOW AS WE'D DO THE SAME IF IT WAS THEIR COUNTRY GETTING DESTROYED.
WHAT'S THIS, THEN? NO FAITH IN ANGLICAN CHARITY?

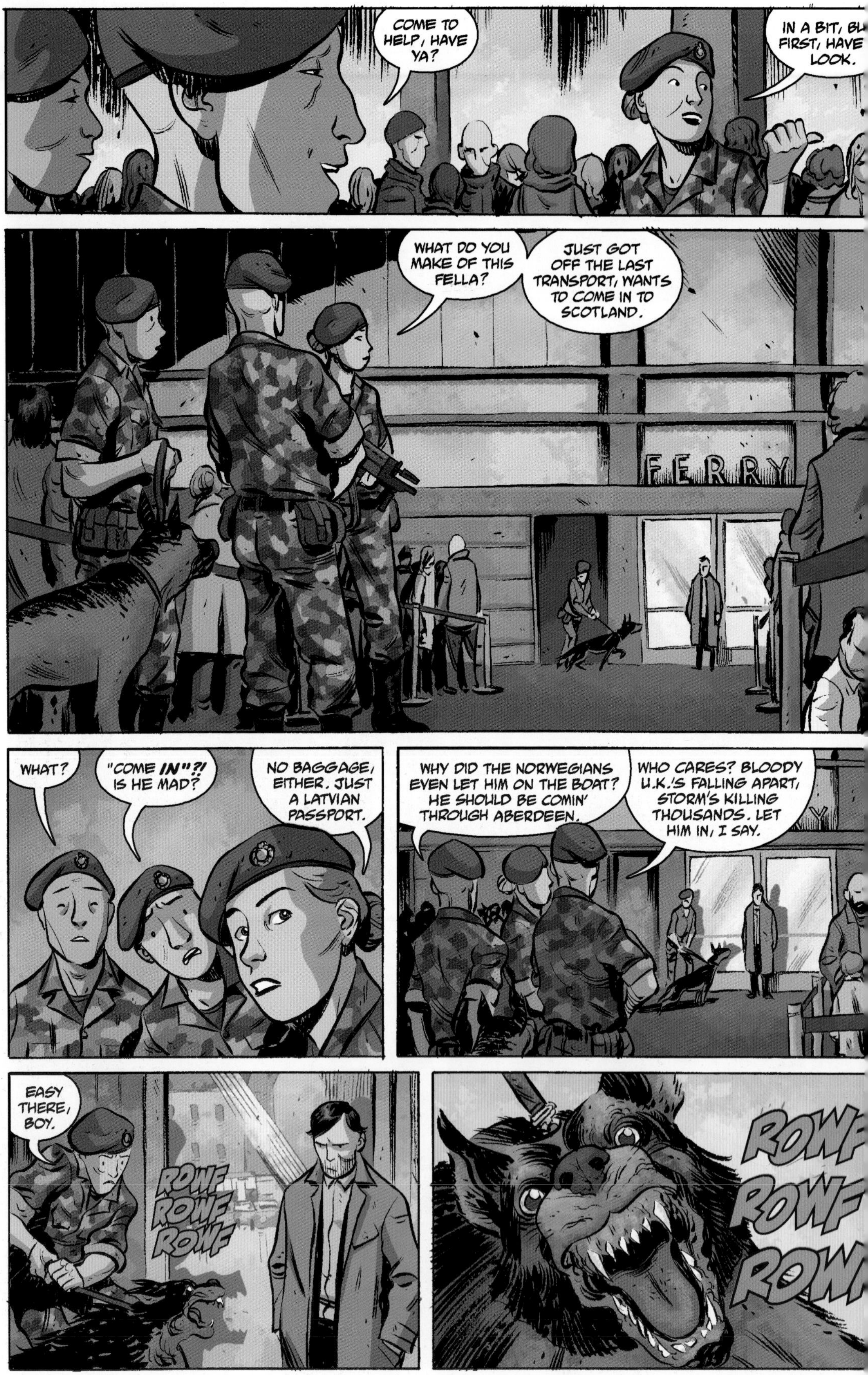
COME TO HELP, HAVE YA?
IN A BIT, FIRST, HAVE LOOK.
WHAT DO YOU MAKE OF THIS FELLA?
JUST GOT OFF THE LAST TRANSPORT, WANTS TO COME IN TO SCOTLAND.
FERRY
WHAT?
"COME IN"?! IS HE MAD?
NO BAGGAGE, EITHER. JUST A LATVIAN PASSPORT.
WHY DID THE NORWEGIANS EVEN LET HIM ON THE BOAT? HE SHOULD BE COMIN' THROUGH ABERDEEN.
WHO CARES? BLOODY U.K.'S FALLING APART, STORM'S KILLING THOUSANDS. LET HIM IN, I SAY.
EASY THERE, BOY.
ROWF ROWF ROWF

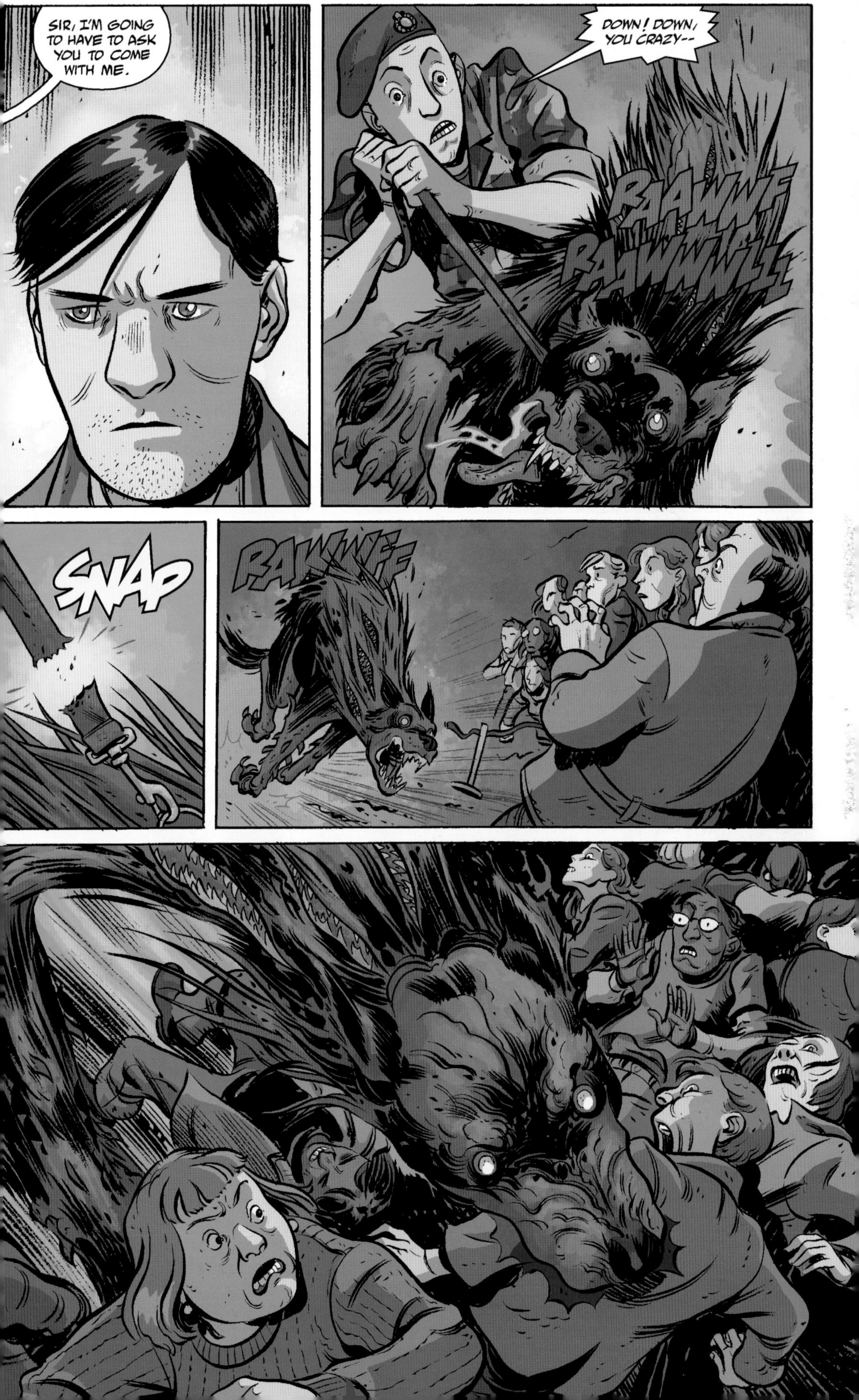
SIR, I'M GOING TO HAVE TO ASK YOU TO COME WITH ME.
DOWN! DOWN, YOU CRAZY--
RAAWWF
RAAWWLL
SNAP
RAWWF

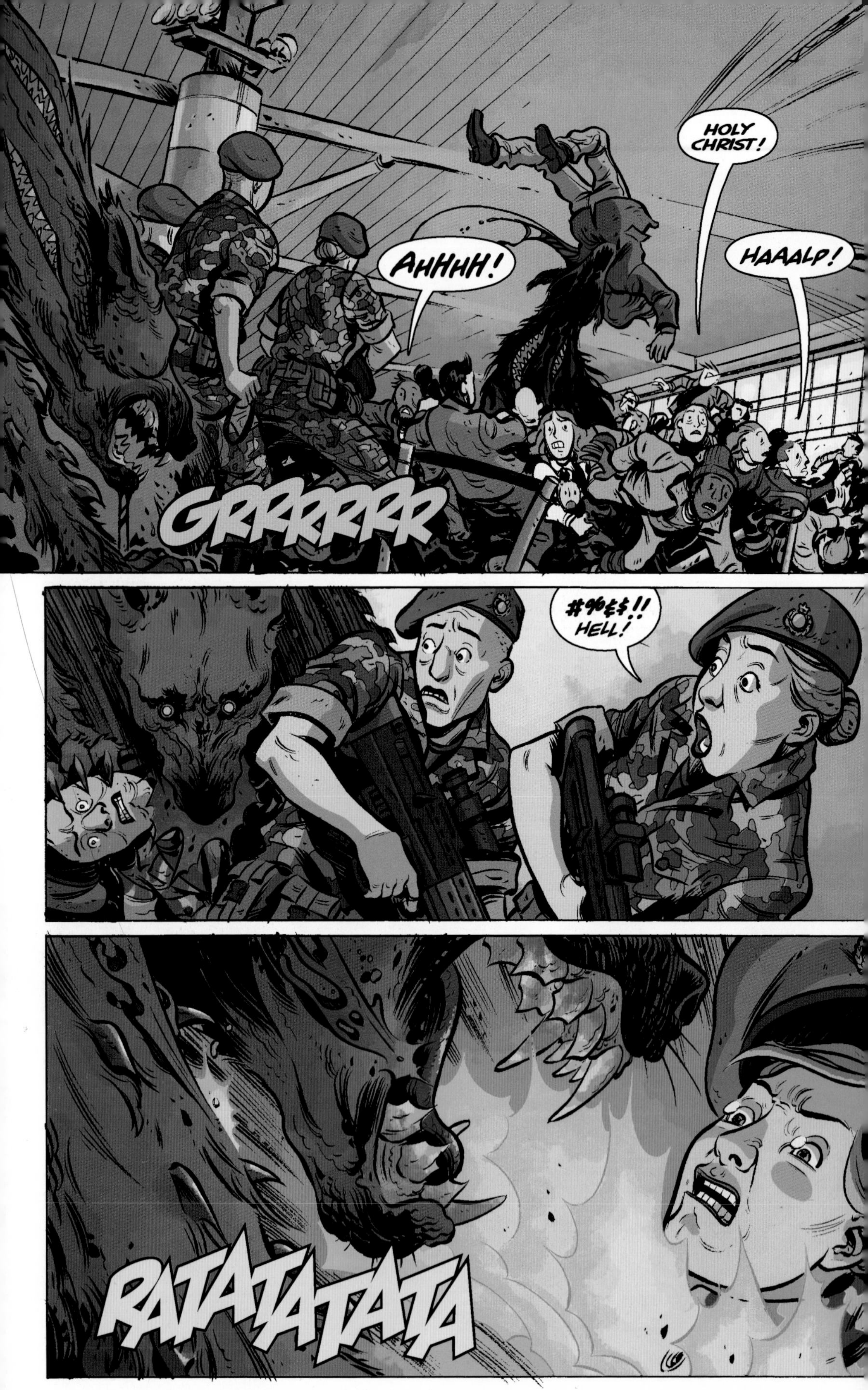
AHHHH!
HOLY CHRIST!
HAAALP!
GRRRRRRR
#%&$!! HELL!
RATATATATA

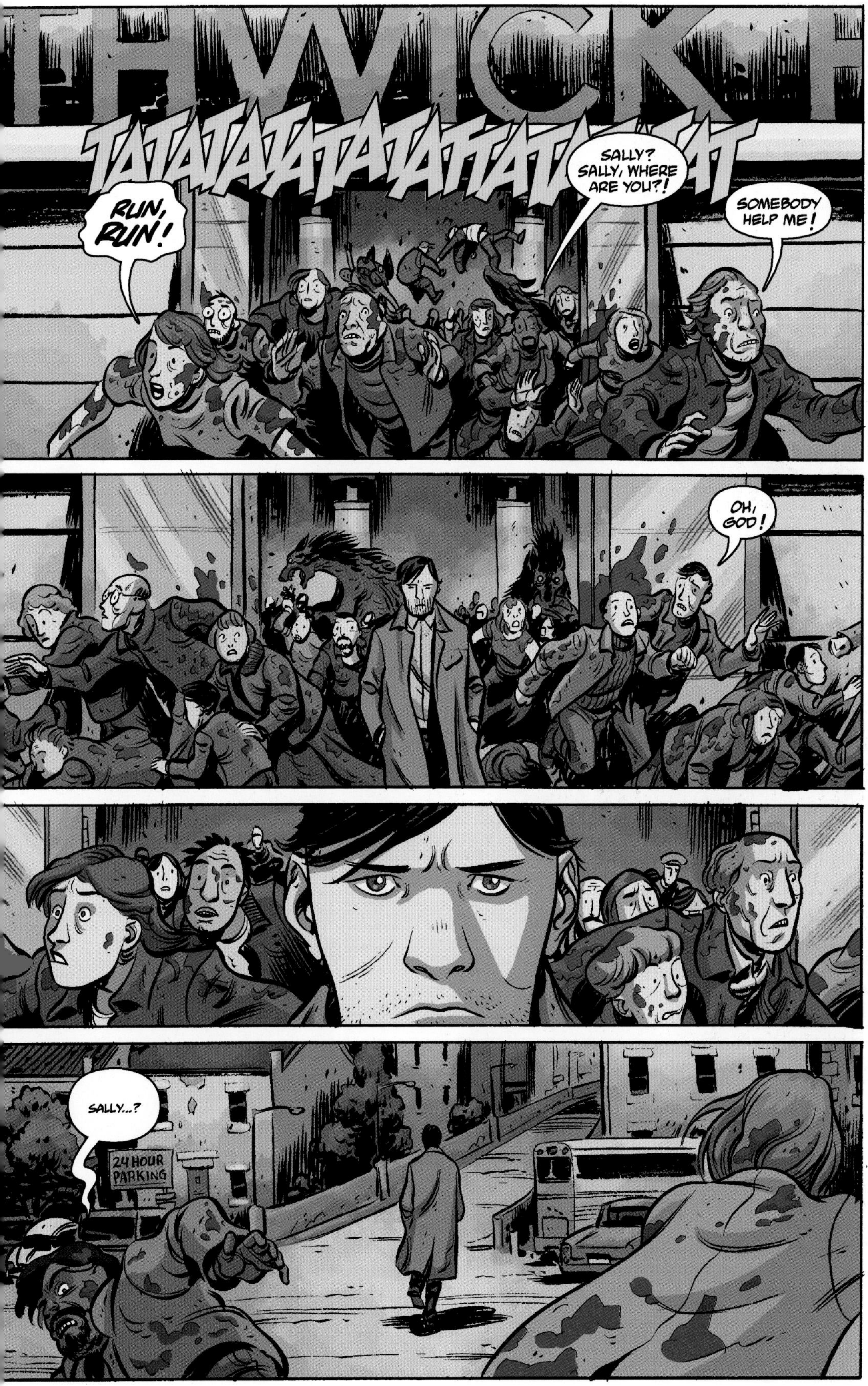
THWICK
TATATATATATATATATATATAT
RUN, RUN!
SALLY? SALLY, WHERE ARE YOU?!
SOMEBODY HELP ME!
OH, GOD!
SALLY...?
24 HOUR PARKING

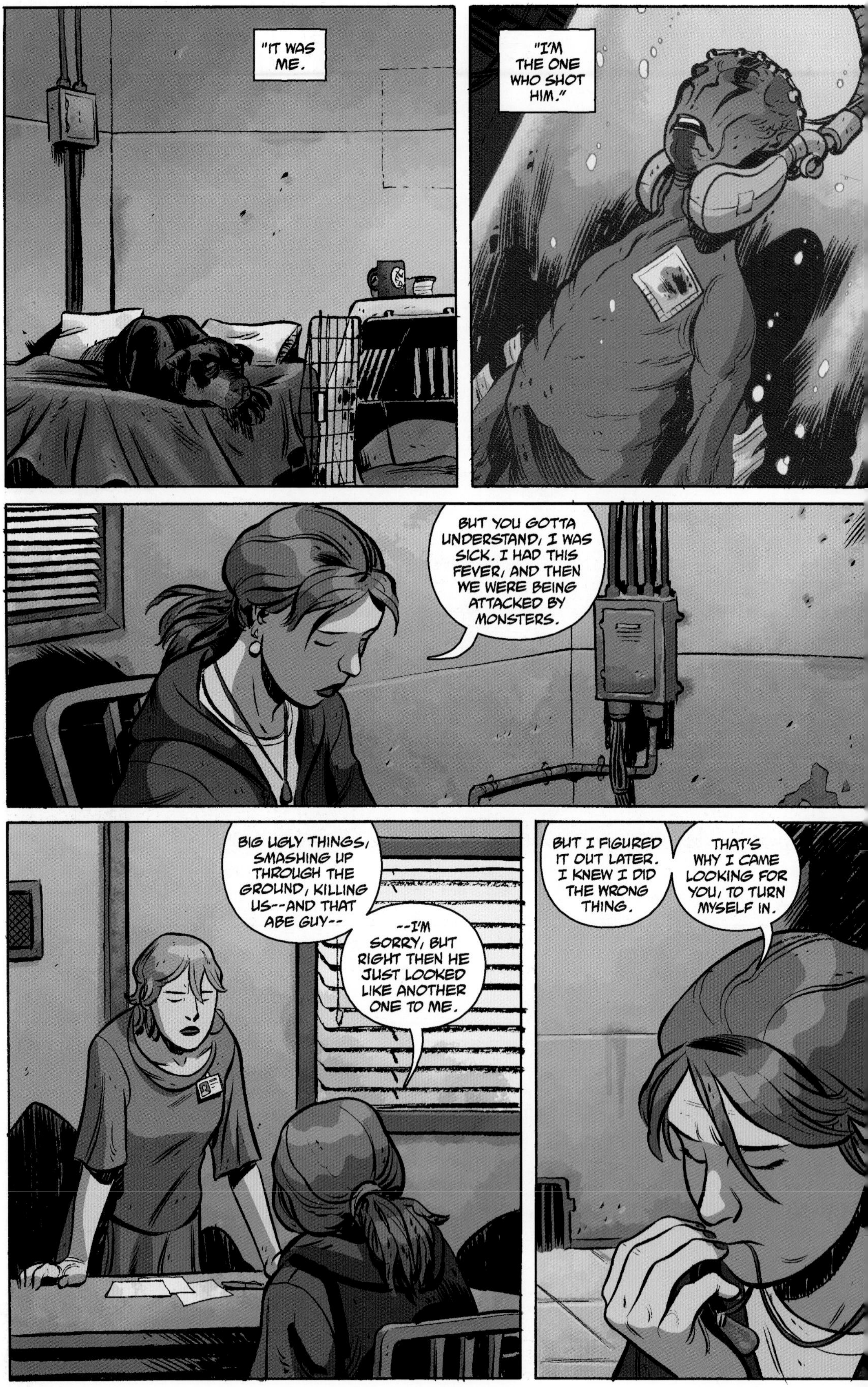
"IT WAS ME.
"I'M THE ONE WHO SHOT HIM."
BUT YOU GOTTA UNDERSTAND, I WAS SICK. I HAD THIS FEVER, AND THEN WE WERE BEING ATTACKED BY MONSTERS.
BIG UGLY THINGS, SMASHING UP THROUGH THE GROUND, KILLING US--AND THAT ABE GUY--
--I'M SORRY, BUT RIGHT THEN HE JUST LOOKED LIKE ANOTHER ONE TO ME.
BUT I FIGURED IT OUT LATER. I KNEW I DID THE WRONG THING.
THAT'S WHY I CAME LOOKING FOR YOU, TO TURN MYSELF IN.

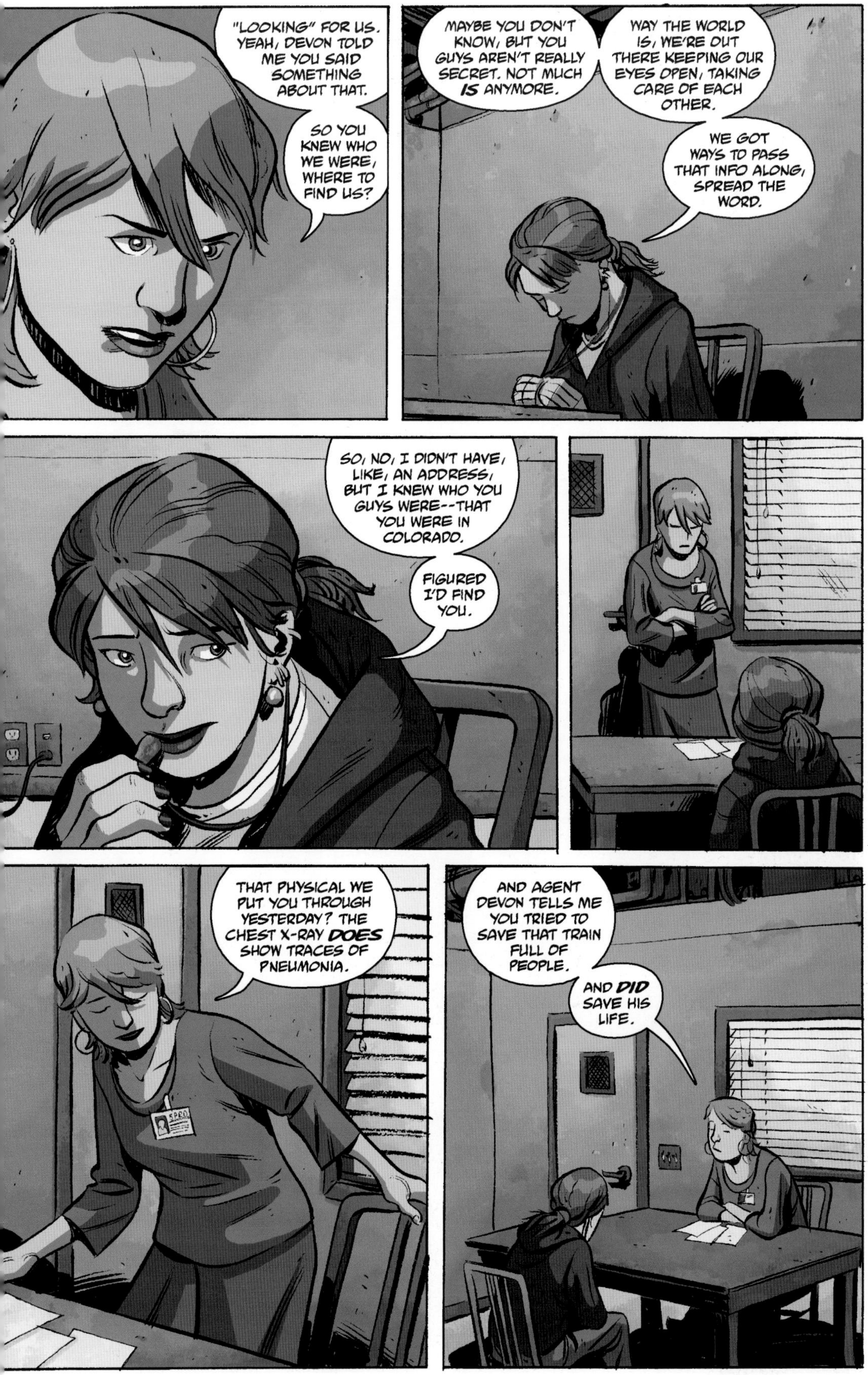
"LOOKING" FOR US. YEAH, DEVON TOLD ME YOU SAID SOMETHING ABOUT THAT.
SO YOU KNEW WHO WE WERE, WHERE TO FIND US?
MAYBE YOU DON'T KNOW, BUT YOU GUYS AREN'T REALLY SECRET. NOT MUCH *IS* ANYMORE.
WAY THE WORLD IS, WE'RE OUT THERE KEEPING OUR EYES OPEN, TAKING CARE OF EACH OTHER.
WE GOT WAYS TO PASS THAT INFO ALONG, SPREAD THE WORD.
SO, NO, I DIDN'T HAVE, LIKE, AN ADDRESS, BUT I KNEW WHO YOU GUYS WERE--THAT YOU WERE IN COLORADO.
FIGURED I'D FIND YOU.
THAT PHYSICAL WE PUT YOU THROUGH YESTERDAY? THE CHEST X-RAY *DOES* SHOW TRACES OF PNEUMONIA.
S.P.R.D.
AND AGENT DEVON TELLS ME YOU TRIED TO SAVE THAT TRAIN FULL OF PEOPLE.
AND *DID* SAVE HIS LIFE.

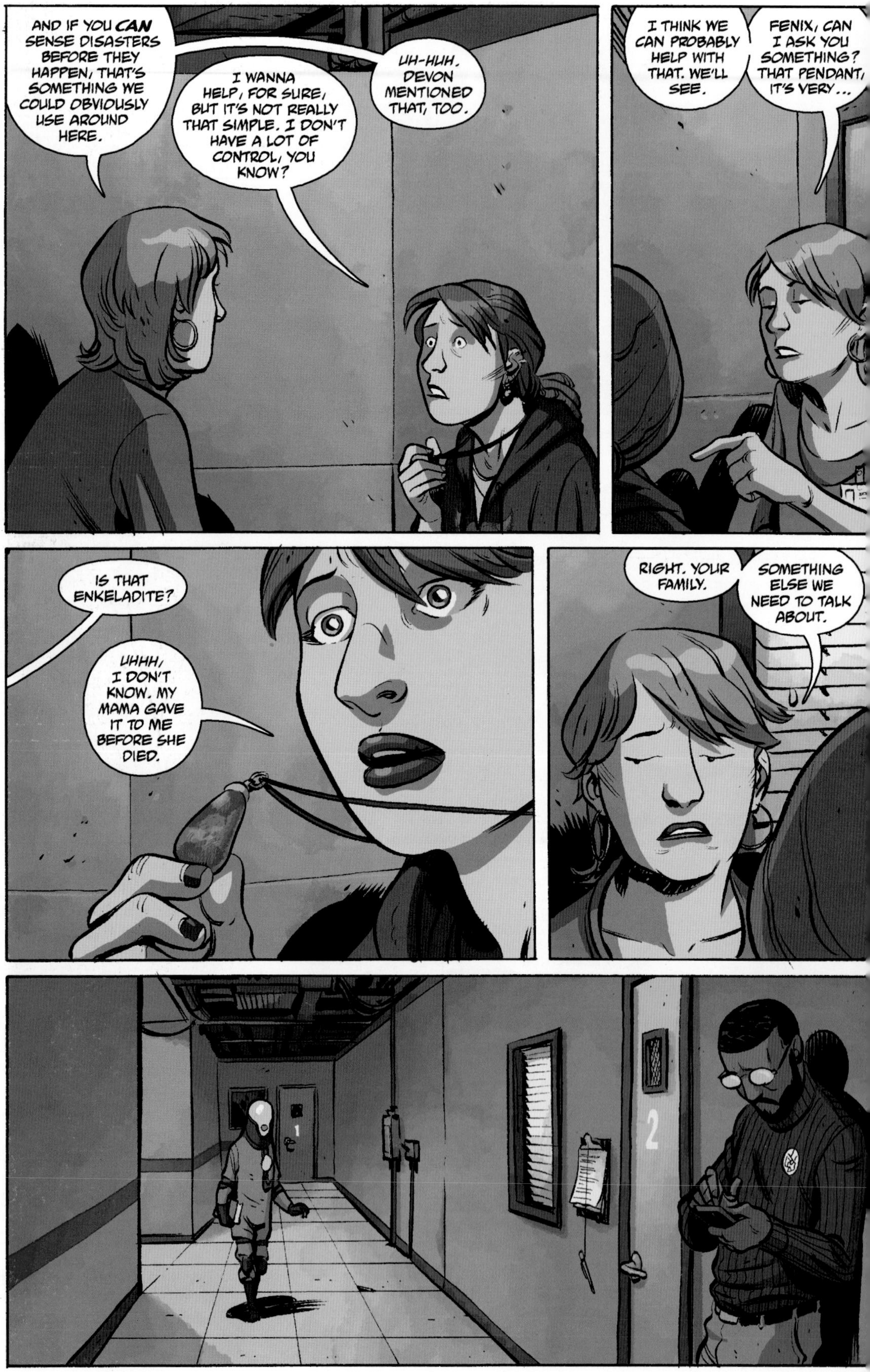
AND IF YOU *CAN* SENSE DISASTERS BEFORE THEY HAPPEN, THAT'S SOMETHING WE COULD OBVIOUSLY USE AROUND HERE.
I WANNA HELP, FOR SURE, BUT IT'S NOT REALLY THAT SIMPLE. I DON'T HAVE A LOT OF CONTROL, YOU KNOW?
UH-HUH. DEVON MENTIONED THAT, TOO.
I THINK WE CAN PROBABLY HELP WITH THAT. WE'LL SEE.
FENIX, CAN I ASK YOU SOMETHING? THAT PENDANT, IT'S VERY...
IS THAT ENKELADITE?
UHHH, I DON'T KNOW. MY MAMA GAVE IT TO ME BEFORE SHE DIED.
RIGHT. YOUR FAMILY.
SOMETHING ELSE WE NEED TO TALK ABOUT.
1
2

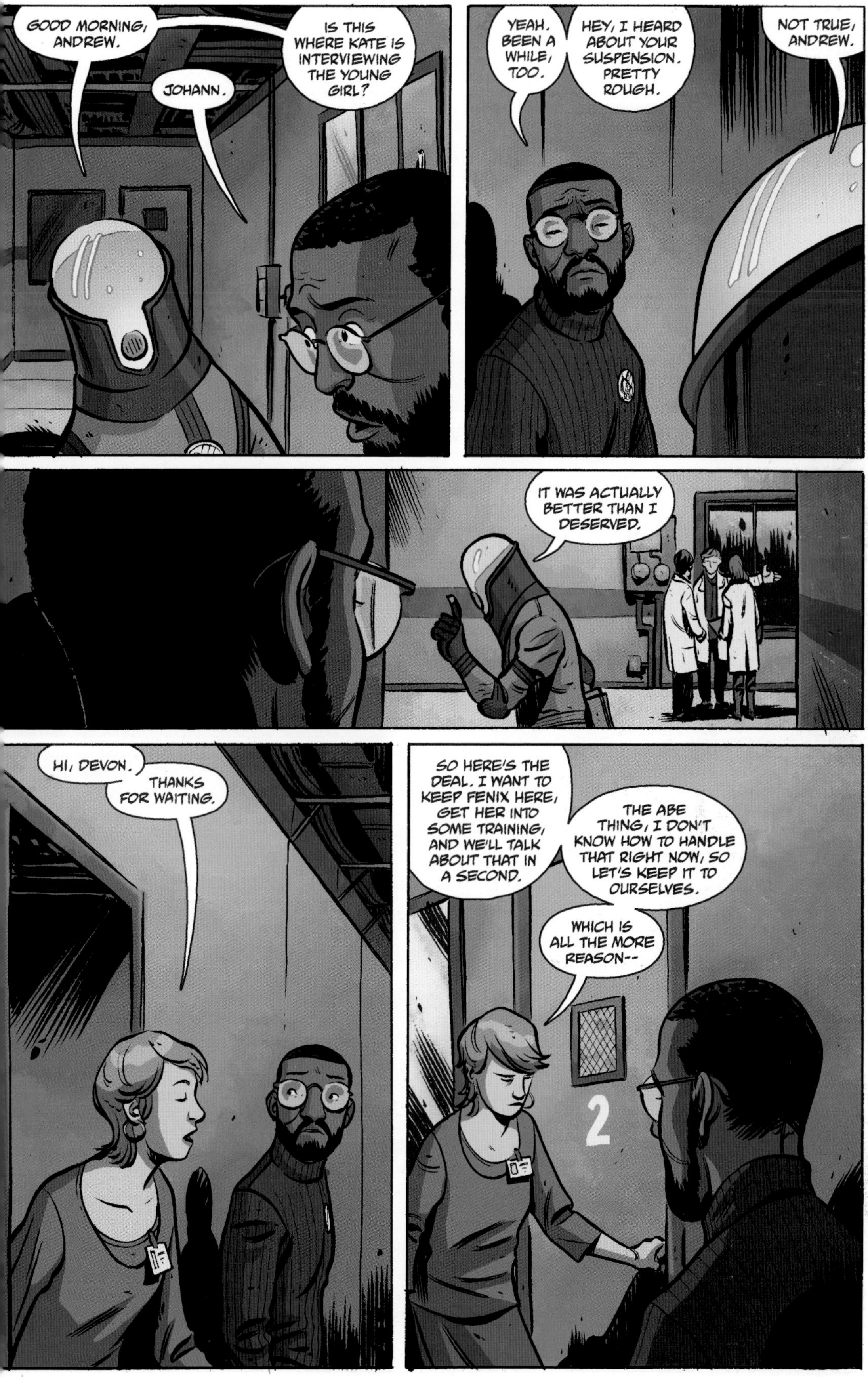
GOOD MORNING, ANDREW.
JOHANN.
IS THIS WHERE KATE IS INTERVIEWING THE YOUNG GIRL?
YEAH. BEEN A WHILE, TOO.
HEY, I HEARD ABOUT YOUR SUSPENSION. PRETTY ROUGH.
NOT TRUE, ANDREW.
IT WAS ACTUALLY BETTER THAN I DESERVED.
HI, DEVON.
THANKS FOR WAITING.
SO HERE'S THE DEAL. I WANT TO KEEP FENIX HERE, GET HER INTO SOME TRAINING, AND WE'LL TALK ABOUT THAT IN A SECOND.
THE ABE THING, I DON'T KNOW HOW TO HANDLE THAT RIGHT NOW, SO LET'S KEEP IT TO OURSELVES.
WHICH IS ALL THE MORE REASON--
2

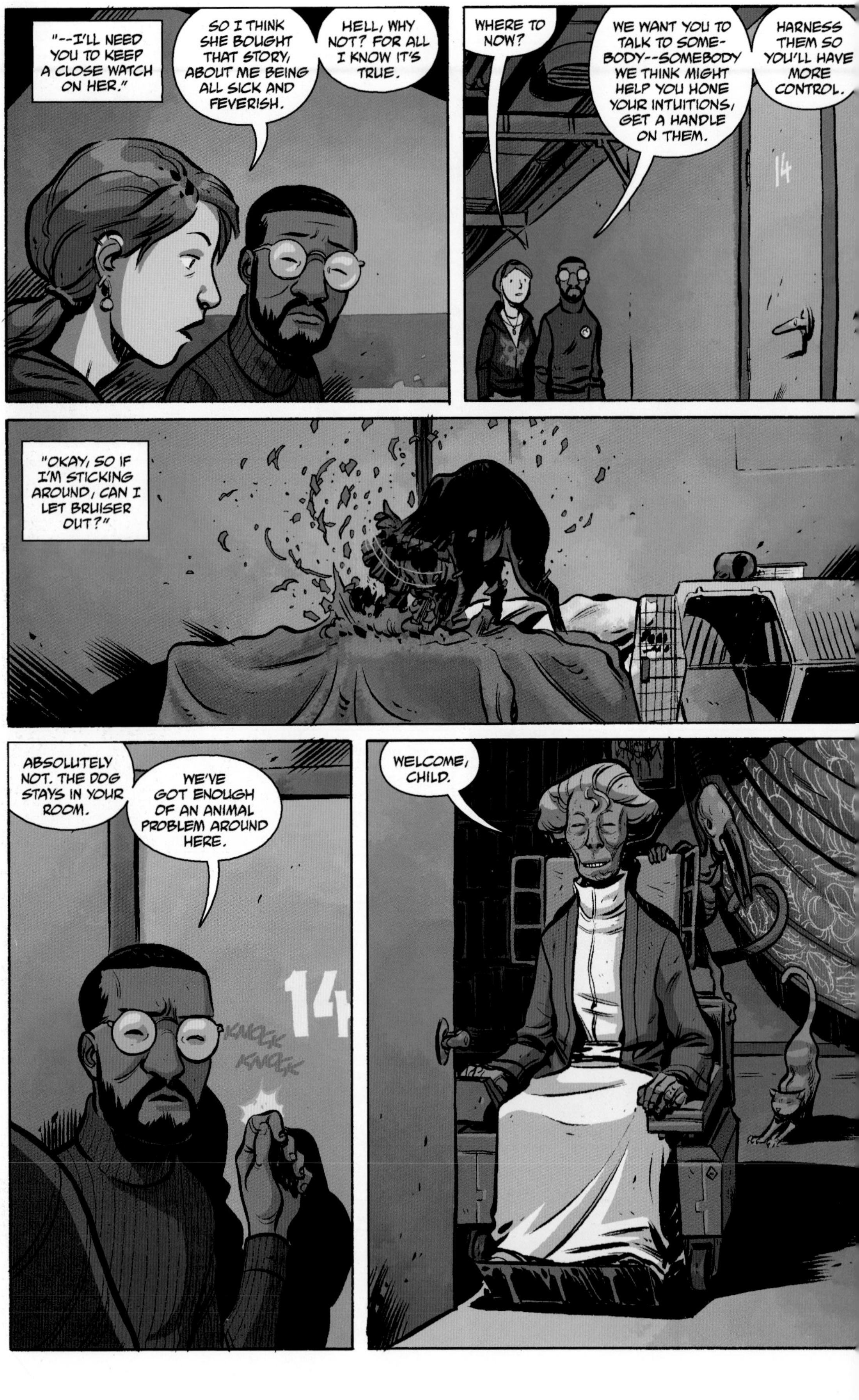
"--I'LL NEED YOU TO KEEP A CLOSE WATCH ON HER."
SO I THINK SHE BOUGHT THAT STORY, ABOUT ME BEING ALL SICK AND FEVERISH.
HELL, WHY NOT? FOR ALL I KNOW IT'S TRUE.
WHERE TO NOW?
WE WANT YOU TO TALK TO SOME-BODY--SOMEBODY WE THINK MIGHT HELP YOU HONE YOUR INTUITIONS, GET A HANDLE ON THEM.
HARNESS THEM SO YOU'LL HAVE MORE CONTROL.
14
"OKAY, SO IF I'M STICKING AROUND, CAN I LET BRUISER OUT?"
ABSOLUTELY NOT. THE DOG STAYS IN YOUR ROOM.
WE'VE GOT ENOUGH OF AN ANIMAL PROBLEM AROUND HERE.
14
KNOCK KNOCK
WELCOME, CHILD.

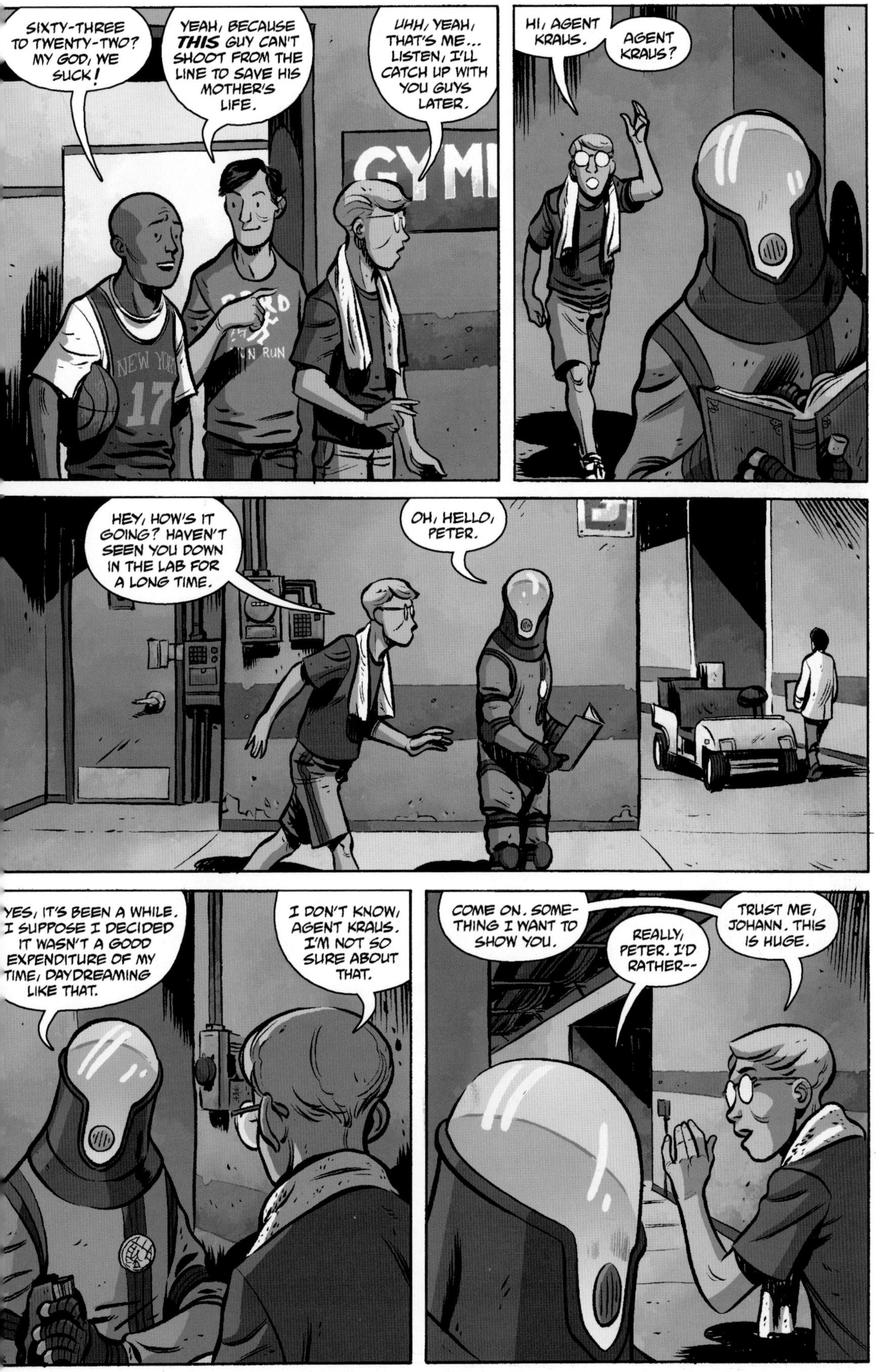
SIXTY-THREE TO TWENTY-TWO? MY GOD, WE SUCK!
YEAH, BECAUSE THIS GUY CAN'T SHOOT FROM THE LINE TO SAVE HIS MOTHER'S LIFE.
UHH, YEAH, THAT'S ME... LISTEN, I'LL CATCH UP WITH YOU GUYS LATER.
GYM
NEW YORK 17
HI, AGENT KRAUS.
AGENT KRAUS?
HEY, HOW'S IT GOING? HAVEN'T SEEN YOU DOWN IN THE LAB FOR A LONG TIME.
OH, HELLO, PETER.
YES, IT'S BEEN A WHILE. I SUPPOSE I DECIDED IT WASN'T A GOOD EXPENDITURE OF MY TIME, DAYDREAMING LIKE THAT.
I DON'T KNOW, AGENT KRAUS. I'M NOT SO SURE ABOUT THAT.
COME ON. SOMETHING I WANT TO SHOW YOU.
REALLY, PETER. I'D RATHER--
TRUST ME, JOHANN. THIS IS HUGE.

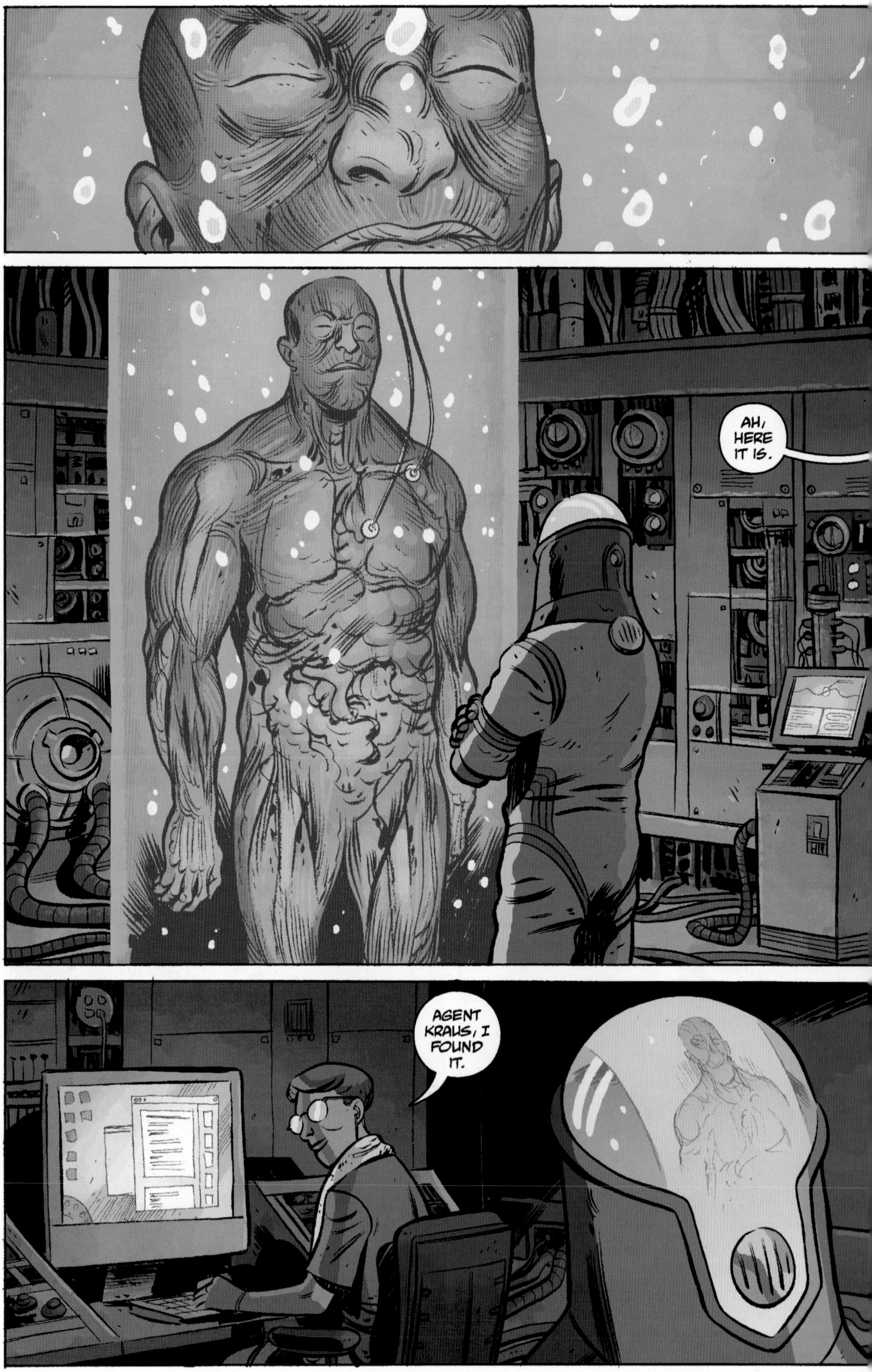
AH, HERE IT IS.
AGENT KRAUS, I FOUND IT.

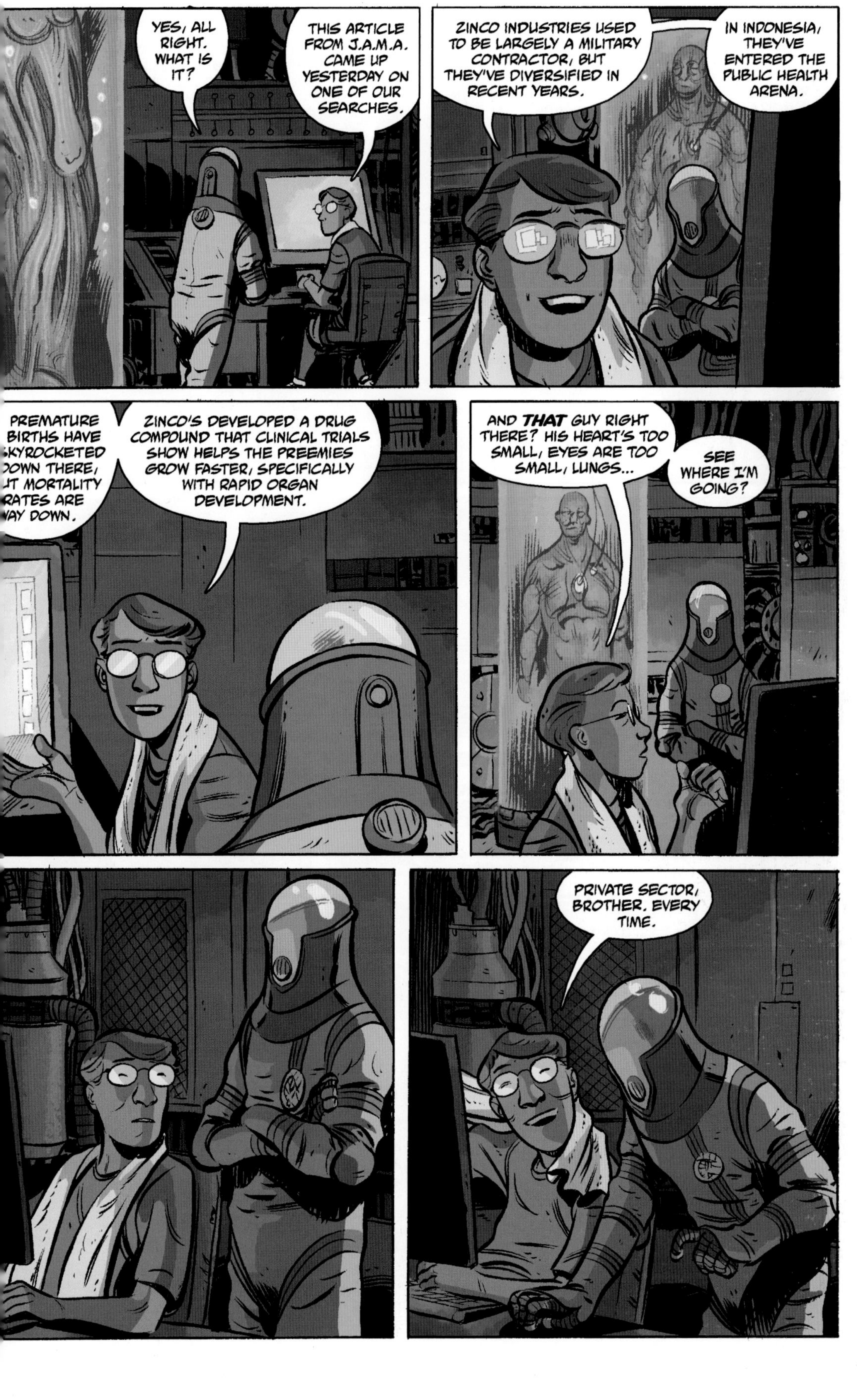
YES, ALL RIGHT. WHAT IS IT?
THIS ARTICLE FROM J.A.M.A. CAME UP YESTERDAY ON ONE OF OUR SEARCHES.
ZINCO INDUSTRIES USED TO BE LARGELY A MILITARY CONTRACTOR, BUT THEY'VE DIVERSIFIED IN RECENT YEARS.
IN INDONESIA, THEY'VE ENTERED THE PUBLIC HEALTH ARENA.
PREMATURE BIRTHS HAVE SKYROCKETED DOWN THERE, UT MORTALITY RATES ARE WAY DOWN.
ZINCO'S DEVELOPED A DRUG COMPOUND THAT CLINICAL TRIALS SHOW HELPS THE PREEMIES GROW FASTER, SPECIFICALLY WITH RAPID ORGAN DEVELOPMENT.
AND ***THAT*** GUY RIGHT THERE? HIS HEART'S TOO SMALL, EYES ARE TOO SMALL, LUNGS...
SEE WHERE I'M GOING?
PRIVATE SECTOR, BROTHER. EVERY TIME.

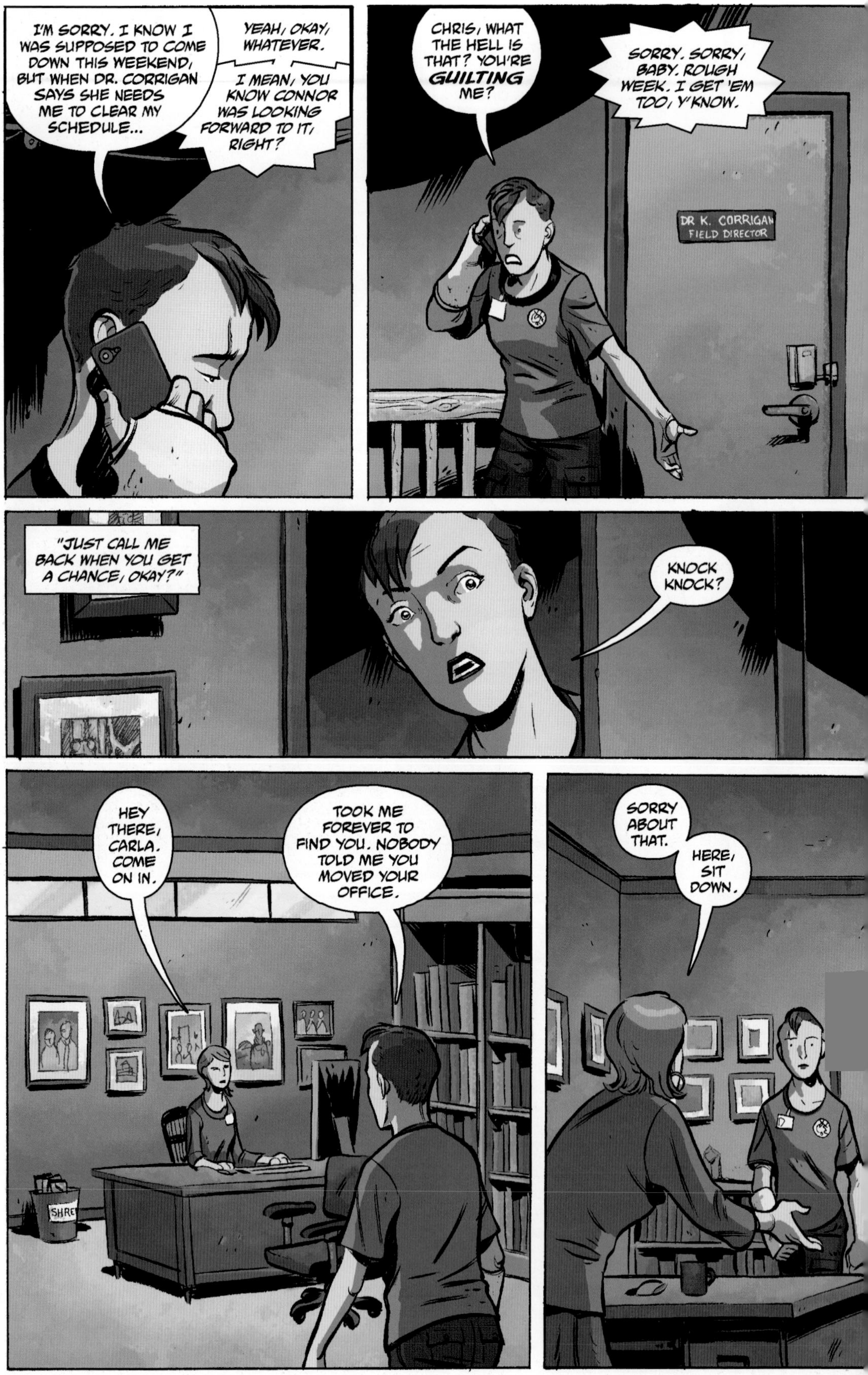

I'M SORRY. I KNOW I WAS SUPPOSED TO COME DOWN THIS WEEKEND, BUT WHEN DR. CORRIGAN SAYS SHE NEEDS ME TO CLEAR MY SCHEDULE...
YEAH, OKAY, WHATEVER.
I MEAN, YOU KNOW CONNOR WAS LOOKING FORWARD TO IT, RIGHT?
CHRIS, WHAT THE HELL IS THAT? YOU'RE GUILTING ME?
SORRY. SORRY, BABY. ROUGH WEEK. I GET 'EM TOO, Y'KNOW.
DR K. CORRIGAN
FIELD DIRECTOR
"JUST CALL ME BACK WHEN YOU GET A CHANCE, OKAY?"
KNOCK KNOCK?
HEY THERE, CARLA. COME ON IN.
TOOK ME FOREVER TO FIND YOU. NOBODY TOLD ME YOU MOVED YOUR OFFICE.
SORRY ABOUT THAT.
HERE, SIT DOWN.

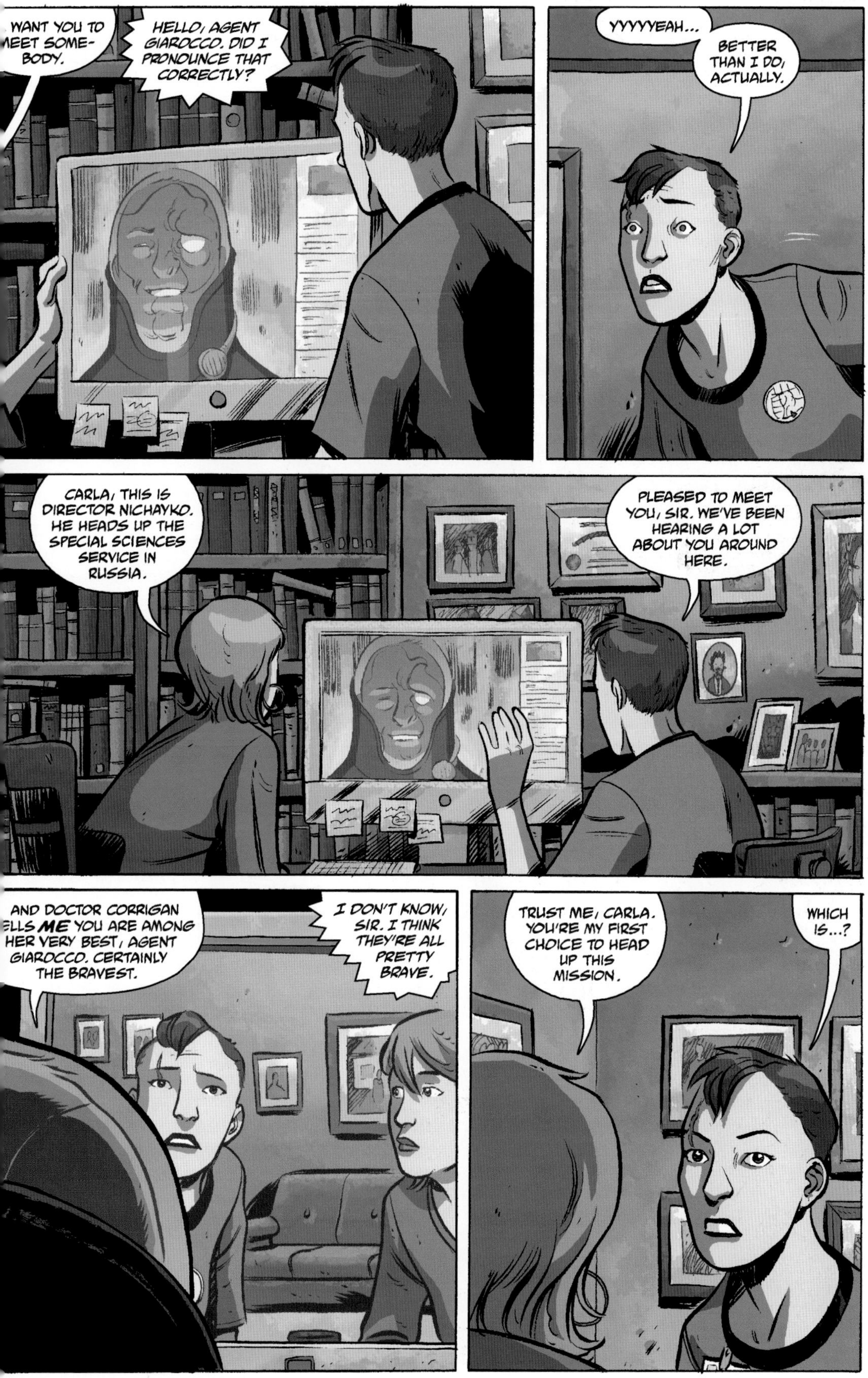
WANT YOU TO
MEET SOME-
BODY.
HELLO, AGENT GIAROCCO. DID I PRONOUNCE THAT CORRECTLY?
YYYYYEAH...
BETTER THAN I DO, ACTUALLY.
CARLA, THIS IS DIRECTOR NICHAYKO. HE HEADS UP THE SPECIAL SCIENCES SERVICE IN RUSSIA.
PLEASED TO MEET YOU, SIR. WE'VE BEEN HEARING A LOT ABOUT YOU AROUND HERE.
AND DOCTOR CORRIGAN
ELLS ME YOU ARE AMONG HER VERY BEST, AGENT GIAROCCO. CERTAINLY THE BRAVEST.
I DON'T KNOW, SIR. I THINK THEY'RE ALL PRETTY BRAVE.
TRUST ME, CARLA. YOU'RE MY FIRST CHOICE TO HEAD UP THIS MISSION.
WHICH IS...?

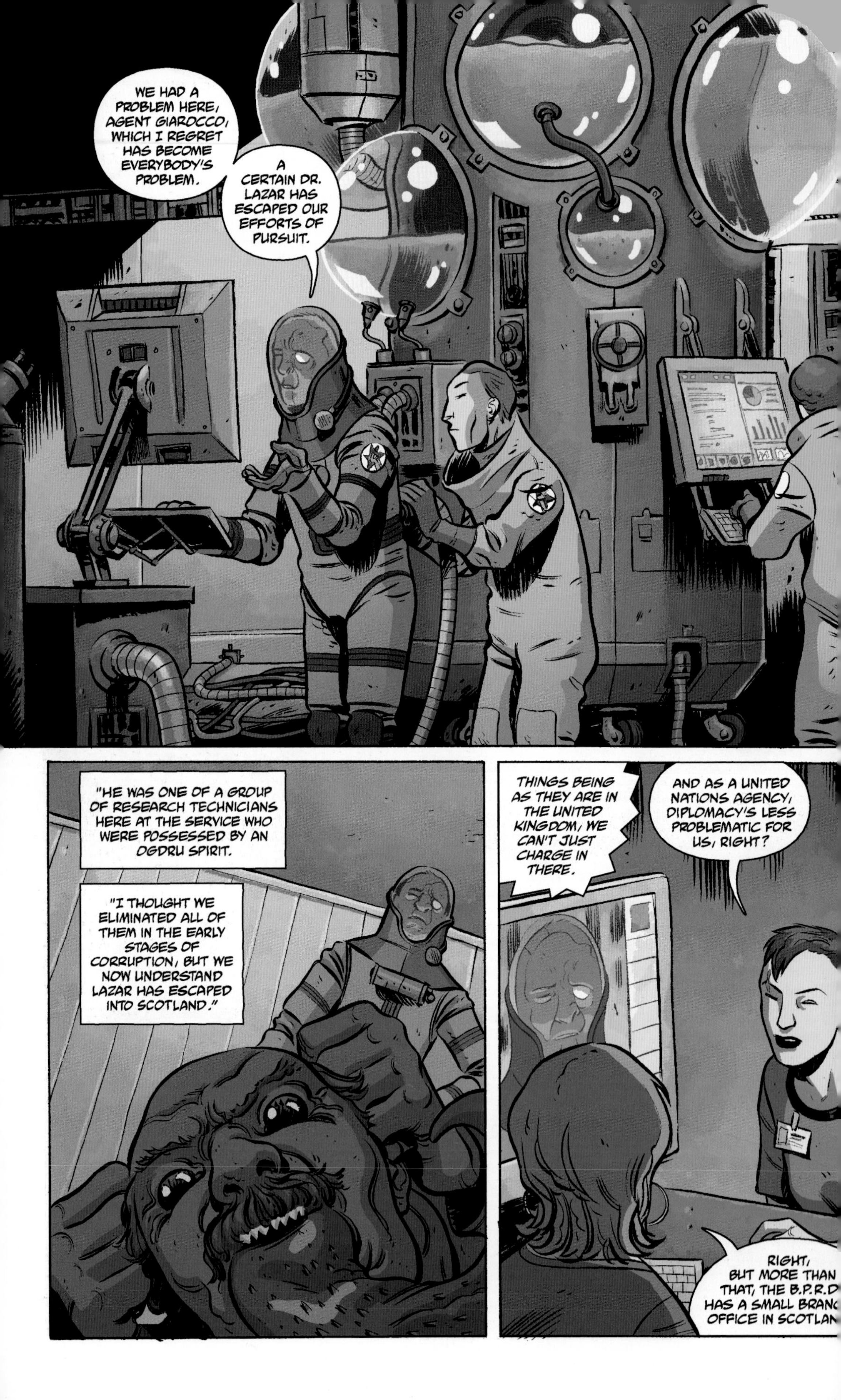
WE HAD A PROBLEM HERE, AGENT GIAROCCO, WHICH I REGRET HAS BECOME EVERYBODY'S PROBLEM.
A CERTAIN DR. LAZAR HAS ESCAPED OUR EFFORTS OF PURSUIT.
"HE WAS ONE OF A GROUP OF RESEARCH TECHNICIANS HERE AT THE SERVICE WHO WERE POSSESSED BY AN OGDRU SPIRIT.
"I THOUGHT WE ELIMINATED ALL OF THEM IN THE EARLY STAGES OF CORRUPTION, BUT WE NOW UNDERSTAND LAZAR HAS ESCAPED INTO SCOTLAND."
THINGS BEING AS THEY ARE IN THE UNITED KINGDOM, WE CAN'T JUST CHARGE IN THERE.
AND AS A UNITED NATIONS AGENCY, DIPLOMACY'S LESS PROBLEMATIC FOR US, RIGHT?
RIGHT, BUT MORE THAN THAT, THE B.P.R.D HAS A SMALL BRANC OFFICE IN SCOTLAN

DOCTOR, AGENT MAROCCO, MY APOLOGIES.

I AM FORCED TO CUT THIS CONFERENCE SHORT. I HAVE HELD OFF ON THIS TRANSFUSION TOO LONG AS IT IS.

YOU HAVE ALL THE FILES. I'LL WAIT FOR WORD FROM YOU TOMORROW.

NOW, HE'S REALLY...

OH, YEAH. HE SURE IS.

AND, UH, "TRANSFUSION"? YIKES!

BUT WE'VE GOT A GOOD RELATIONSHIP WITH THE S.S.S., AND THIS IS SOMETHING WE REALLY NEED TO FOLLOW UP ON.

LOTS OF INTERNET CHATTER ABOUT SCOTLAND AND THE RISE OF A "MESSIAH."

FROM WHAT I'VE HEARD--AND CAN SEE--I'D THINK 'CHAYKO WOULD PREFER KRAUS TO ME ON THIS MISSION.

EXCEPT JOHANN'S STILL ON SUSPENSION FROM ACTIVE DUTY FOR WHAT HAPPENED IN CANADA.

SO THIS IS *YOUR* MISSION-- ALONG WITH A CO-CAPTAIN ONCE YOU GET TO SCOTLAND.

CO-CAPTAIN?

COME ON. I'LL TELL YOU MORE OVER DINNER.

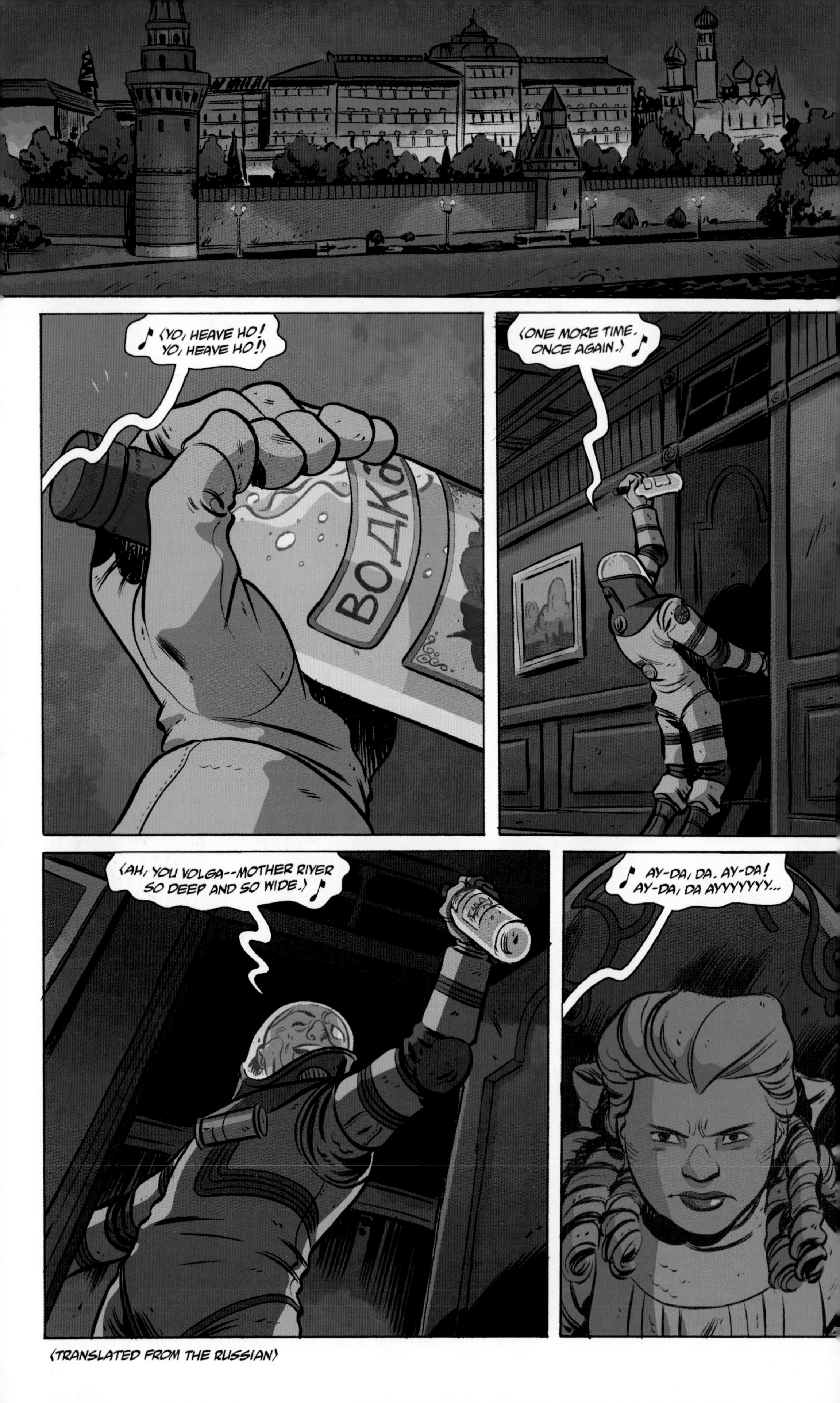

♪ ‹YO, HEAVE HO! YO, HEAVE HO!›
‹ONE MORE TIME. ONCE AGAIN.› ♪
‹AH, YOU VOLGA--MOTHER RIVER SO DEEP AND SO WIDE.› ♪
♪ AY-DA, DA. AY-DA! AY-DA, DA AYYYYYYY...


‹TRANSLATED FROM THE RUSSIAN›

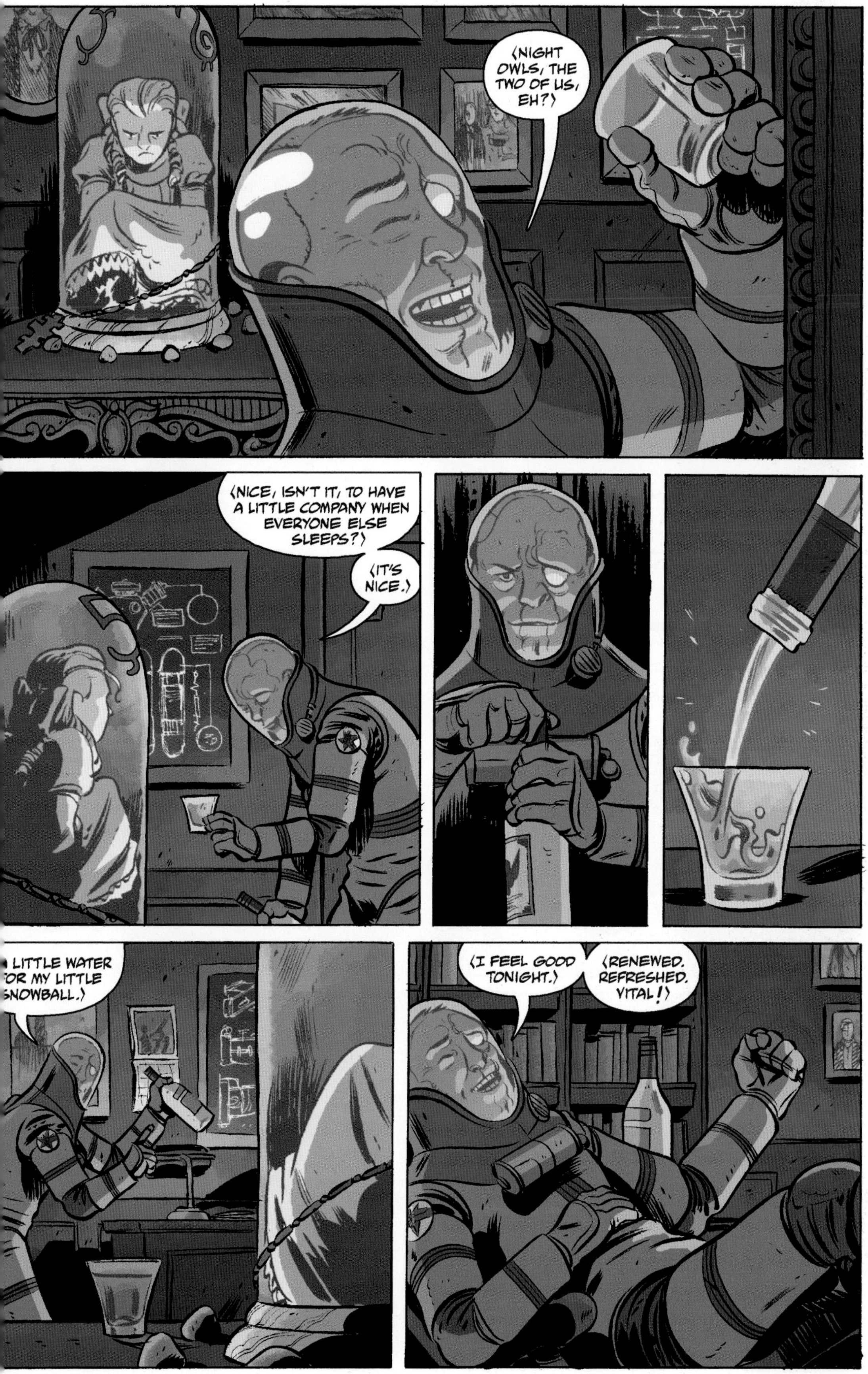

‹NIGHT OWLS, THE TWO OF US, EH?›
‹NICE, ISN'T IT, TO HAVE A LITTLE COMPANY WHEN EVERYONE ELSE SLEEPS?›
‹IT'S NICE.›
LITTLE WATER OR MY LITTLE SNOWBALL.›
‹I FEEL GOOD TONIGHT.›
‹RENEWED. REFRESHED. VITAL!›

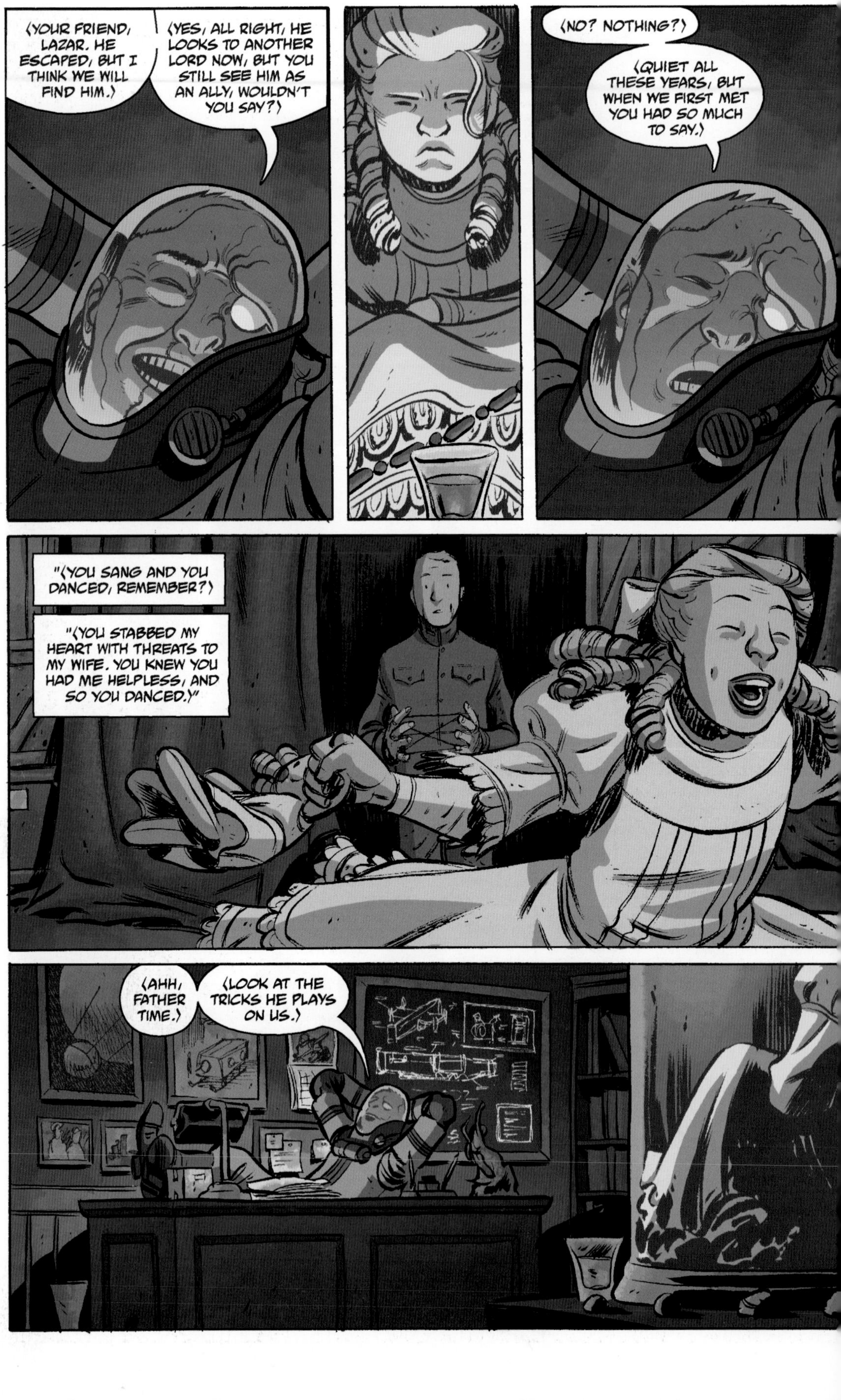
⟨YOUR FRIEND, LAZAR. HE ESCAPED, BUT I THINK WE WILL FIND HIM.⟩
⟨YES, ALL RIGHT, HE LOOKS TO ANOTHER LORD NOW, BUT YOU STILL SEE HIM AS AN ALLY, WOULDN'T YOU SAY?⟩
⟨NO? NOTHING?⟩
⟨QUIET ALL THESE YEARS, BUT WHEN WE FIRST MET YOU HAD SO MUCH TO SAY.⟩
"⟨YOU SANG AND YOU DANCED, REMEMBER?⟩
"⟨YOU STABBED MY HEART WITH THREATS TO MY WIFE. YOU KNEW YOU HAD ME HELPLESS, AND SO YOU DANCED.⟩"
⟨AHH, FATHER TIME.⟩
⟨LOOK AT THE TRICKS HE PLAYS ON US.⟩

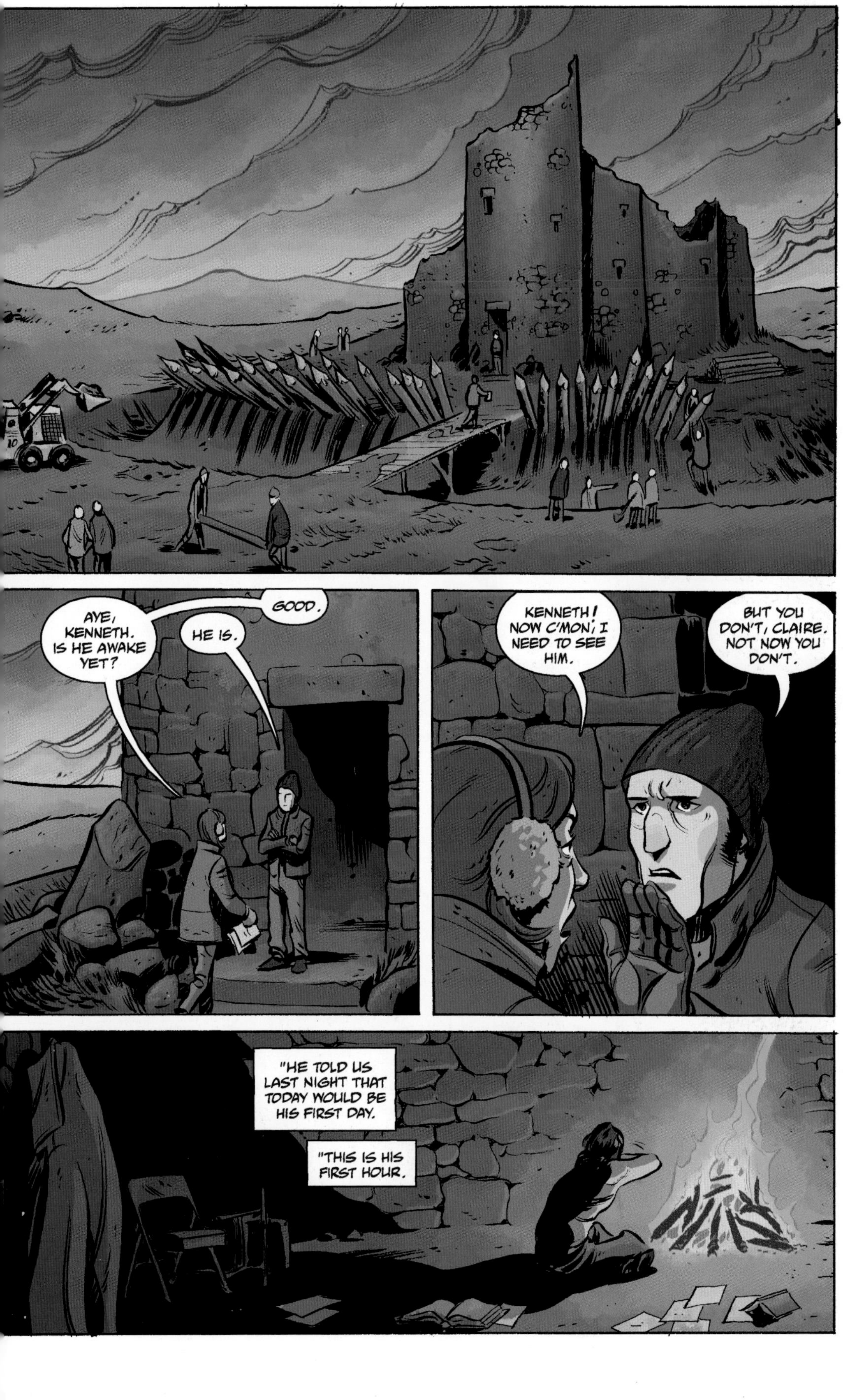
AYE, KENNETH. IS HE AWAKE YET?
HE IS.
GOOD.
KENNETH! NOW C'MON; I NEED TO SEE HIM.
BUT YOU DON'T, CLAIRE. NOT NOW YOU DON'T.
"HE TOLD US LAST NIGHT THAT TODAY WOULD BE HIS FIRST DAY.
"THIS IS HIS FIRST HOUR.

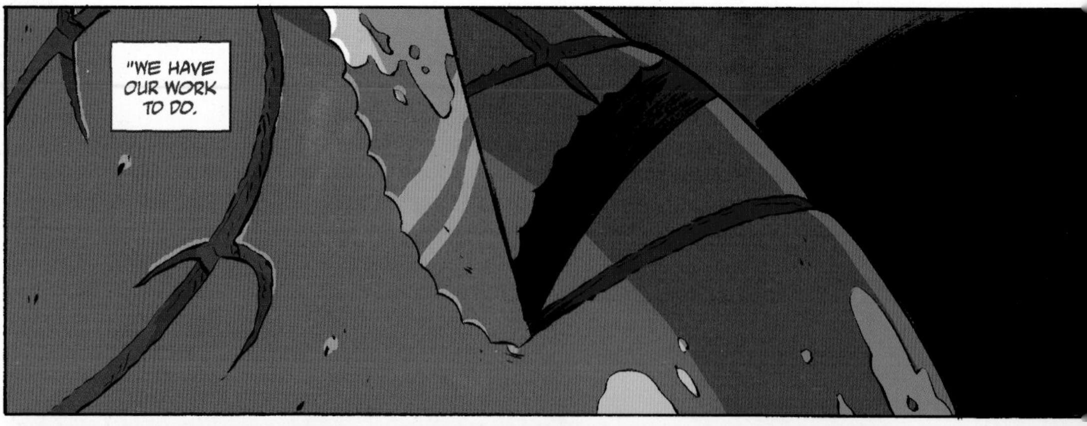
"WE HAVE OUR WORK TO DO.

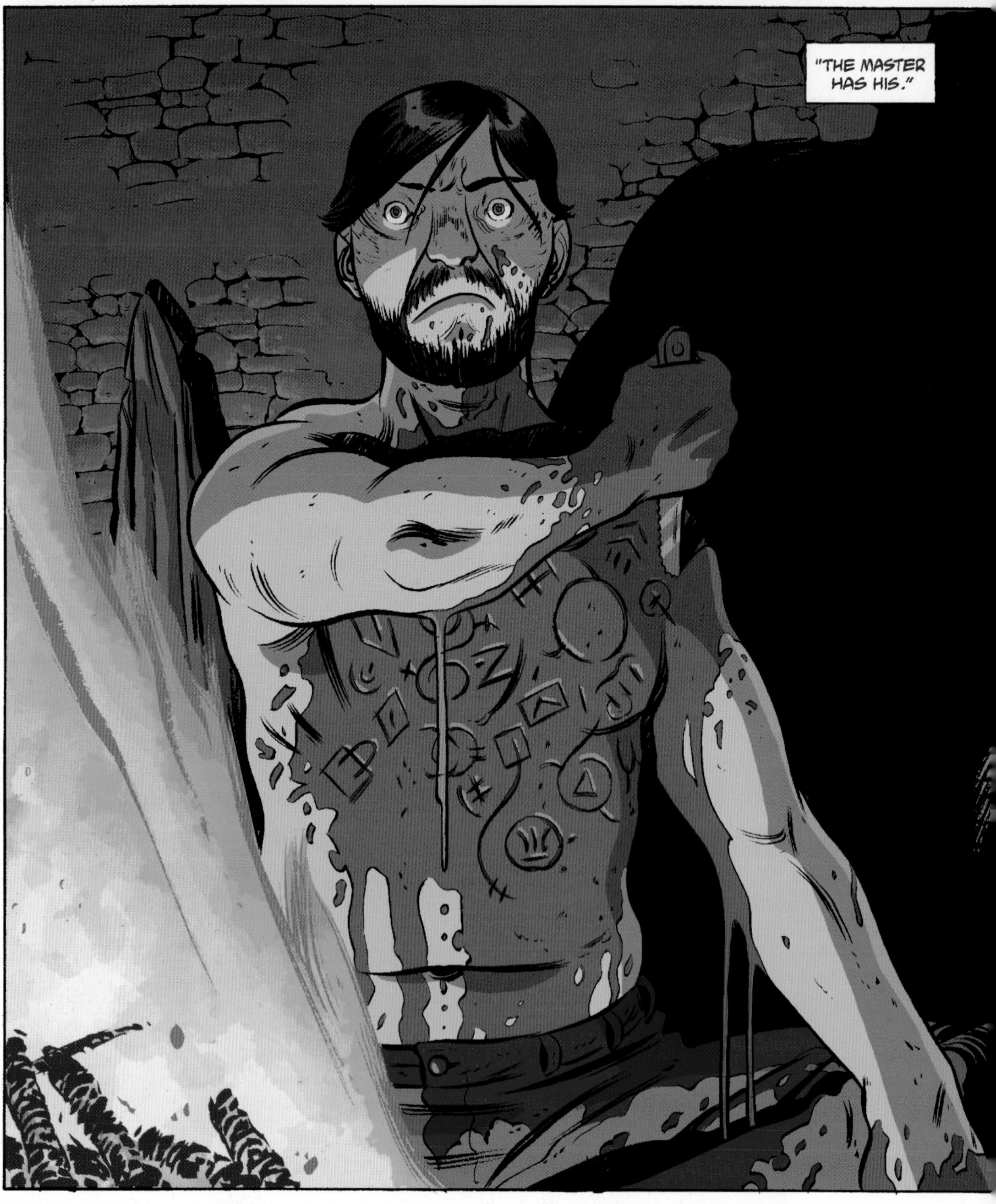
"THE MASTER HAS HIS."

# THE RETURN OF THE MASTER CHAPTER TWO

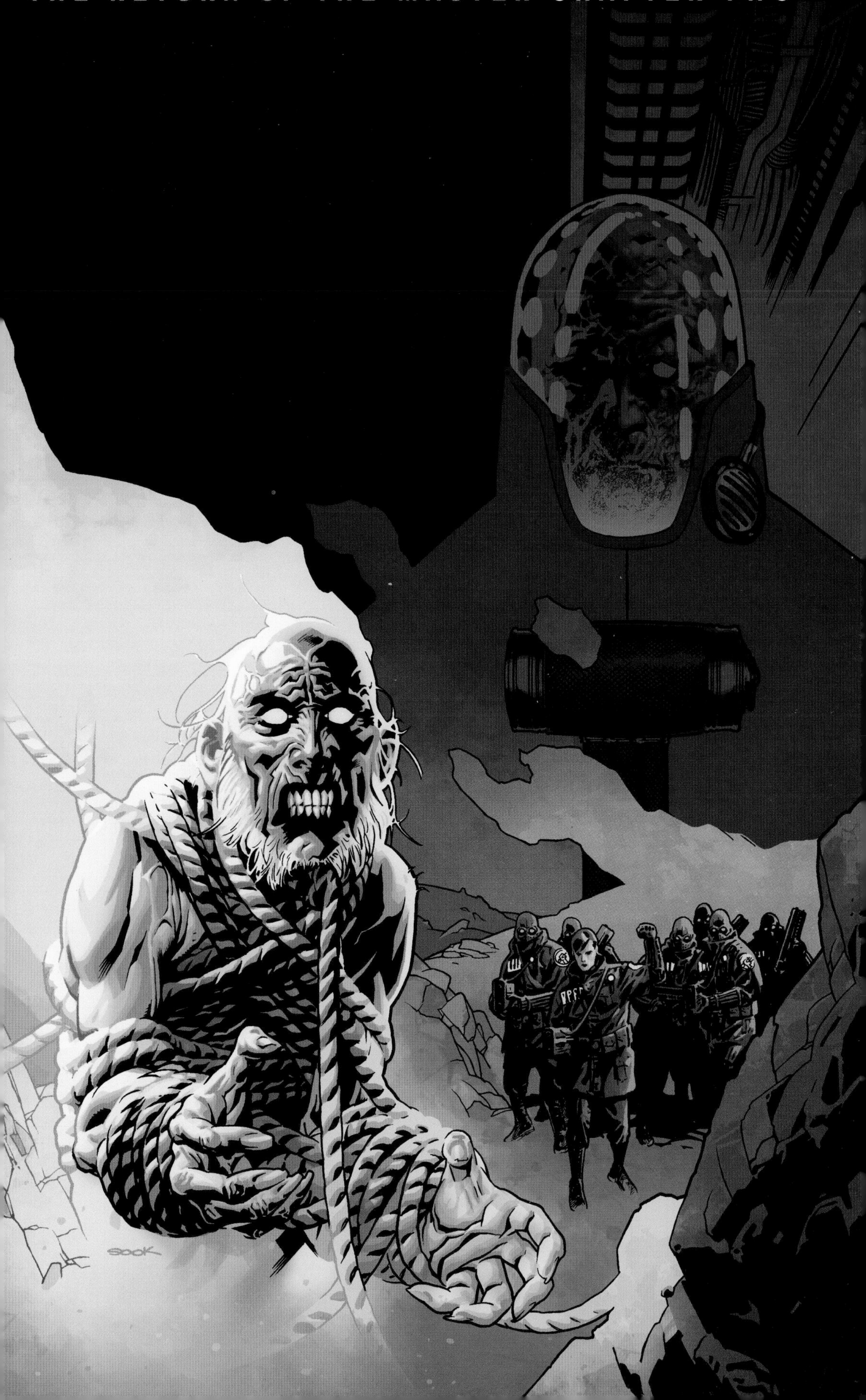
SOOK

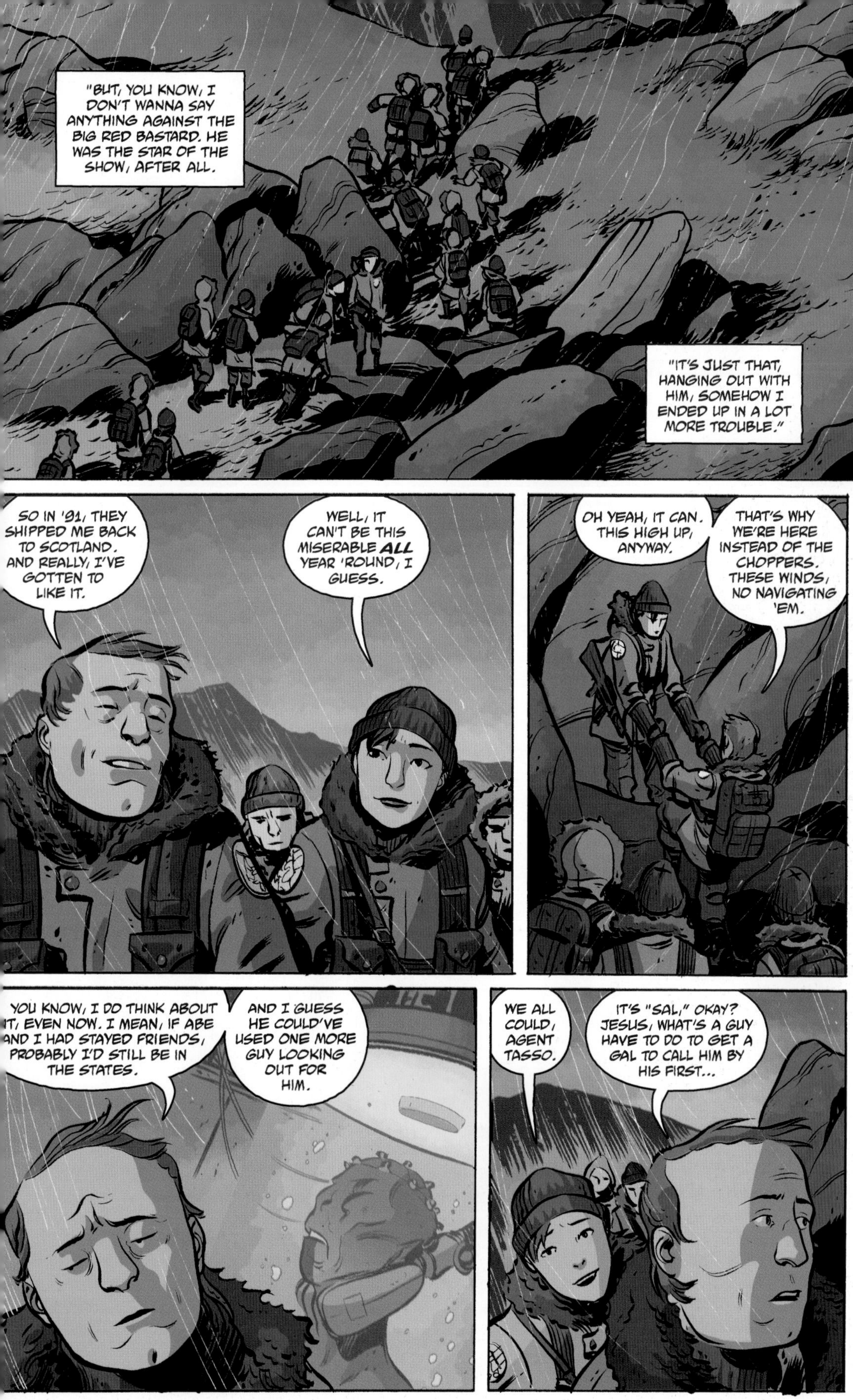
"BUT, YOU KNOW, I DON'T WANNA SAY ANYTHING AGAINST THE BIG RED BASTARD. HE WAS THE STAR OF THE SHOW, AFTER ALL.
"IT'S JUST THAT, HANGING OUT WITH HIM, SOMEHOW I ENDED UP IN A LOT MORE TROUBLE."
SO IN '91, THEY SHIPPED ME BACK TO SCOTLAND. AND REALLY, I'VE GOTTEN TO LIKE IT.
WELL, IT CAN'T BE THIS MISERABLE ALL YEAR 'ROUND, I GUESS.
OH YEAH, IT CAN. THIS HIGH UP, ANYWAY.
THAT'S WHY WE'RE HERE INSTEAD OF THE CHOPPERS. THESE WINDS, NO NAVIGATING 'EM.
YOU KNOW, I DO THINK ABOUT IT, EVEN NOW. I MEAN, IF ABE AND I HAD STAYED FRIENDS, PROBABLY I'D STILL BE IN THE STATES.
AND I GUESS HE COULD'VE USED ONE MORE GUY LOOKING OUT FOR HIM.
WE ALL COULD, AGENT TASSO.
IT'S "SAL," OKAY? JESUS, WHAT'S A GUY HAVE TO DO TO GET A GAL TO CALL HIM BY HIS FIRST...

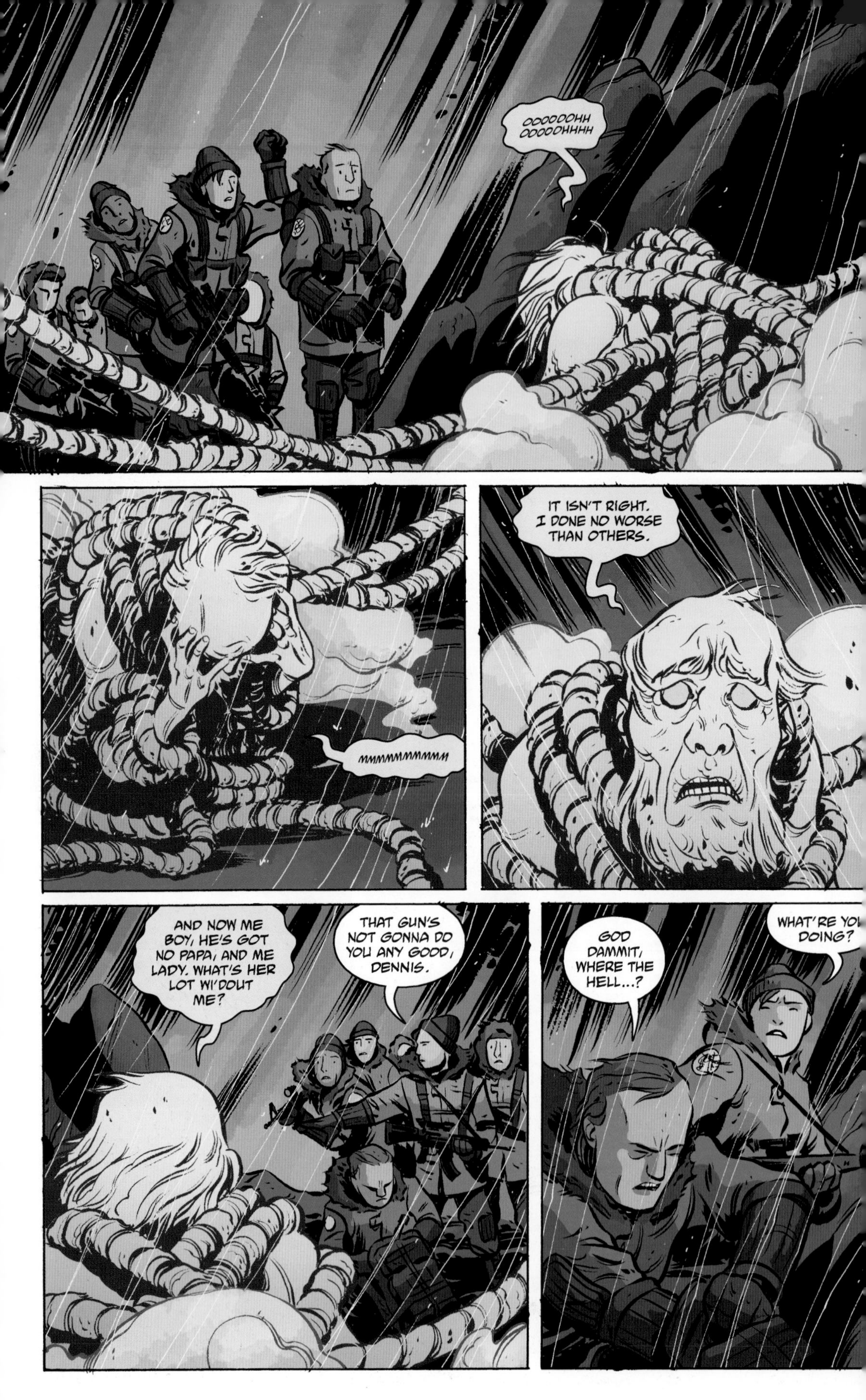
OOOOOOHH OOOOOHHHH
MMMMMMMMMMM
IT ISN'T RIGHT. I DONE NO WORSE THAN OTHERS.
AND NOW ME BOY, HE'S GOT NO PAPA, AND ME LADY. WHAT'S HER LOT WI'DOUT ME?
THAT GUN'S NOT GONNA DO YOU ANY GOOD, DENNIS.
GOD DAMMIT, WHERE THE HELL...?
WHAT'RE YOU DOING?

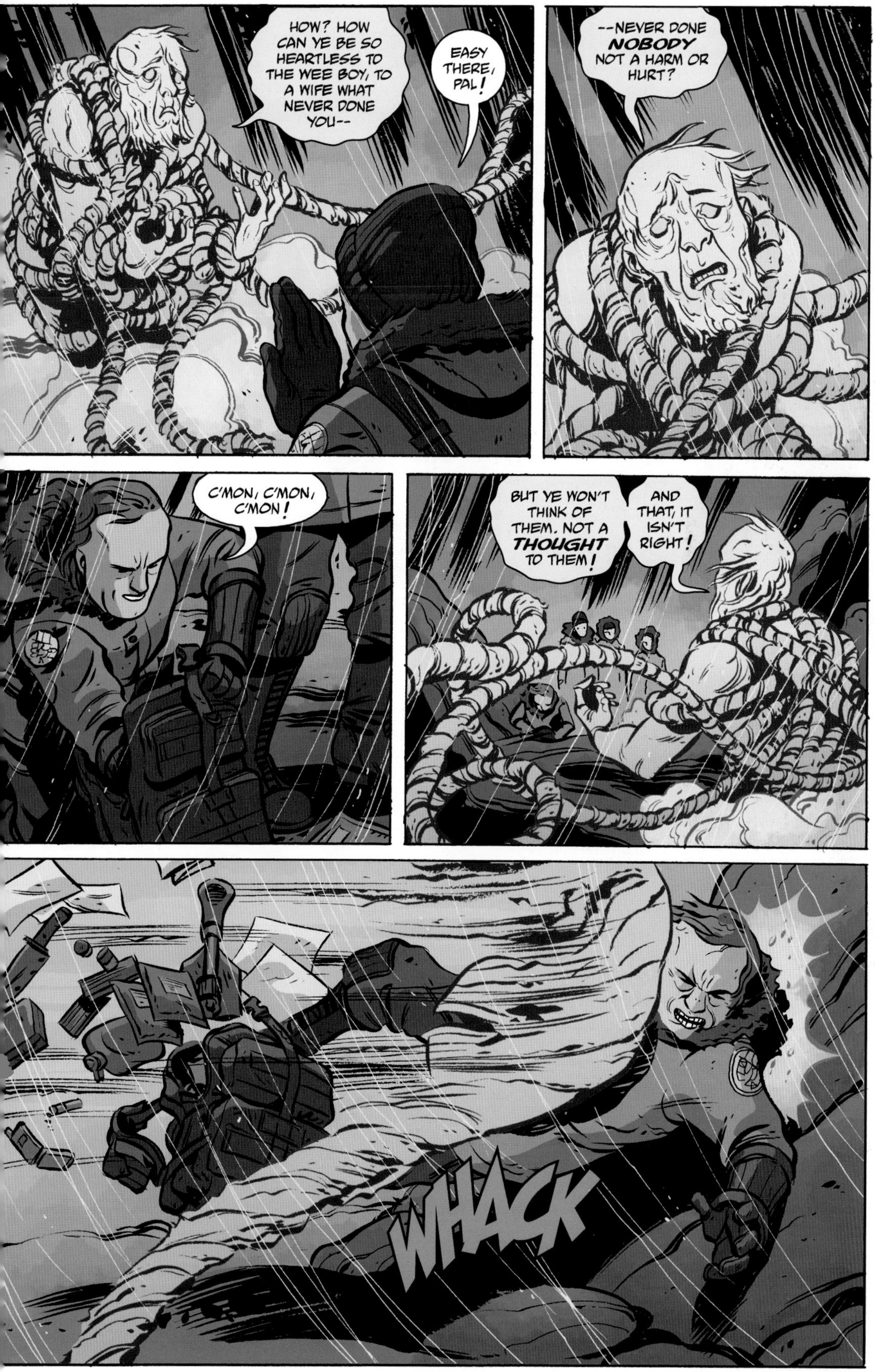

HOW? HOW CAN YE BE SO HEARTLESS TO THE WEE BOY, TO A WIFE WHAT NEVER DONE YOU--
EASY THERE, PAL!
--NEVER DONE NOBODY NOT A HARM OR HURT?
C'MON, C'MON, C'MON!
BUT YE WON'T THINK OF THEM. NOT A THOUGHT TO THEM!
AND THAT, IT ISN'T RIGHT!
WHACK

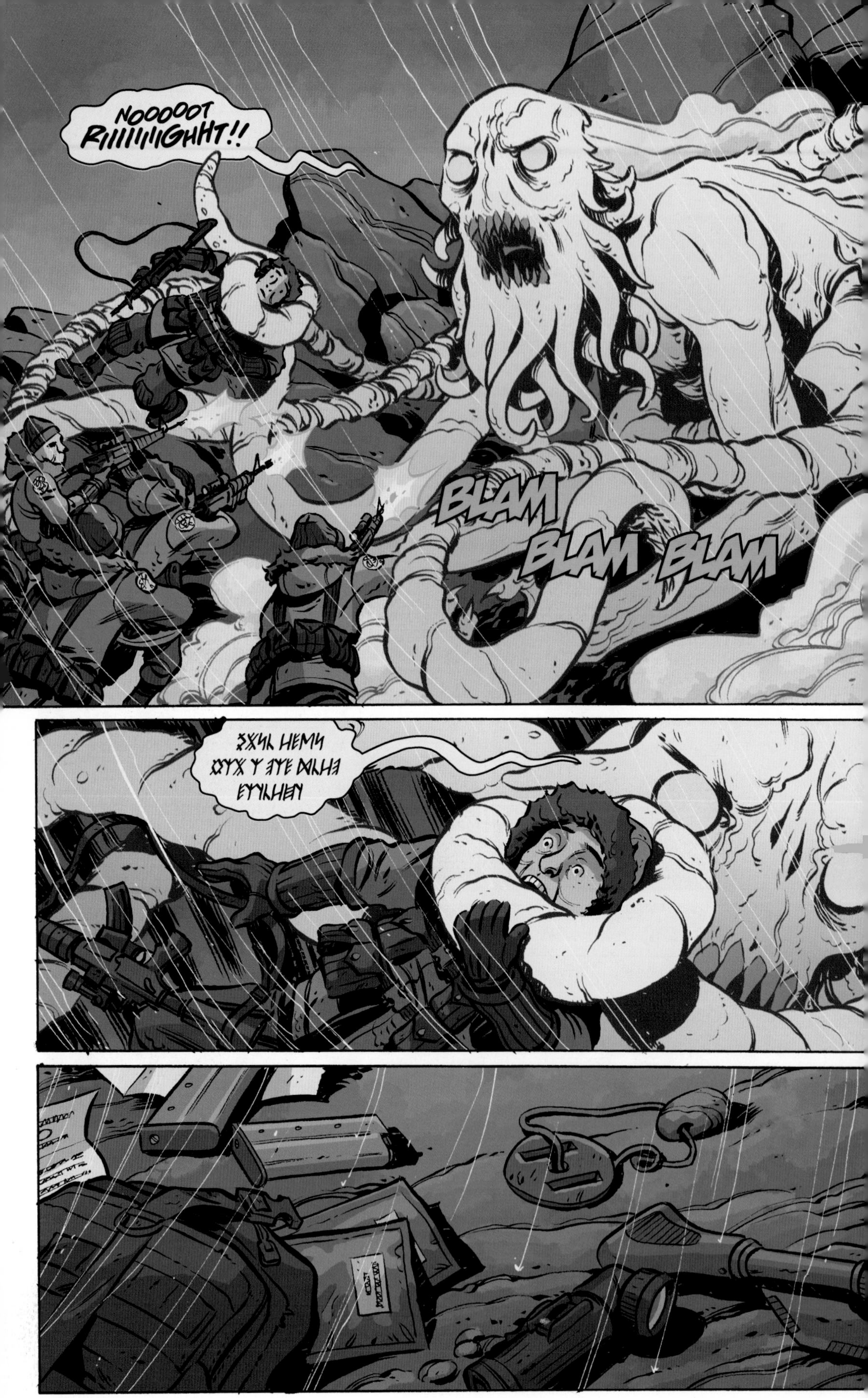
NOOOOOT RIIIIIIIGHHT!!
BLAM
BLAM
BLAM

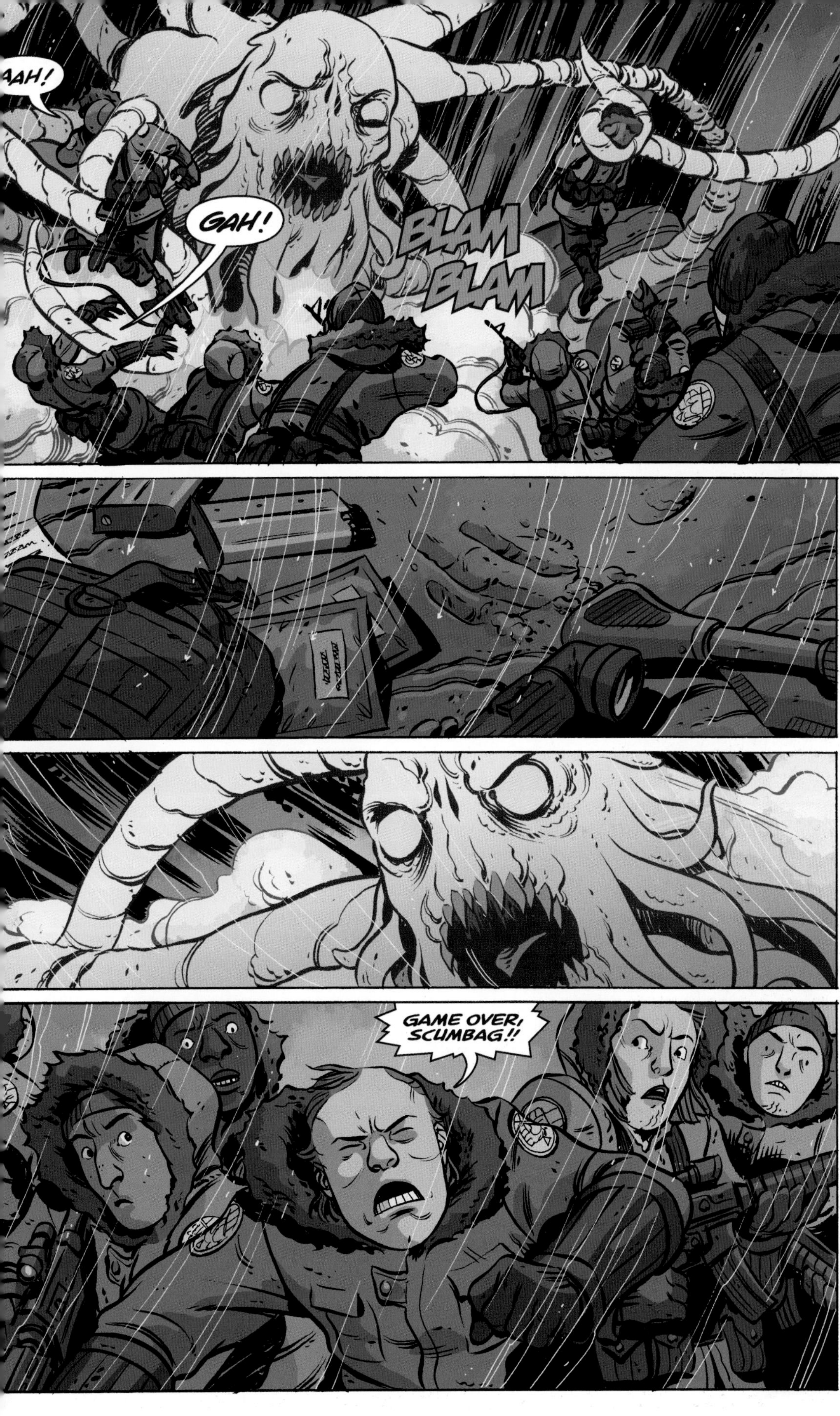
AAH!
GAH!
BLAM BLAM
GAME OVER, SCUMBAG!!

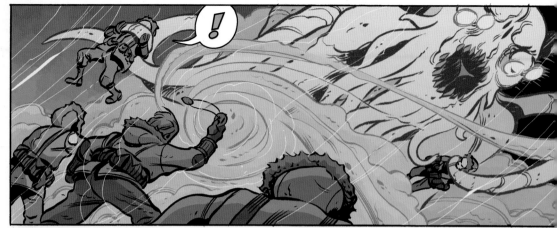

KRACK

IF THAT'S THE BEST THIS "MAD RUSSIAN" CAN DO, SOME OF US MIGHT JUST LIVE THROUGH THIS.

THAT LITTLE...*THAT* KILLED OUR MONSTER?

SOME HAUNTINGS, YOU REALLY JUST NEED THE RIGHT CHARM. AND THIS ONE'S A DOOZY.

HELLBOY, HE GAVE IT TO ME AS A GOING AWAY GIFT WHEN HE HEARD I WAS HEADED BACK TO SCOTLAND.

MUCH TROUBLE AS HE GOT ME INTO, GOT ME OUTTA *LOTS* MORE.

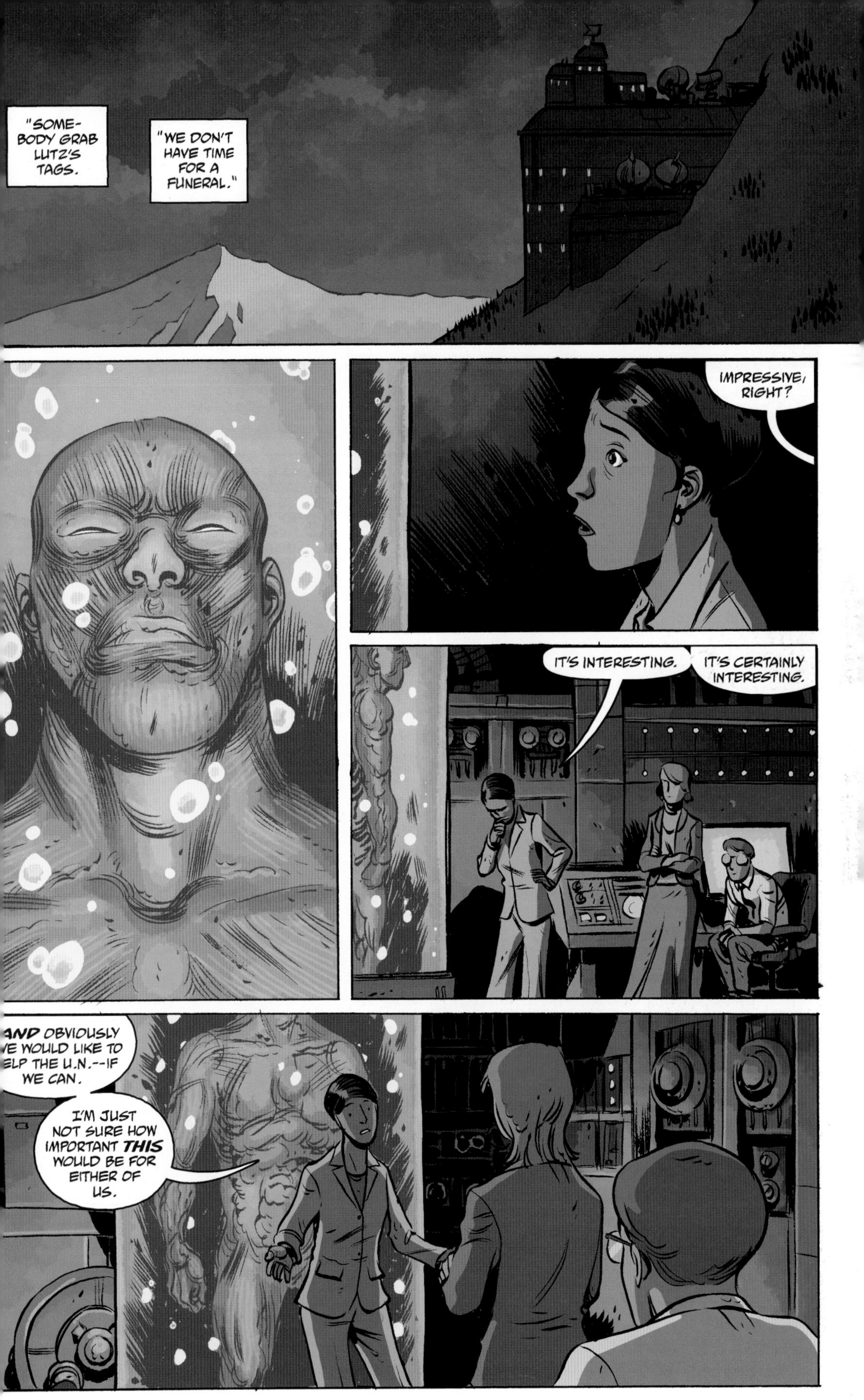
"SOME-BODY GRAB LUTZ'S TAGS.
"WE DON'T HAVE TIME FOR A FUNERAL."
IMPRESSIVE, RIGHT?
IT'S INTERESTING.
IT'S CERTAINLY INTERESTING.
AND OBVIOUSLY WE WOULD LIKE TO HELP THE U.N.--IF WE CAN.
I'M JUST NOT SURE HOW IMPORTANT THIS WOULD BE FOR EITHER OF US.

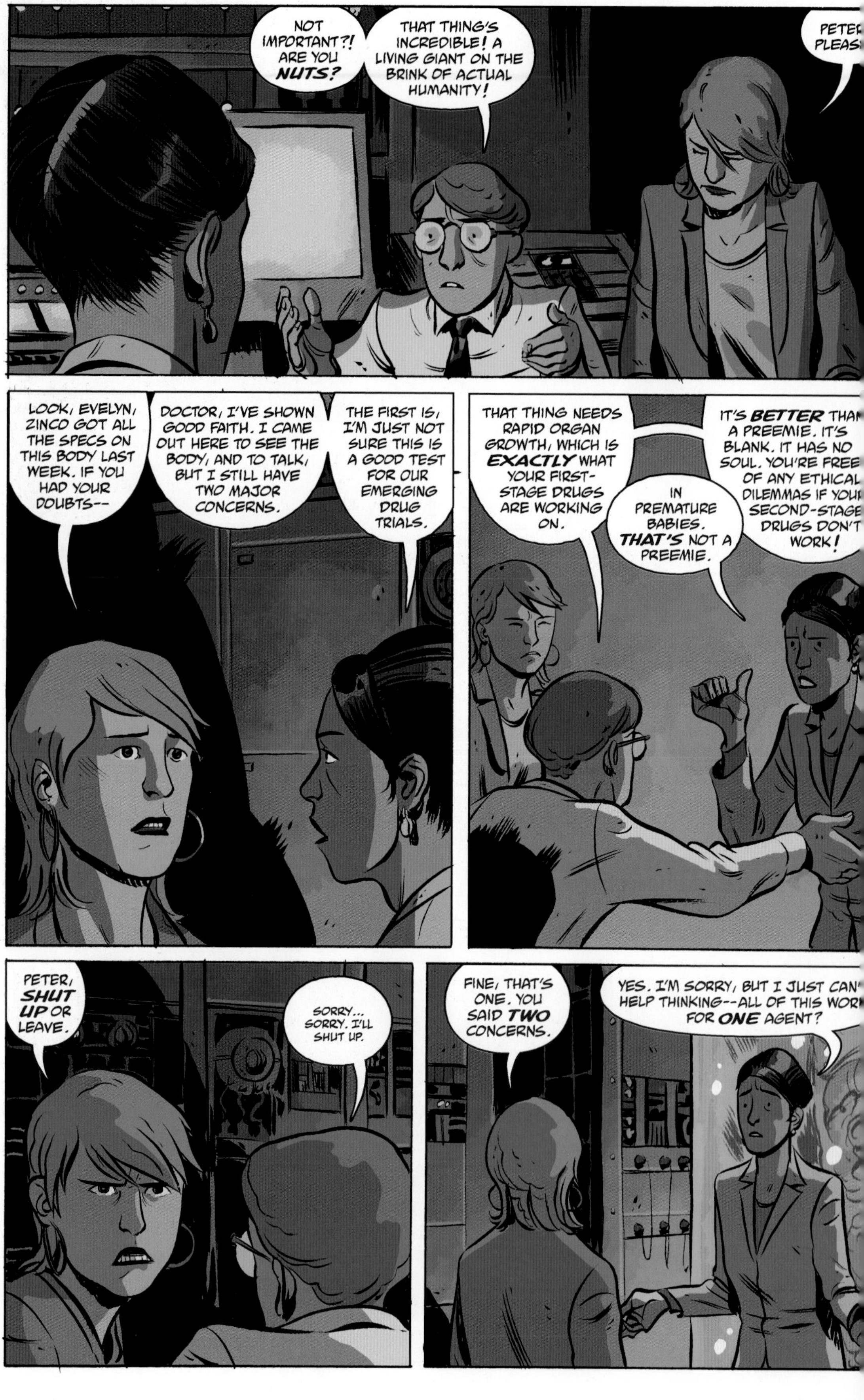
NOT IMPORTANT?! ARE YOU NUTS?
THAT THING'S INCREDIBLE! A LIVING GIANT ON THE BRINK OF ACTUAL HUMANITY!
PETE
PLEAS
LOOK, EVELYN, ZINCO GOT ALL THE SPECS ON THIS BODY LAST WEEK. IF YOU HAD YOUR DOUBTS--
DOCTOR, I'VE SHOWN GOOD FAITH. I CAME OUT HERE TO SEE THE BODY, AND TO TALK, BUT I STILL HAVE TWO MAJOR CONCERNS.
THE FIRST IS, I'M JUST NOT SURE THIS IS A GOOD TEST FOR OUR EMERGING DRUG TRIALS.
THAT THING NEEDS RAPID ORGAN GROWTH, WHICH IS EXACTLY WHAT YOUR FIRST-STAGE DRUGS ARE WORKING ON.
IN PREMATURE BABIES. THAT'S NOT A PREEMIE.
IT'S BETTER THA
A PREEMIE. IT'S BLANK. IT HAS NO SOUL. YOU'RE FREE
OF ANY ETHICAL DILEMMAS IF YOU
SECOND-STAGE DRUGS DON'T WORK!
PETER, SHUT UP OR LEAVE.
SORRY... SORRY. I'LL SHUT UP.
FINE, THAT'S ONE. YOU SAID TWO CONCERNS.
YES. I'M SORRY, BUT I JUST CAN
HELP THINKING--ALL OF THIS WOR
FOR ONE AGENT?

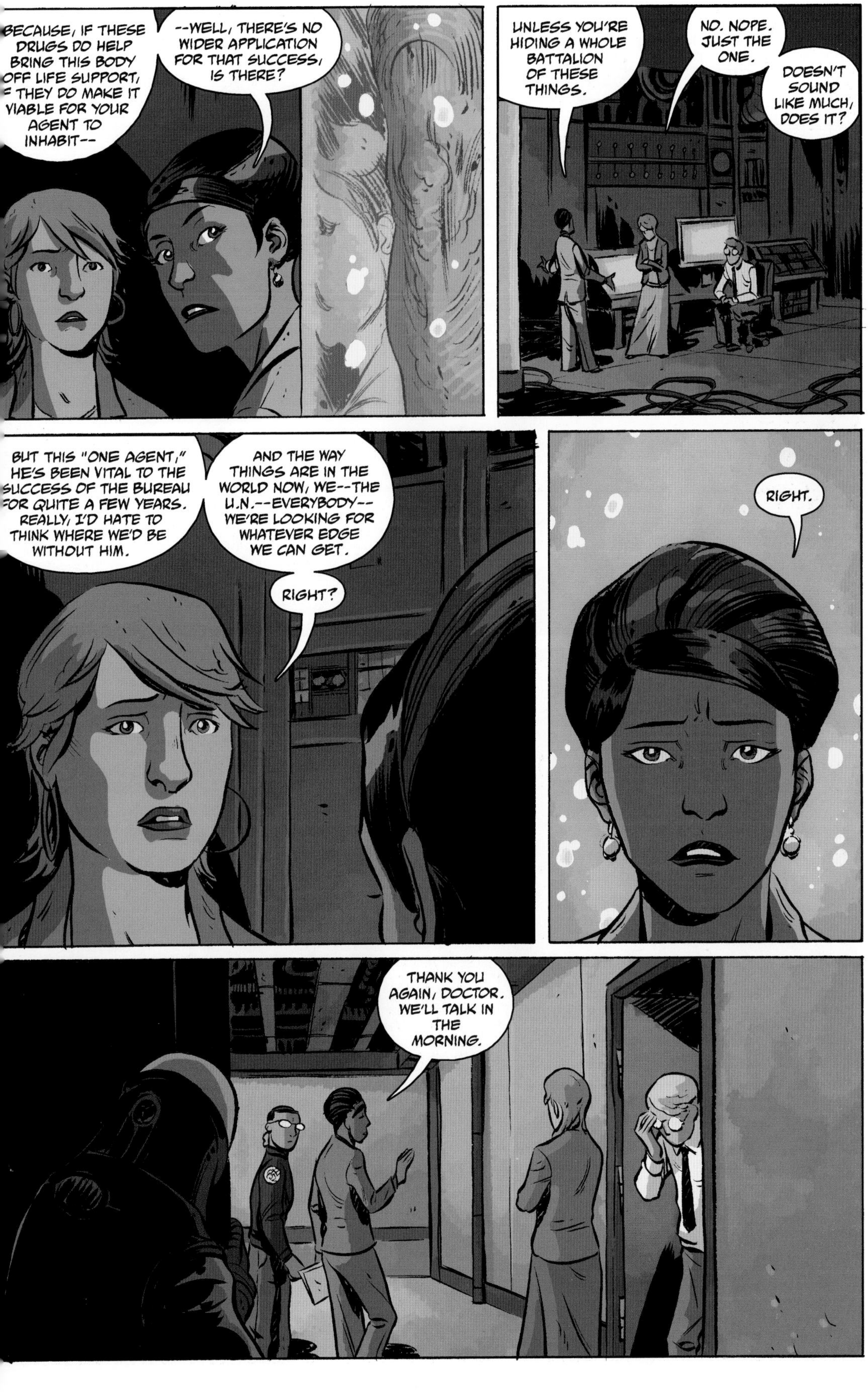
BECAUSE, IF THESE DRUGS DO HELP BRING THIS BODY OFF LIFE SUPPORT, IF THEY DO MAKE IT VIABLE FOR YOUR AGENT TO INHABIT--
--WELL, THERE'S NO WIDER APPLICATION FOR THAT SUCCESS, IS THERE?
UNLESS YOU'RE HIDING A WHOLE BATTALION OF THESE THINGS.
NO. NOPE. JUST THE ONE.
DOESN'T SOUND LIKE MUCH, DOES IT?
BUT THIS "ONE AGENT," HE'S BEEN VITAL TO THE SUCCESS OF THE BUREAU FOR QUITE A FEW YEARS. REALLY, I'D HATE TO THINK WHERE WE'D BE WITHOUT HIM.
AND THE WAY THINGS ARE IN THE WORLD NOW, WE--THE U.N.--EVERYBODY--WE'RE LOOKING FOR WHATEVER EDGE WE CAN GET.
RIGHT?
RIGHT.
THANK YOU AGAIN, DOCTOR. WE'LL TALK IN THE MORNING.

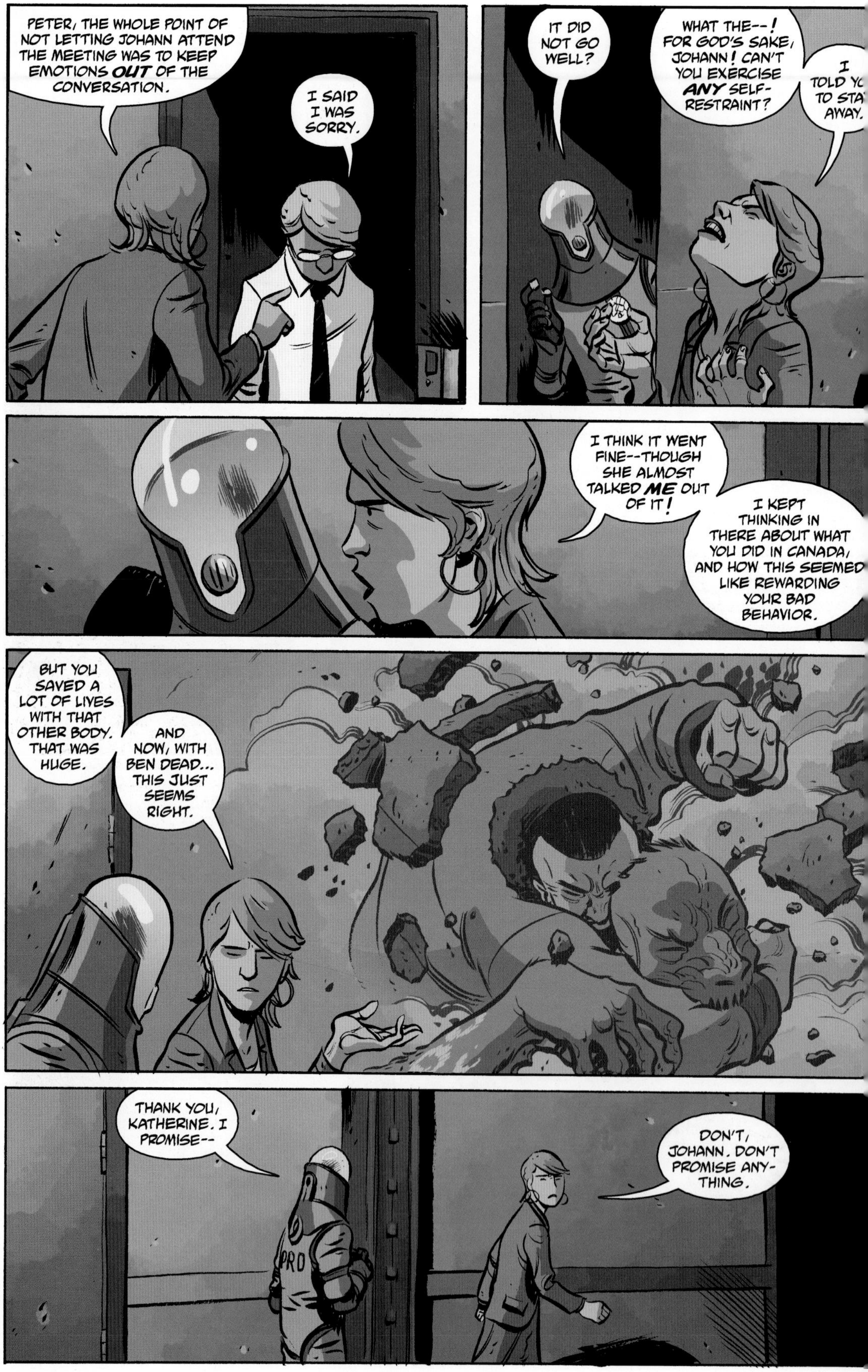
PETER, THE WHOLE POINT OF NOT LETTING JOHANN ATTEND THE MEETING WAS TO KEEP EMOTIONS OUT OF THE CONVERSATION.
I SAID I WAS SORRY.
IT DID NOT GO WELL?
WHAT THE--! FOR GOD'S SAKE, JOHANN! CAN'T YOU EXERCISE ANY SELF-RESTRAINT?
I TOLD YO TO STA AWAY.
I THINK IT WENT FINE--THOUGH SHE ALMOST TALKED ME OUT OF IT!
I KEPT THINKING IN THERE ABOUT WHAT YOU DID IN CANADA, AND HOW THIS SEEMED LIKE REWARDING YOUR BAD BEHAVIOR.
BUT YOU SAVED A LOT OF LIVES WITH THAT OTHER BODY. THAT WAS HUGE.
AND NOW, WITH BEN DEAD... THIS JUST SEEMS RIGHT.
THANK YOU, KATHERINE. I PROMISE--
DON'T, JOHANN. DON'T PROMISE ANY-THING.
PRD

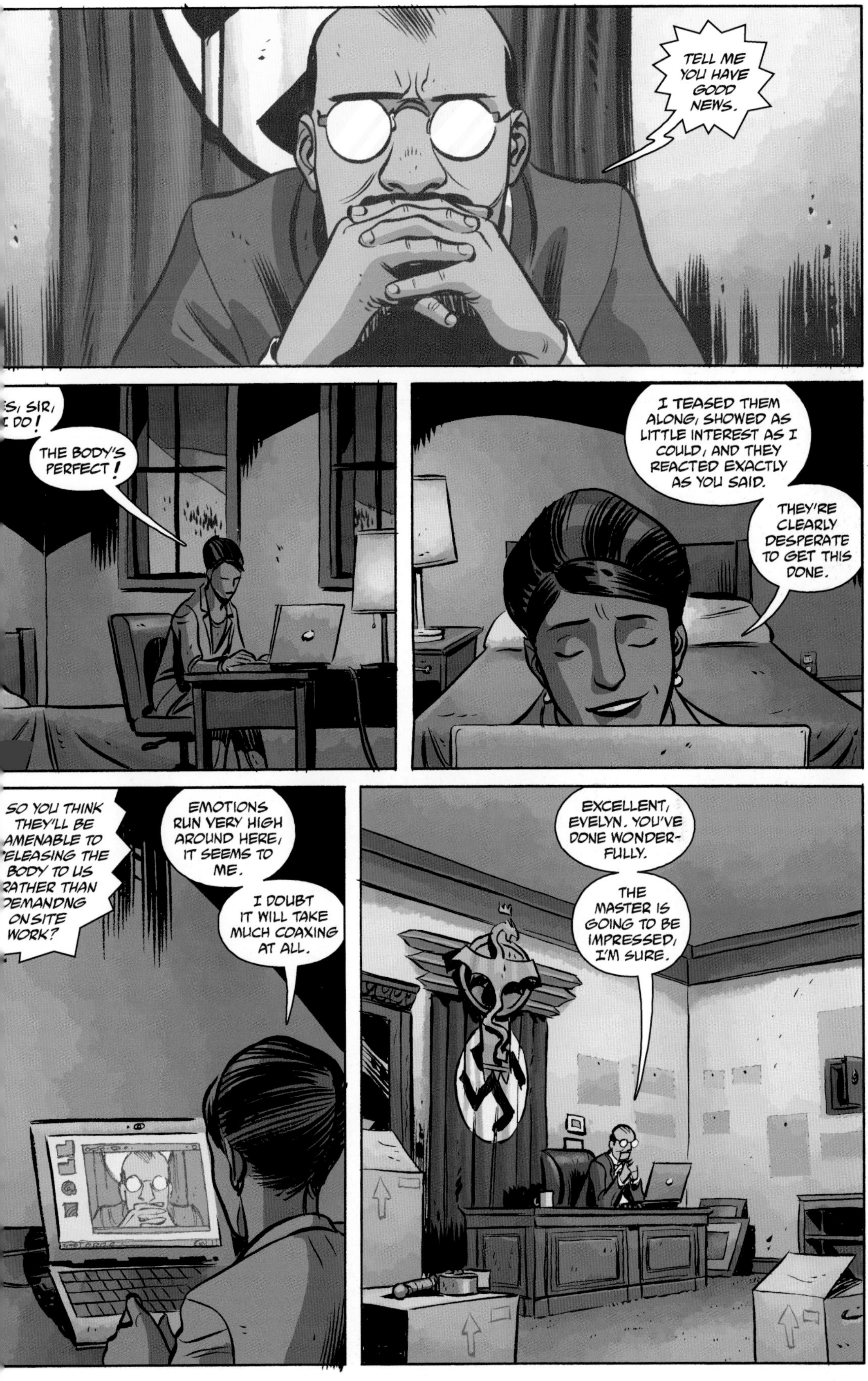
TELL ME YOU HAVE GOOD NEWS.
S, SIR, DO!
THE BODY'S PERFECT!
I TEASED THEM ALONG, SHOWED AS LITTLE INTEREST AS I COULD, AND THEY REACTED EXACTLY AS YOU SAID.
THEY'RE CLEARLY DESPERATE TO GET THIS DONE.
SO YOU THINK THEY'LL BE AMENABLE TO ELEASING THE BODY TO US RATHER THAN DEMANDNG ONSITE WORK?
EMOTIONS RUN VERY HIGH AROUND HERE, IT SEEMS TO ME.
I DOUBT IT WILL TAKE MUCH COAXING AT ALL.
EXCELLENT, EVELYN. YOU'VE DONE WONDER-FULLY.
THE MASTER IS GOING TO BE IMPRESSED, I'M SURE.

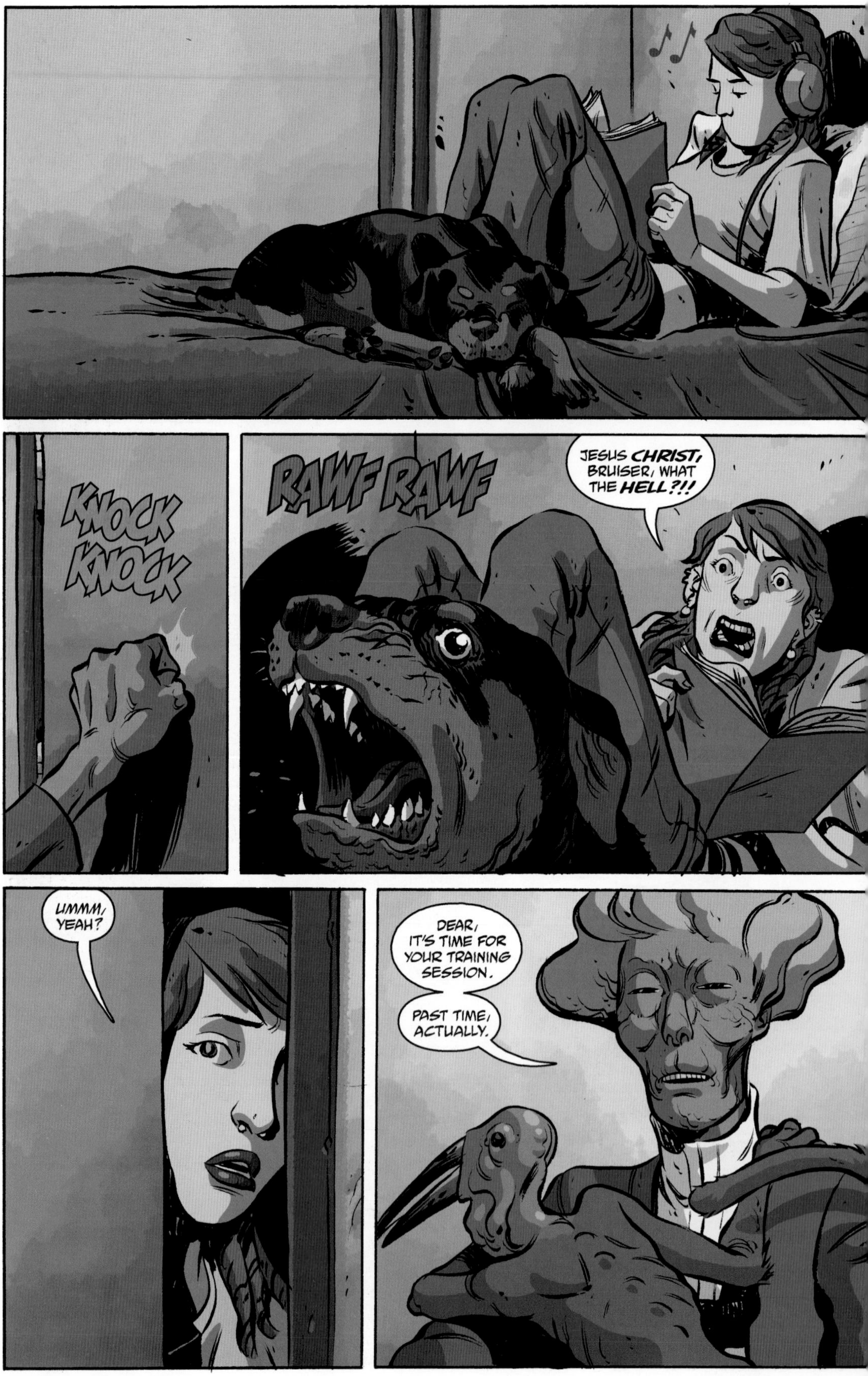

KNOCK KNOCK
RAWF RAWF
JESUS CHRIST, BRUISER, WHAT THE HELL?!!
UMMM, YEAH?
DEAR, IT'S TIME FOR YOUR TRAINING SESSION.
PAST TIME, ACTUALLY.

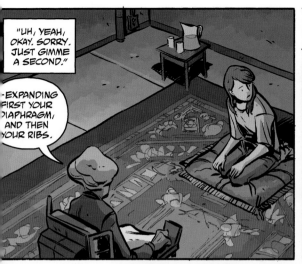

"UH, YEAH, OKAY. SORRY. JUST GIMME A SECOND."

--EXPANDING FIRST YOUR DIAPHRAGM, AND THEN YOUR RIBS.

HOW DEEP ARE WE? THAT ELEVATOR JUST KEPT GOING--

*FOCUS, GIRL!*

SLOWLY NOW, ON THE OUTWARD BREATH...

...OPEN YOUR MIND.

AND LET THE ANXIETIES PASS FROM YOUR HEART, TO YOUR EYES.

NO...NO, I DON'T LIKE IT.

THERE'S NOTHING TO BE AFRAID OF, DARLING. THEY ARE JUST YOUR FEELINGS GIVEN FORM. ONLY POSSIBILITIES, NOT REAL.

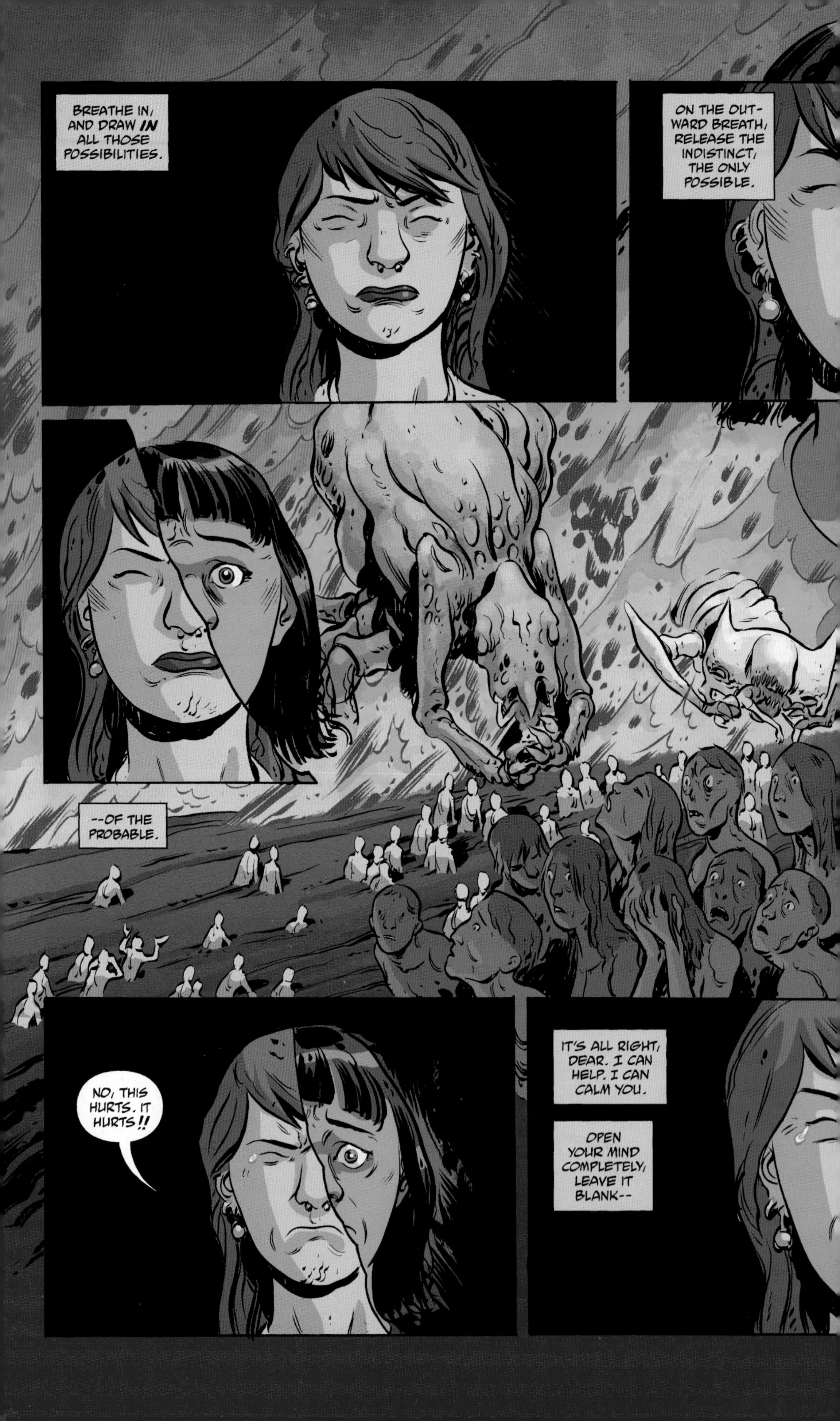
BREATHE IN, AND DRAW *IN* ALL THOSE POSSIBILITIES.
ON THE OUT-WARD BREATH, RELEASE THE INDISTINCT, THE ONLY POSSIBLE.
--OF THE PROBABLE.
NO, THIS HURTS. IT HURTS!!
IT'S ALL RIGHT, DEAR. I CAN HELP. I CAN CALM YOU.
OPEN YOUR MIND COMPLETELY, LEAVE IT BLANK--

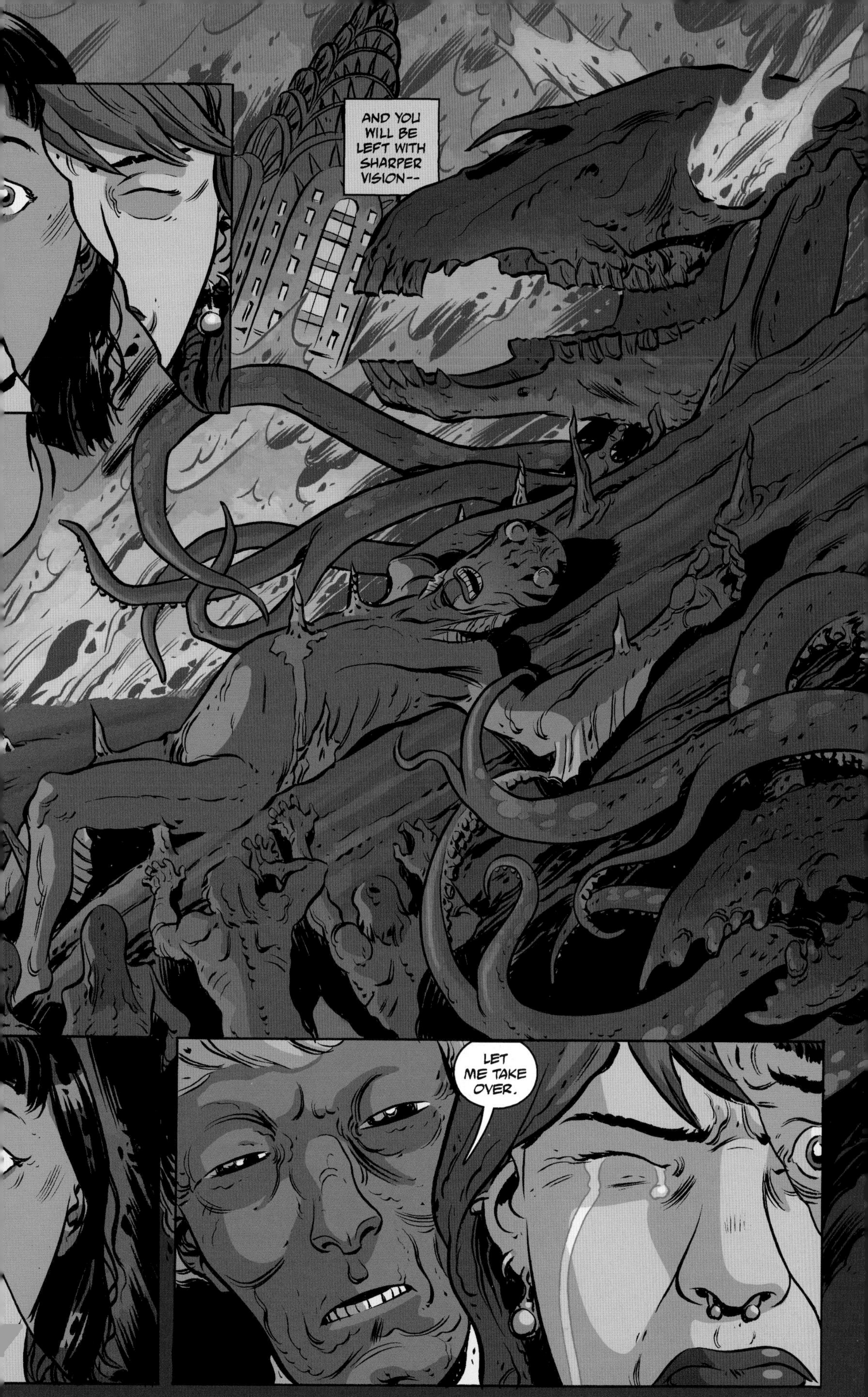
AND YOU WILL BE LEFT WITH SHARPER VISION--
LET ME TAKE OVER.

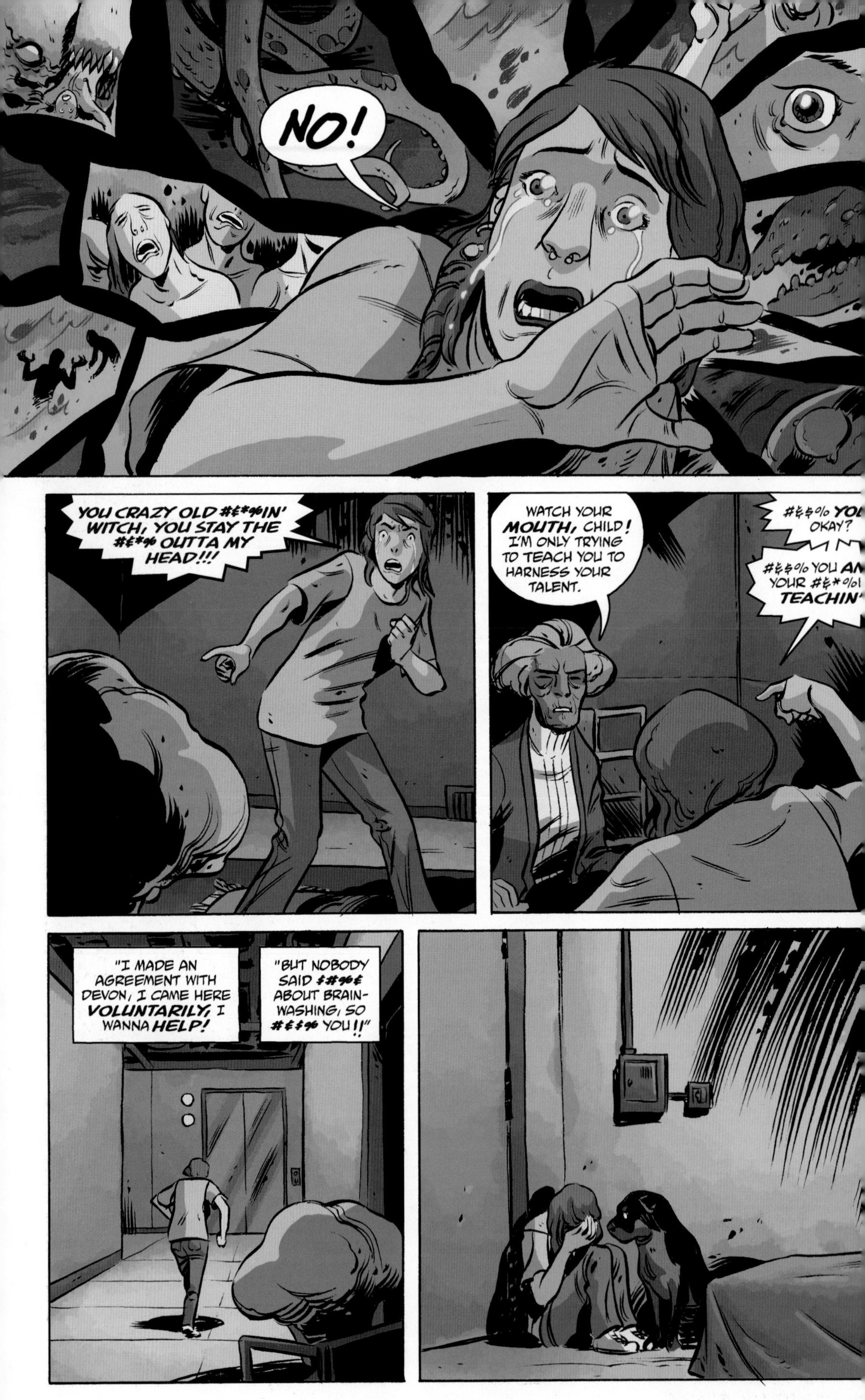

NO!
YOU CRAZY OLD #€*%IN' WITCH, YOU STAY THE #€*% OUTTA MY HEAD!!!
WATCH YOUR MOUTH, CHILD! I'M ONLY TRYING TO TEACH YOU TO HARNESS YOUR TALENT.
#€$% YOU OKAY?
#€$% YOU AN YOUR #€*%! TEACHIN'
"I MADE AN AGREEMENT WITH DEVON, I CAME HERE VOLUNTARILY, I WANNA HELP!
"BUT NOBODY SAID $#%€ ABOUT BRAIN-WASHING, SO #€$% YOU!!"

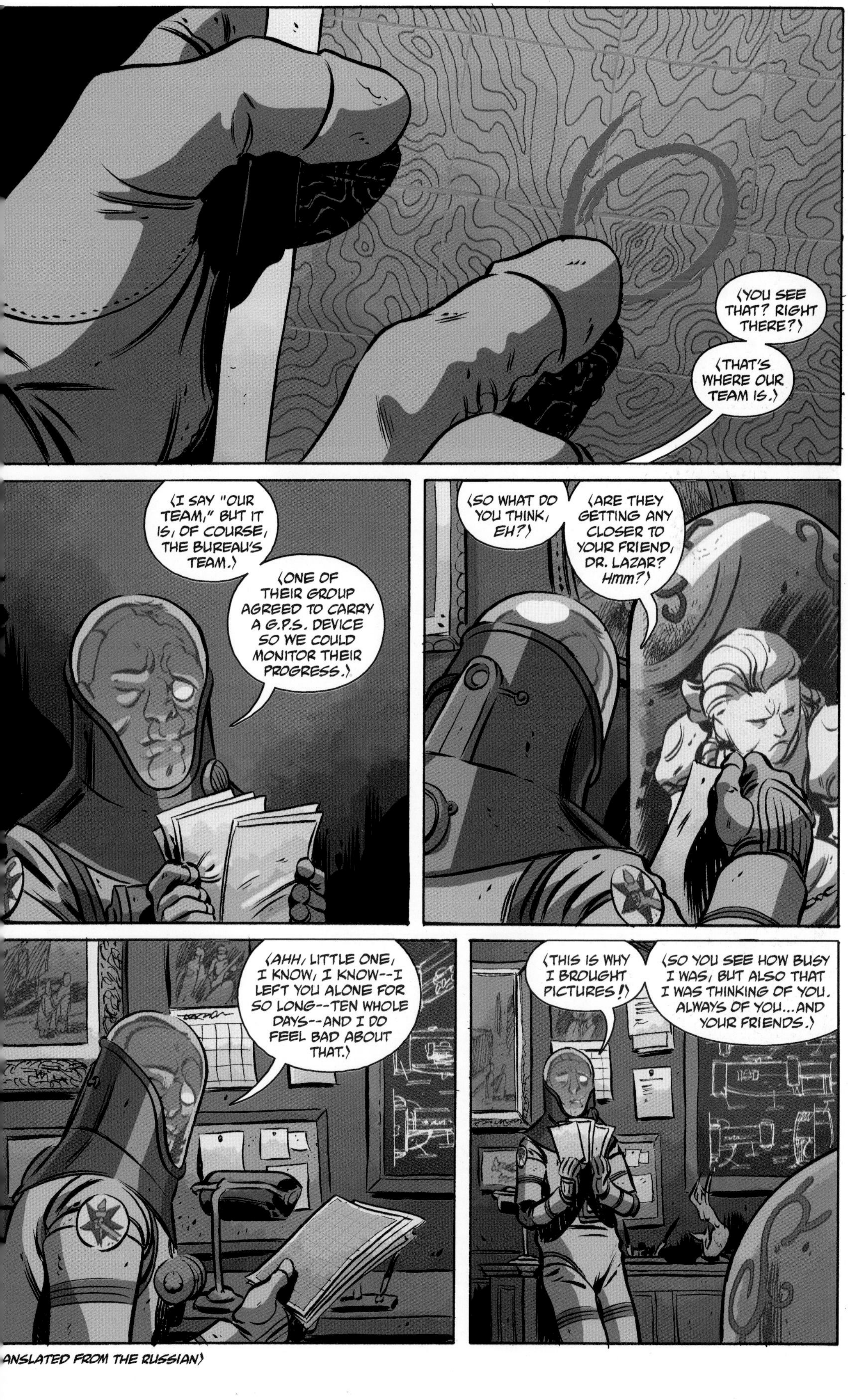
⟨YOU SEE THAT? RIGHT THERE?⟩
⟨THAT'S WHERE OUR TEAM IS.⟩
⟨I SAY "OUR TEAM," BUT IT IS, OF COURSE, THE BUREAU'S TEAM.⟩
⟨ONE OF THEIR GROUP AGREED TO CARRY A G.P.S. DEVICE SO WE COULD MONITOR THEIR PROGRESS.⟩
⟨SO WHAT DO YOU THINK, EH?⟩
⟨ARE THEY GETTING ANY CLOSER TO YOUR FRIEND, DR. LAZAR? Hmm?⟩
⟨AHH, LITTLE ONE, I KNOW, I KNOW--I LEFT YOU ALONE FOR SO LONG--TEN WHOLE DAYS--AND I DO FEEL BAD ABOUT THAT.⟩
⟨THIS IS WHY I BROUGHT PICTURES!⟩
⟨SO YOU SEE HOW BUSY I WAS, BUT ALSO THAT I WAS THINKING OF YOU. ALWAYS OF YOU...AND YOUR FRIENDS.⟩

ANSLATED FROM THE RUSSIAN⟩

⟨THEY ARE MARCHING, MARCHING ACROSS SCOTLAND, SNOW-FLAKE.⟩

⟨AND THEY WILL FIND LAZAR, I THINK.⟩

⟨THE B.P.R.D., THEY ARE VERY GOOD AT THEIR JOBS, AND I THINK THEY WILL FIND HIM.⟩

⟨BUT *WHAT* WILL THEY FIND?⟩

⟨HE IS SUCH A LITTLE MAN, A NOBODY, BUT OUR INTELLIGENCE SUGGESTS THAT HE'S GATHERING A FOLLOWING THERE, SOMEWHERE IN SCOTLAND.⟩

⟨I WONDER WHO THEY THINK *HE* IS.⟩

⟨I WONDER EVEN WHO HE THINKS HE IS.⟩

⟨TELL ME, SNOW-FLAKE.⟩

⟨WHO DO *YOU* THINK HE IS?⟩

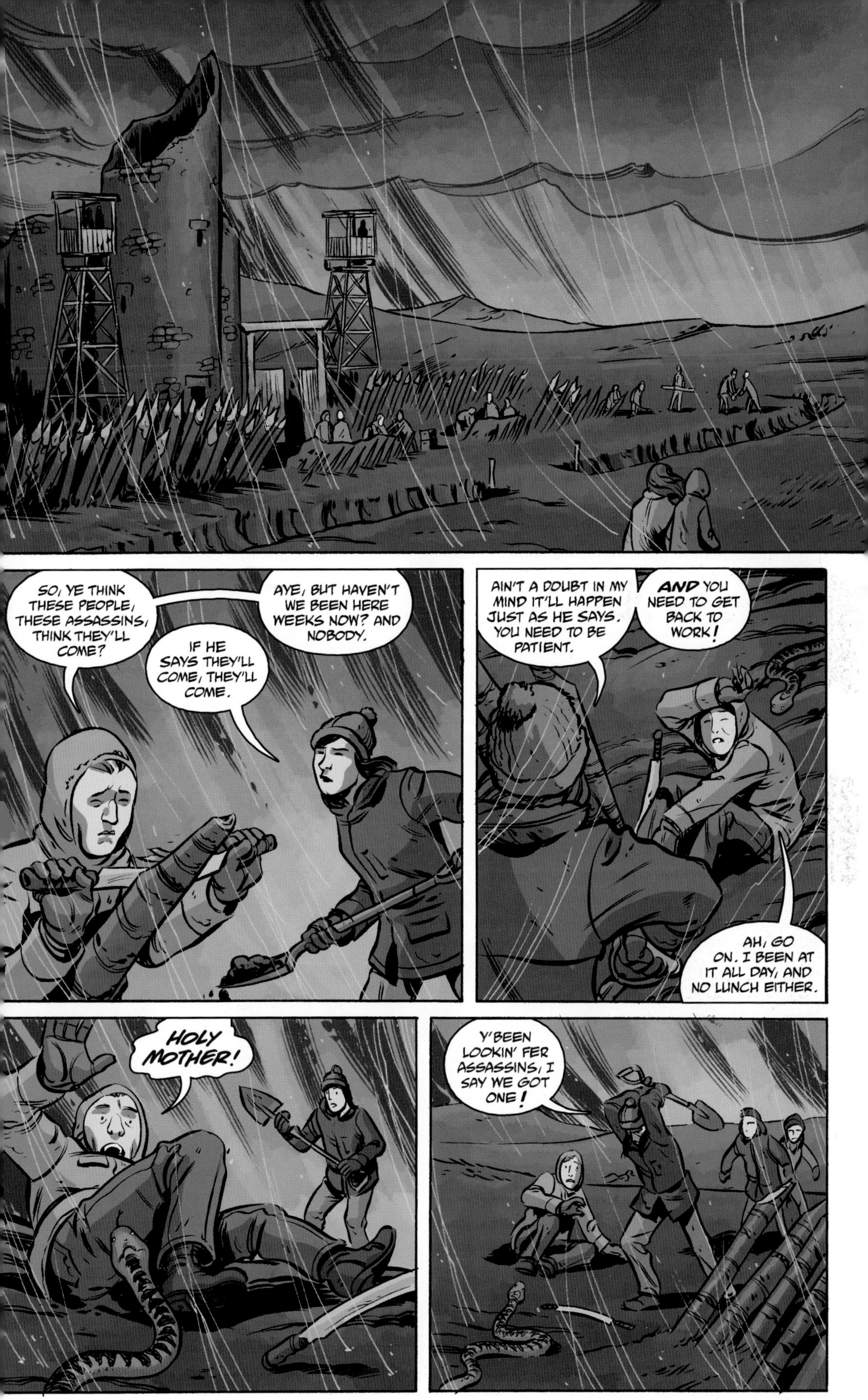
SO, YE THINK THESE PEOPLE, THESE ASSASSINS, THINK THEY'LL COME?
IF HE SAYS THEY'LL COME, THEY'LL COME.
AYE, BUT HAVEN'T WE BEEN HERE WEEKS NOW? AND NOBODY.
AIN'T A DOUBT IN MY MIND IT'LL HAPPEN JUST AS HE SAYS. YOU NEED TO BE PATIENT.
AND YOU NEED TO GET BACK TO WORK!
AH, GO ON. I BEEN AT IT ALL DAY, AND NO LUNCH EITHER.
HOLY MOTHER!
Y'BEEN LOOKIN' FER ASSASSINS, I SAY WE GOT ONE!

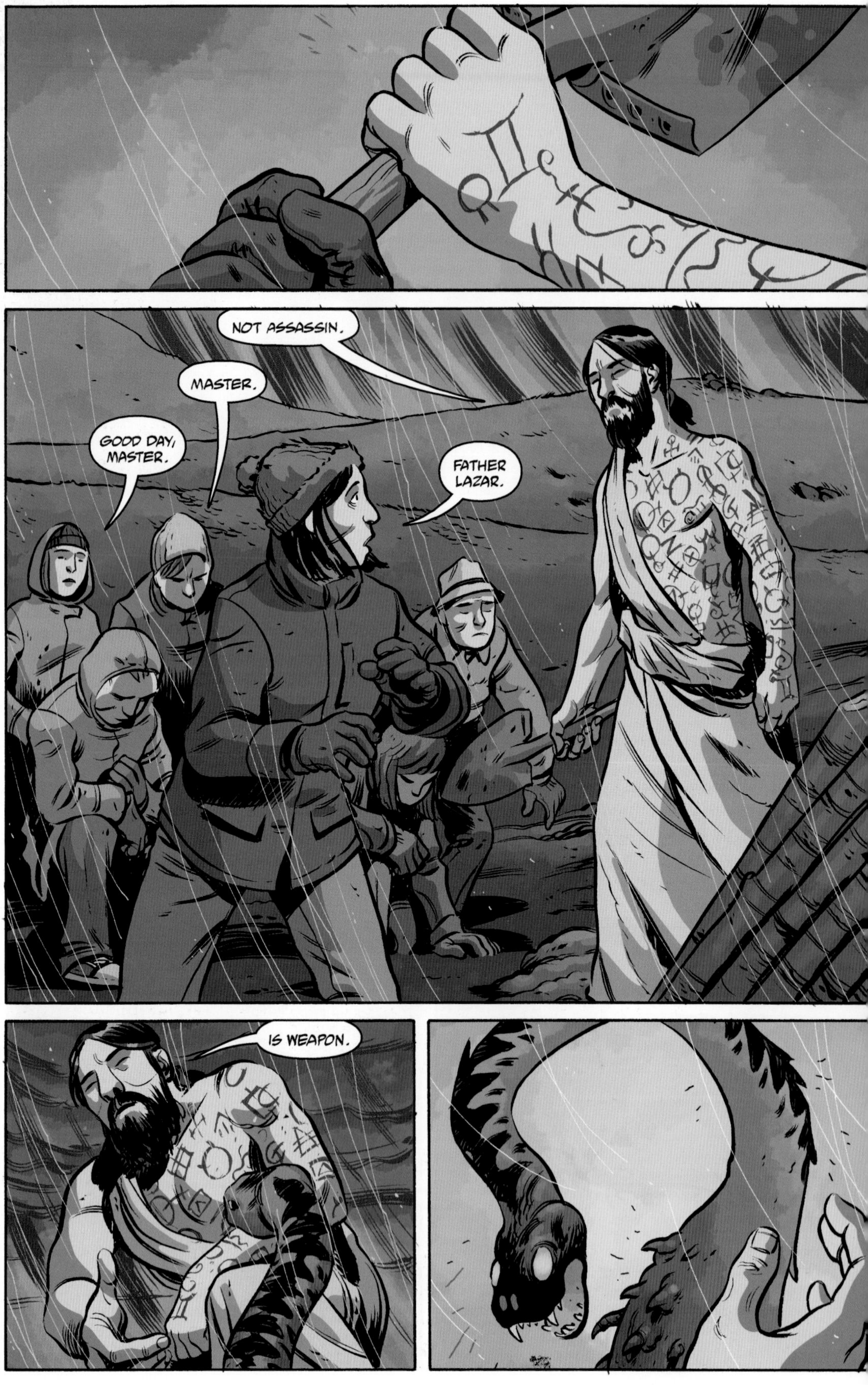
NOT ASSASSIN.
MASTER.
GOOD DAY, MASTER.
FATHER LAZAR.
IS WEAPON.

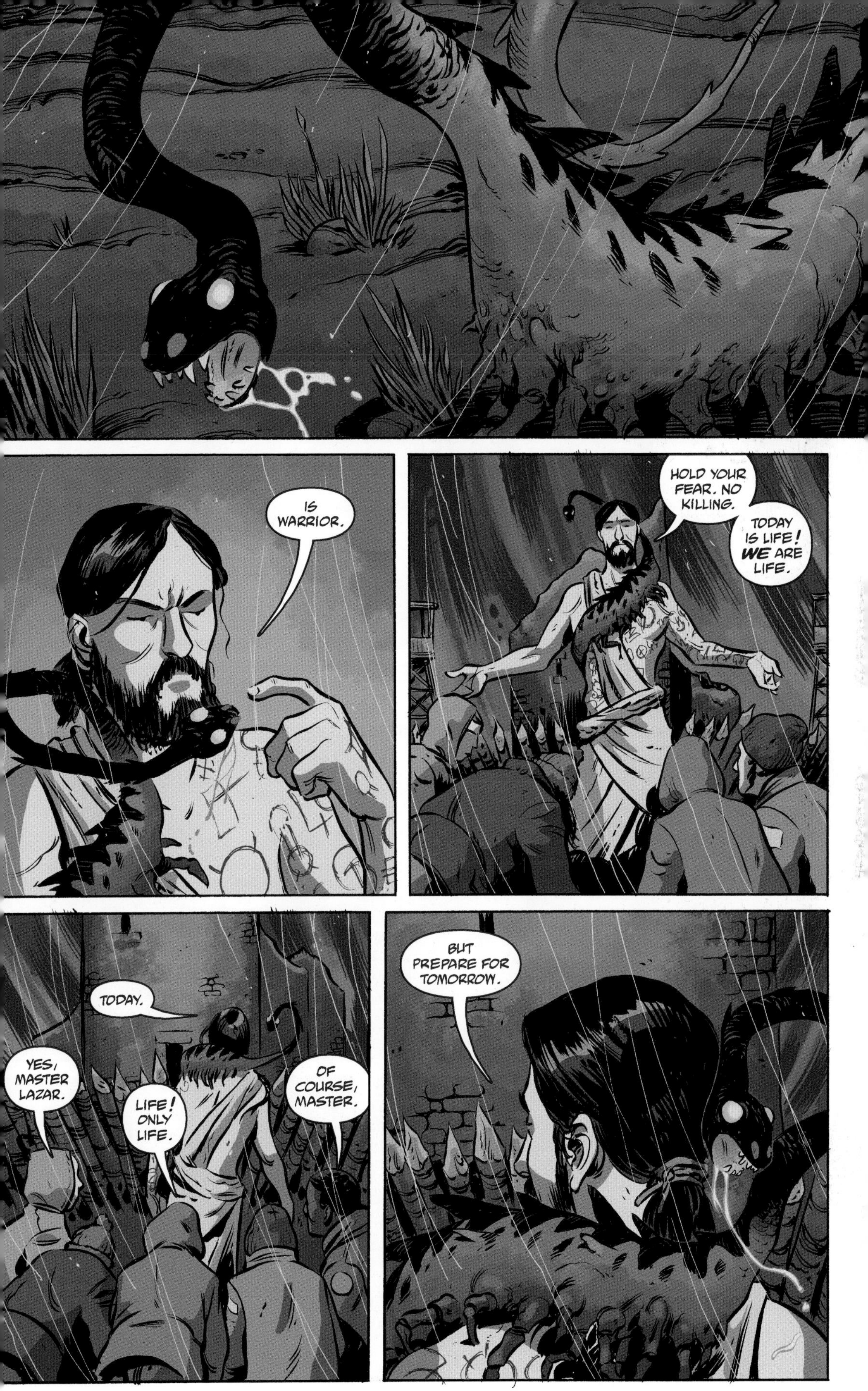
IS WARRIOR.
HOLD YOUR FEAR. NO KILLING.
TODAY IS LIFE! WE ARE LIFE.
TODAY.
YES, MASTER LAZAR.
LIFE! ONLY LIFE.
OF COURSE, MASTER.
BUT PREPARE FOR TOMORROW.

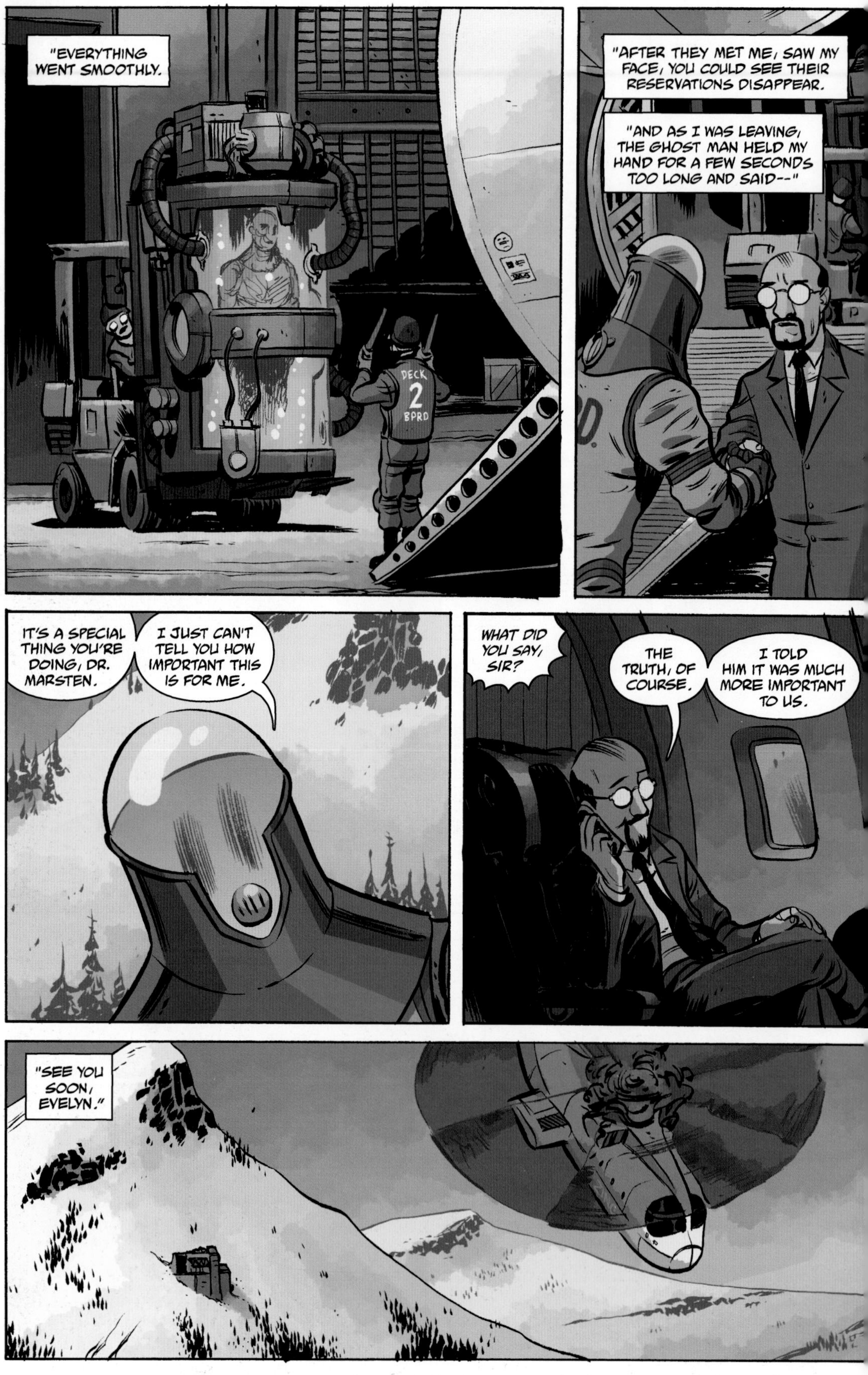
"EVERYTHING WENT SMOOTHLY.
DECK 2 BPRD
"AFTER THEY MET ME, SAW MY FACE, YOU COULD SEE THEIR RESERVATIONS DISAPPEAR.
"AND AS I WAS LEAVING, THE GHOST MAN HELD MY HAND FOR A FEW SECONDS TOO LONG AND SAID--"
IT'S A SPECIAL THING YOU'RE DOING, DR. MARSTEN.
I JUST CAN'T TELL YOU HOW IMPORTANT THIS IS FOR ME.
WHAT DID YOU SAY, SIR?
THE TRUTH, OF COURSE.
I TOLD HIM IT WAS MUCH MORE IMPORTANT TO US.
"SEE YOU SOON, EVELYN."

# THE RETURN OF THE MASTER **CHAPTER THREE**

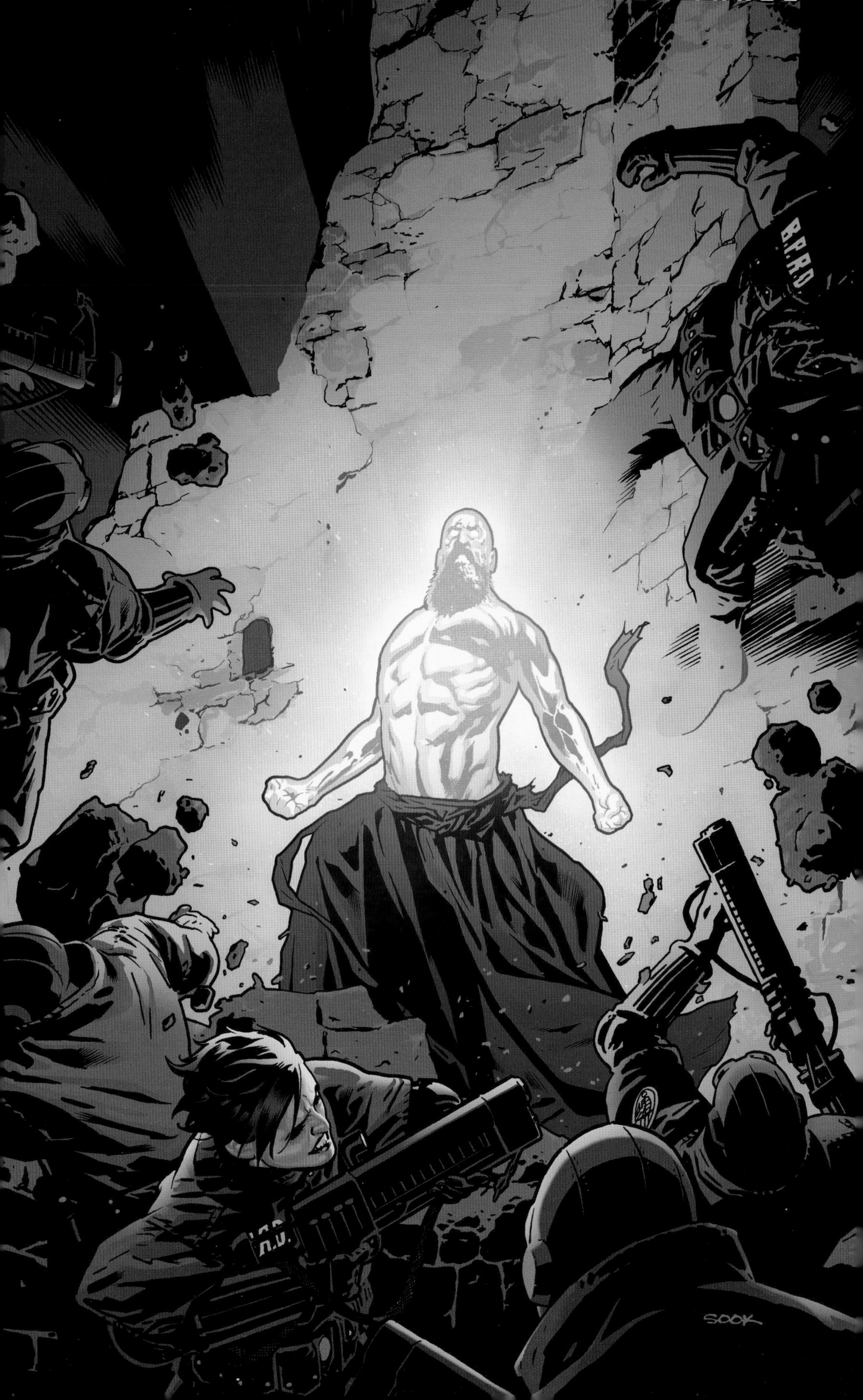
B.P.R.D.
SOOK

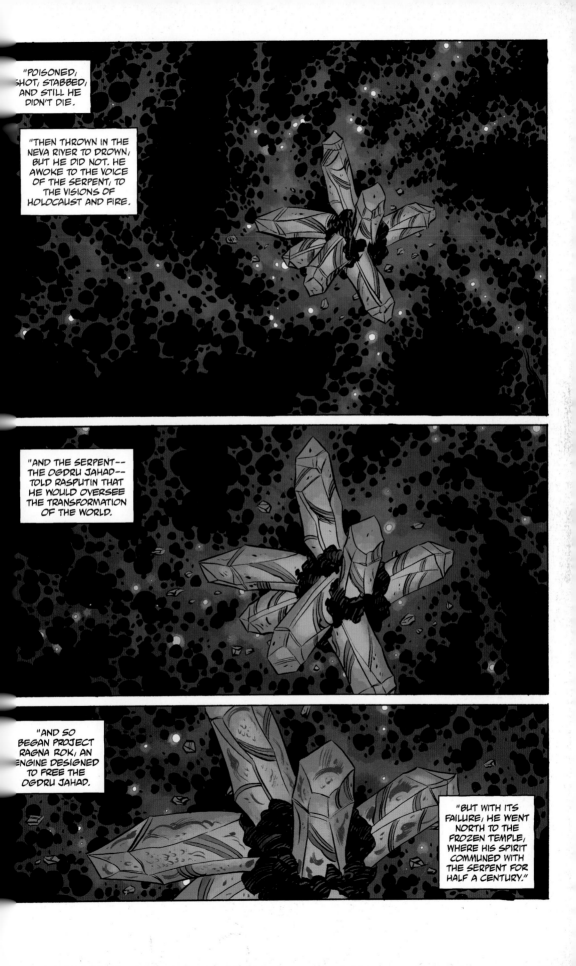

"POISONED, SHOT, STABBED, AND STILL HE DIDN'T DIE.

"THEN THROWN IN THE NEVA RIVER TO DROWN, BUT HE DID NOT. HE AWOKE TO THE VOICE OF THE SERPENT, TO THE VISIONS OF HOLOCAUST AND FIRE.

"AND THE SERPENT-- THE OGDRU JAHAD-- TOLD RASPUTIN THAT HE WOULD OVERSEE THE TRANSFORMATION OF THE WORLD.

"AND SO BEGAN PROJECT RAGNA ROK, AN ENGINE DESIGNED TO FREE THE OGDRU JAHAD.

"BUT WITH ITS FAILURE, HE WENT NORTH TO THE FROZEN TEMPLE, WHERE HIS SPIRIT COMMUNED WITH THE SERPENT FOR HALF A CENTURY."

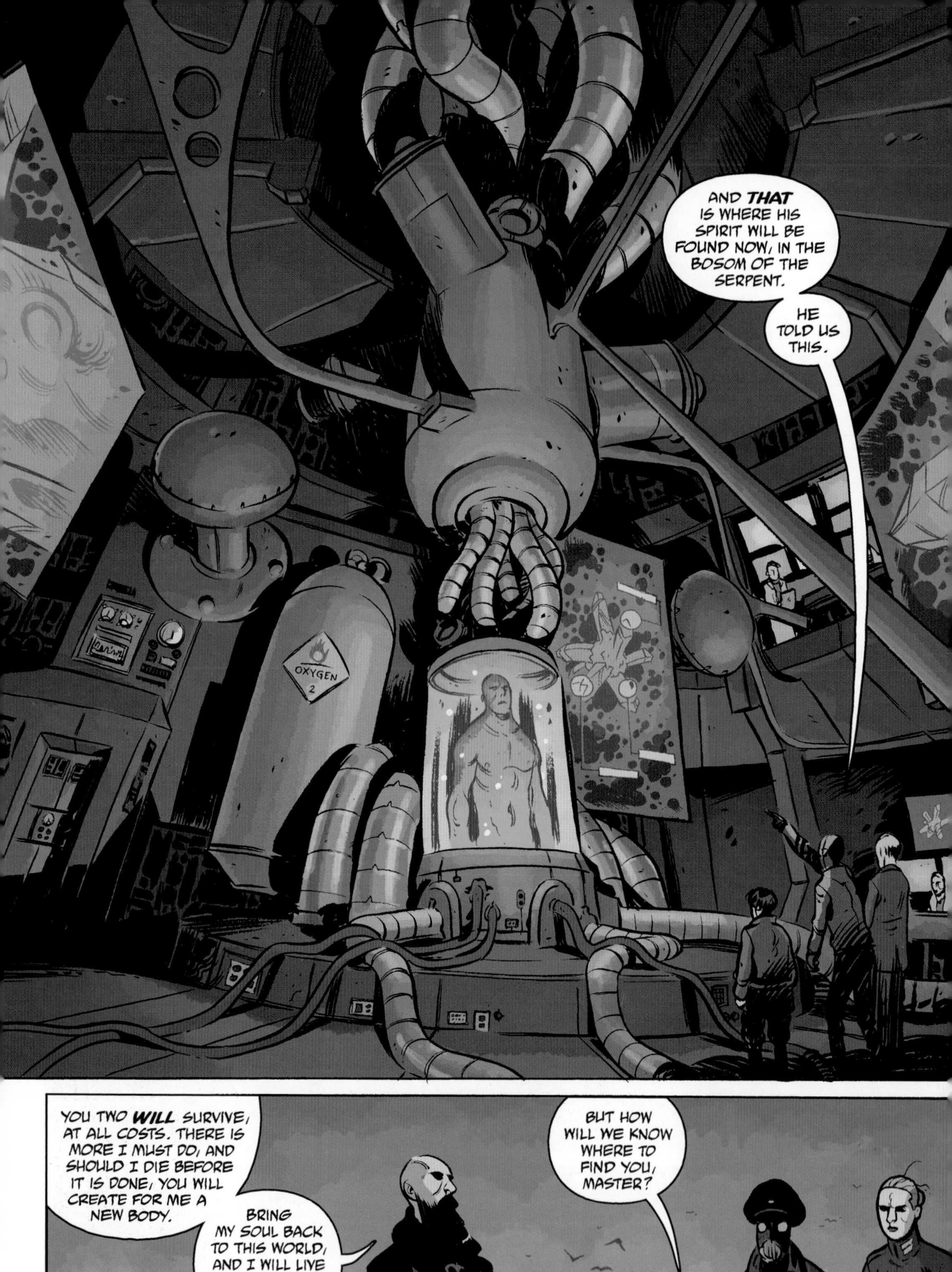
OXYGEN 2
AND THAT IS WHERE HIS SPIRIT WILL BE FOUND NOW, IN THE BOSOM OF THE SERPENT.
HE TOLD US THIS.

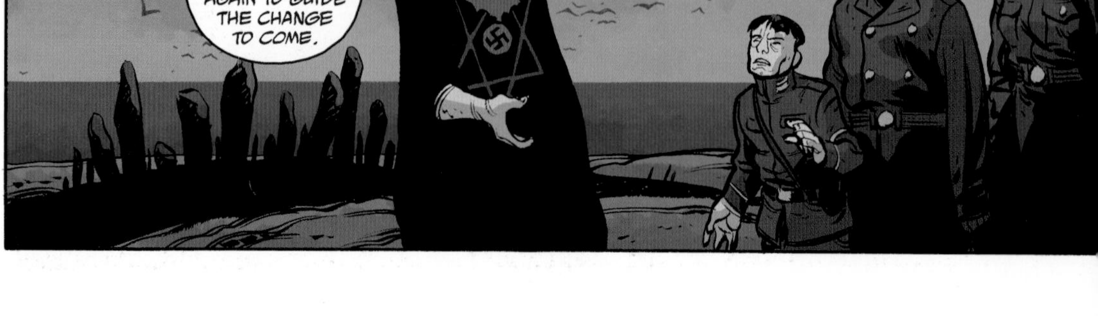
YOU TWO WILL SURVIVE, AT ALL COSTS. THERE IS MORE I MUST DO, AND SHOULD I DIE BEFORE IT IS DONE, YOU WILL CREATE FOR ME A NEW BODY.
BRING MY SOUL BACK TO THIS WORLD, AND I WILL LIVE AGAIN TO GUIDE THE CHANGE TO COME.
BUT HOW WILL WE KNOW WHERE TO FIND YOU, MASTER?

WITH **MY** MASTER, WITH THE DRAGON.

THERE WILL BE A SIGN, AND YOU WILL KNOW IT IS TIME.

WELL, ISN'T THAT EXACTLY WHAT WE'VE DONE?

WE HAVE A NEW, POWERFUL BODY AND WE'VE FOUND THE OGDRU JAHAD'S PRISON.

ONCE WE ISOLATE A HUMAN SOUL AMONG ALL THE ENERGY SIGNATURES RADIATING FROM THOSE CRYSTALS, WE'LL PULL HIM BACK.

IT **IS** IMPRESSIVE, HERR MARSTEN. BUT IS THERE NO APPREHENSION ABOUT OUTSOURCING **THIS** CRUCIAL COMPONENT OF THE PROCESS? IF LEOPOLD AND I HAD ONLY A BIT MORE TIME--

OXYGEN 2

KARL, WHAT HAPPENED WAS **MY** FAULT. YOU DIDN'T HAVE THE RIGHT EQUIPMENT. IT'S NO REFLECTION ON YOUR ABILITIES.

AND WE'RE ON A TIMETABLE, AREN'T WE?

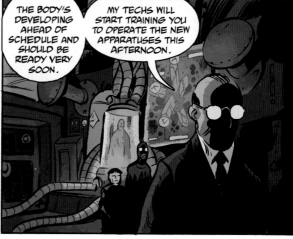

THE BODY'S DEVELOPING AHEAD OF SCHEDULE AND SHOULD BE READY VERY SOON.

MY TECHS WILL START TRAINING YOU TO OPERATE THE NEW APPARATUSES THIS AFTERNOON.

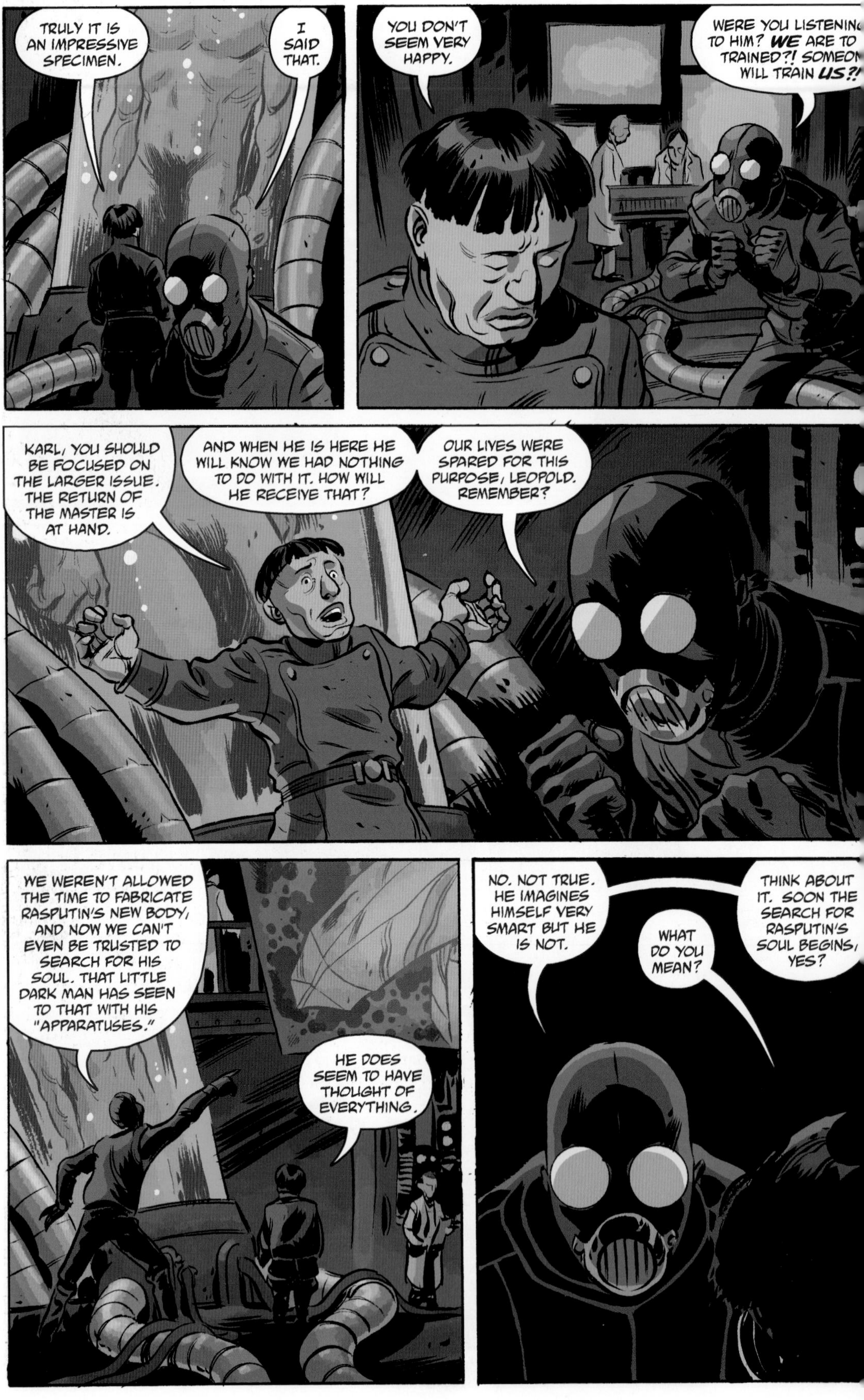
TRULY IT IS AN IMPRESSIVE SPECIMEN.
I SAID THAT.
YOU DON'T SEEM VERY HAPPY.
WERE YOU LISTENIN
TO HIM? WE ARE TO
TRAINED?! SOMEO
WILL TRAIN US?!
KARL, YOU SHOULD BE FOCUSED ON THE LARGER ISSUE. THE RETURN OF THE MASTER IS AT HAND.
AND WHEN HE IS HERE HE WILL KNOW WE HAD NOTHING TO DO WITH IT. HOW WILL HE RECEIVE THAT?
OUR LIVES WERE SPARED FOR THIS PURPOSE, LEOPOLD. REMEMBER?
WE WEREN'T ALLOWED THE TIME TO FABRICATE RASPUTIN'S NEW BODY, AND NOW WE CAN'T EVEN BE TRUSTED TO SEARCH FOR HIS SOUL. THAT LITTLE DARK MAN HAS SEEN TO THAT WITH HIS "APPARATUSES."
HE DOES SEEM TO HAVE THOUGHT OF EVERYTHING.
THINK ABOUT IT. SOON THE SEARCH FOR RASPUTIN'S SOUL BEGINS, YES?
WHAT DO YOU MEAN?
NO. NOT TRUE. HE IMAGINES HIMSELF VERY SMART BUT HE IS NOT.

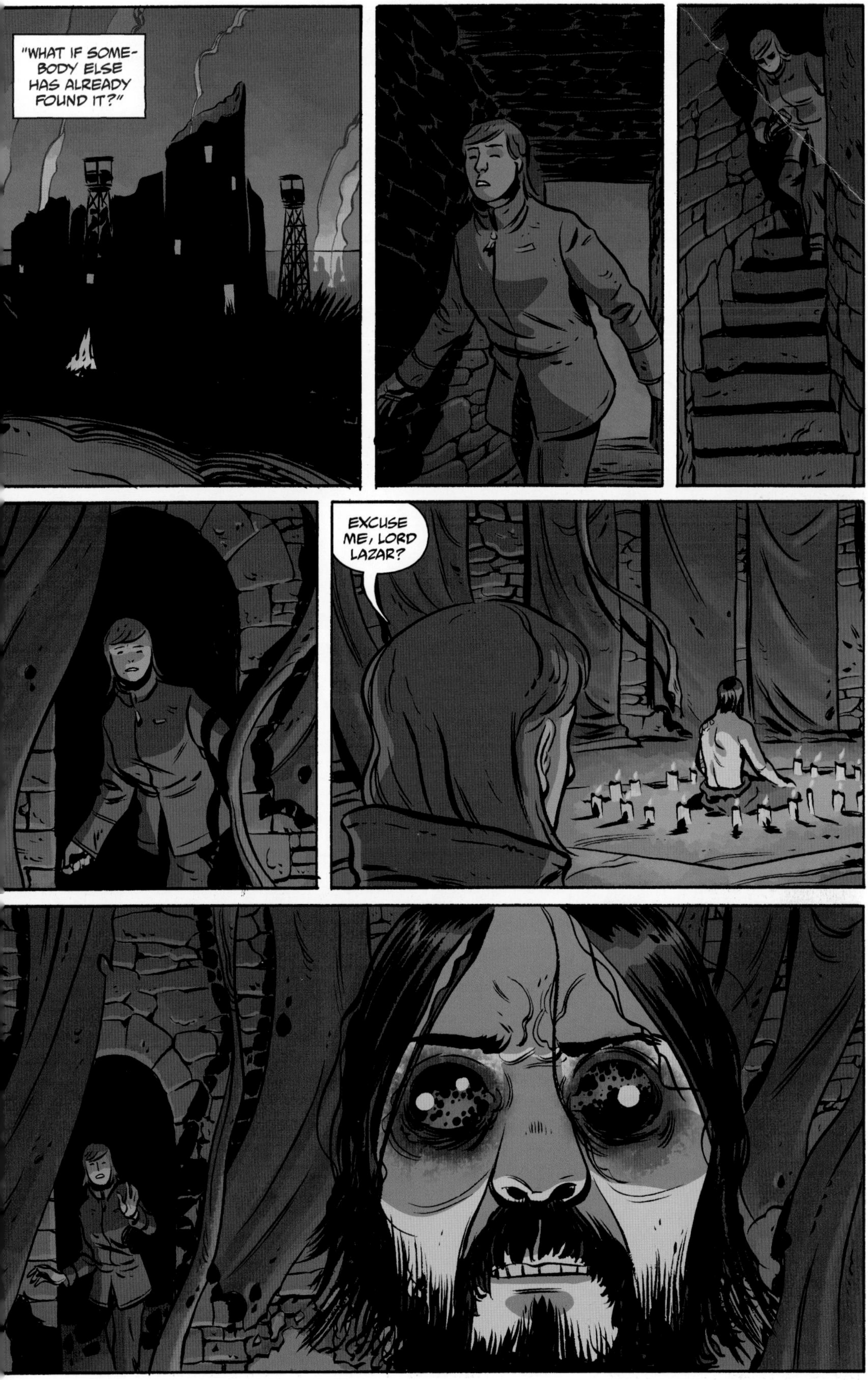
"WHAT IF SOMEBODY ELSE HAS ALREADY FOUND IT?"
EXCUSE ME, LORD LAZAR?

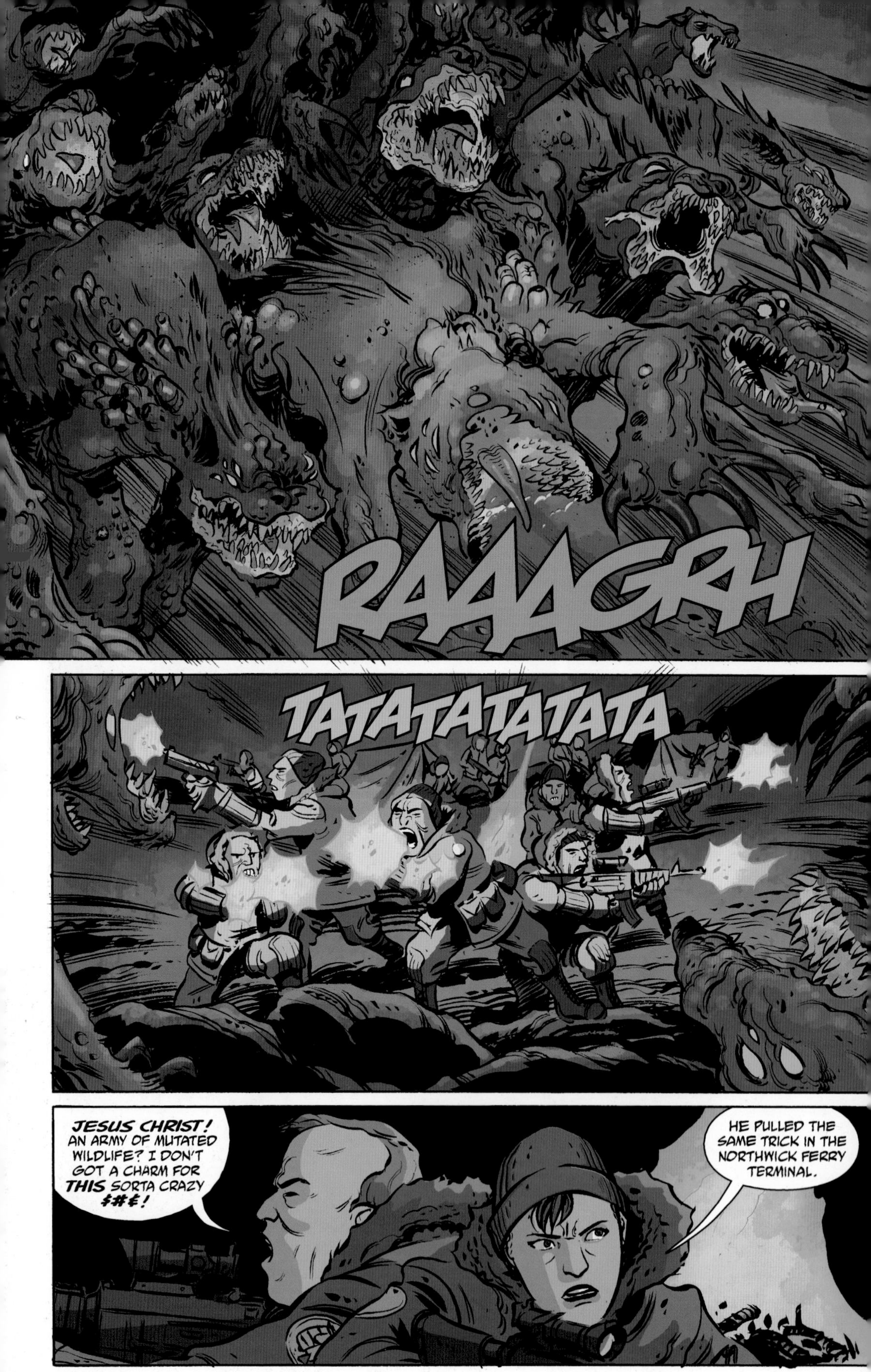
RAAAGRH
TATATATATATA
JESUS CHRIST! AN ARMY OF MUTATED WILDLIFE? I DON'T GOT A CHARM FOR THIS SORTA CRAZY $#€!
HE PULLED THE SAME TRICK IN THE NORTHWICK FERRY TERMINAL.

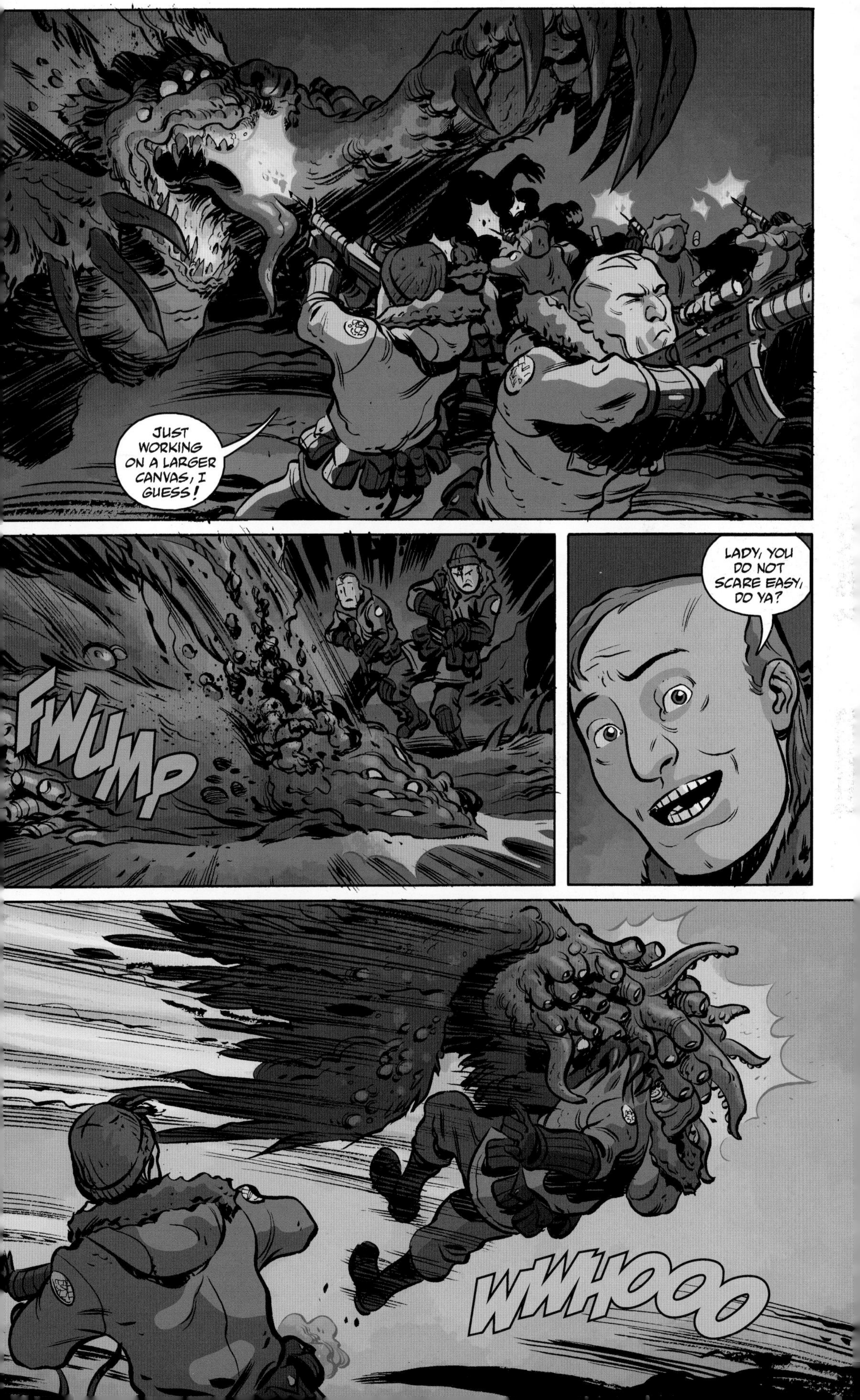
JUST WORKING ON A LARGER CANVAS, I GUESS!
FWUMP
LADY, YOU DO NOT SCARE EASY, DO YA?
WWHOOO

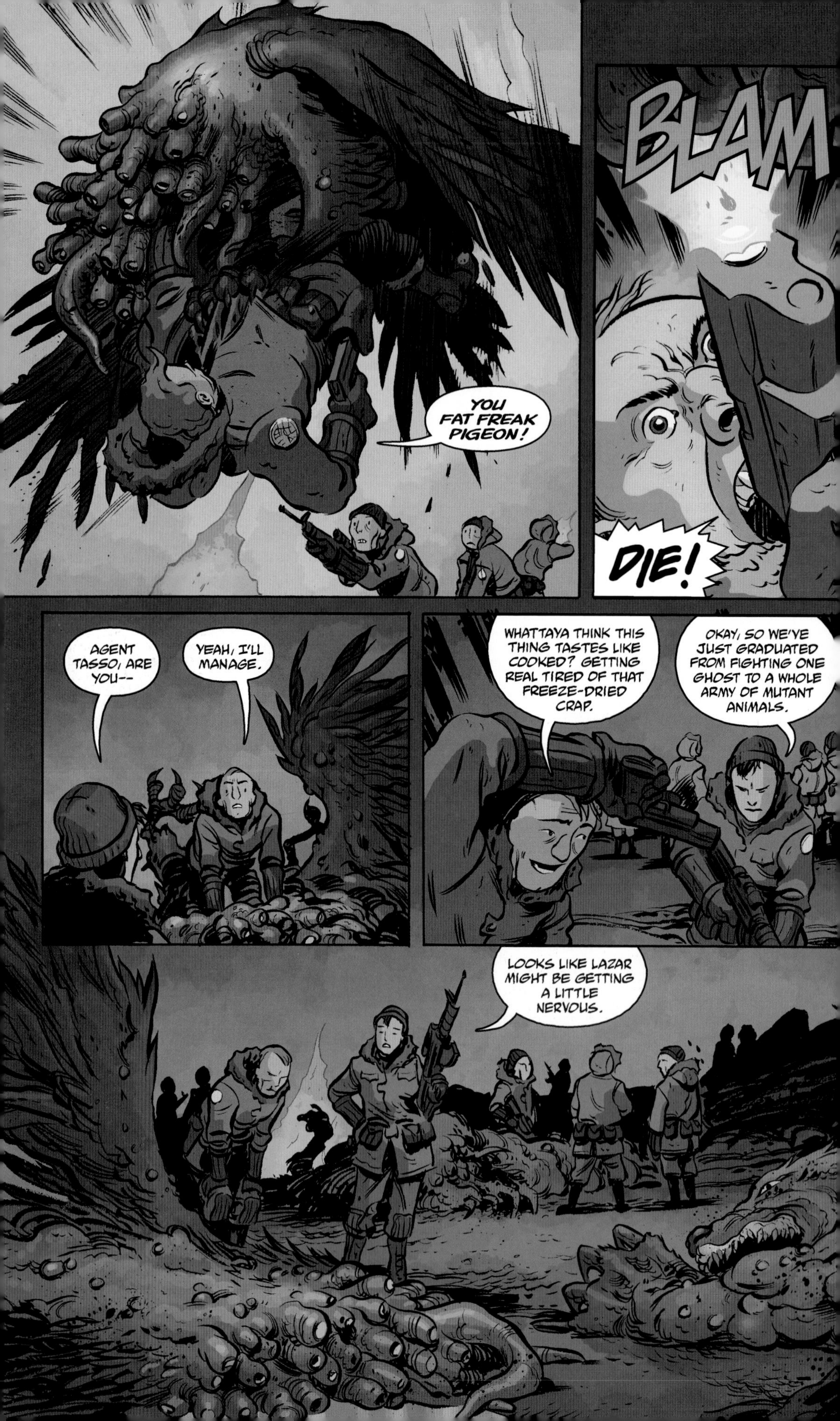

YOU FAT FREAK PIGEON!
BLAM
DIE!
AGENT TASSO, ARE YOU--
YEAH, I'LL MANAGE.
WHATTAYA THINK THIS THING TASTES LIKE COOKED? GETTING REAL TIRED OF THAT FREEZE-DRIED CRAP.
OKAY, SO WE'VE JUST GRADUATED FROM FIGHTING ONE GHOST TO A WHOLE ARMY OF MUTANT ANIMALS.
LOOKS LIKE LAZAR MIGHT BE GETTING A LITTLE NERVOUS.

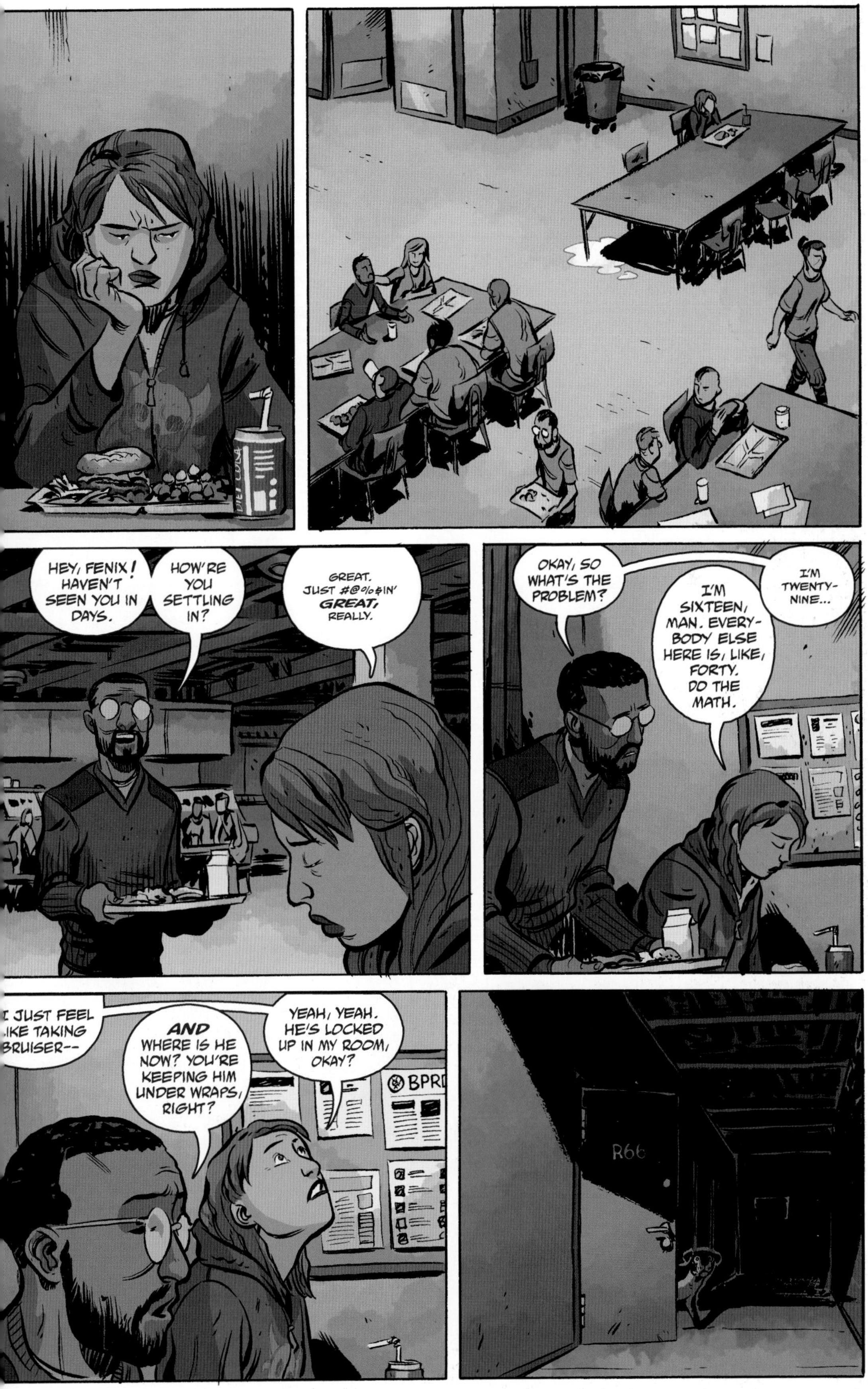
DIET COLA
HEY, FENIX! HAVEN'T SEEN YOU IN DAYS.
HOW'RE YOU SETTLING IN?
GREAT. JUST #@%$IN' GREAT, REALLY.
OKAY, SO WHAT'S THE PROBLEM?
I'M SIXTEEN, MAN. EVERYBODY ELSE HERE IS, LIKE, FORTY. DO THE MATH.
I'M TWENTY-NINE...
I JUST FEEL IKE TAKING RUISER--
AND WHERE IS HE NOW? YOU'RE KEEPING HIM UNDER WRAPS, RIGHT?
YEAH, YEAH. HE'S LOCKED UP IN MY ROOM, OKAY?
BPRD
R66

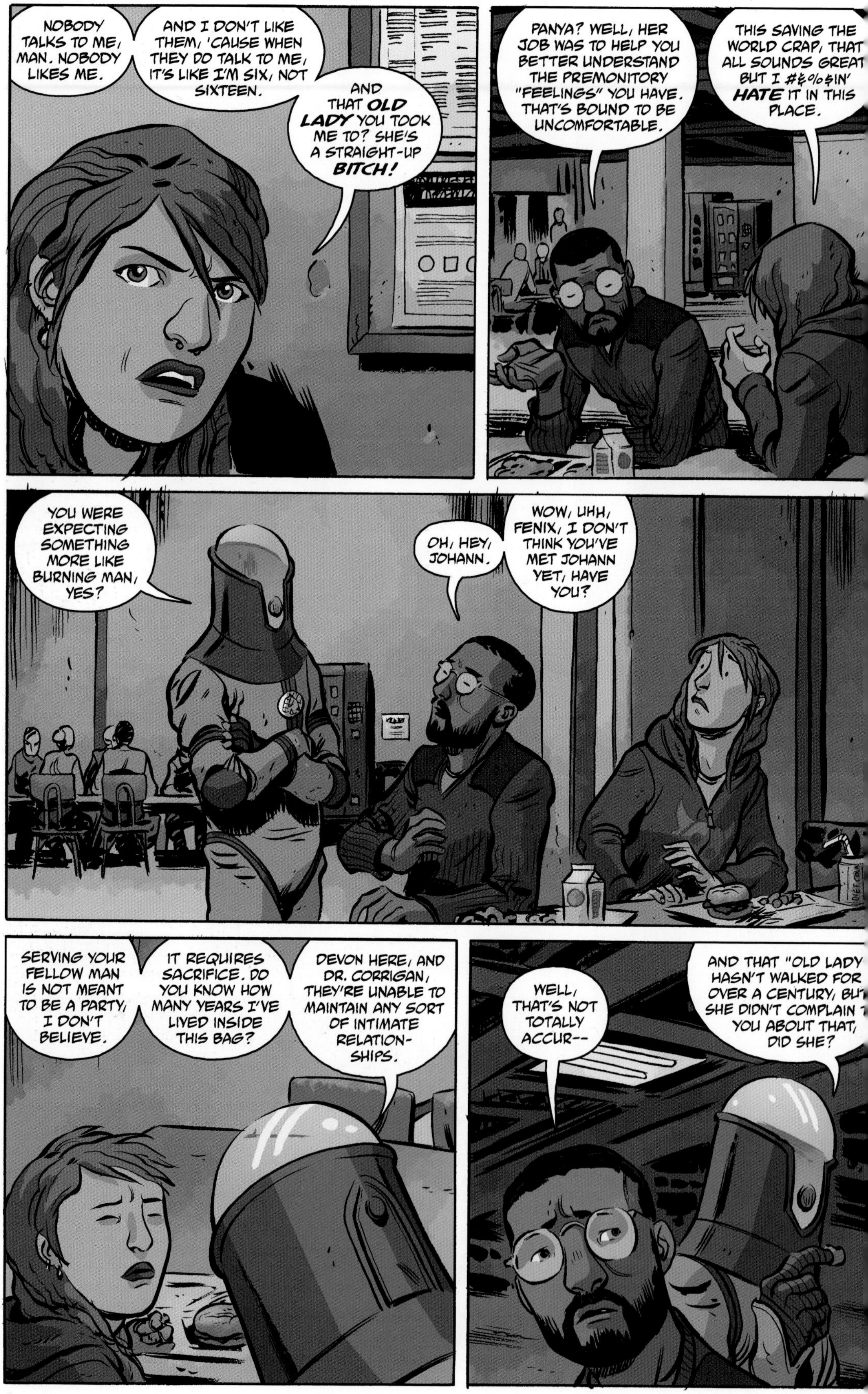
NOBODY TALKS TO ME, MAN. NOBODY LIKES ME.
AND I DON'T LIKE THEM, 'CAUSE WHEN THEY DO TALK TO ME, IT'S LIKE I'M SIX, NOT SIXTEEN.
AND THAT OLD LADY YOU TOOK ME TO? SHE'S A STRAIGHT-UP BITCH!
PANYA? WELL, HER JOB WAS TO HELP YOU BETTER UNDERSTAND THE PREMONITORY "FEELINGS" YOU HAVE. THAT'S BOUND TO BE UNCOMFORTABLE.
THIS SAVING THE WORLD CRAP, THAT ALL SOUNDS GREAT BUT I #&%$IN' HATE IT IN THIS PLACE.
YOU WERE EXPECTING SOMETHING MORE LIKE BURNING MAN, YES?
OH, HEY, JOHANN.
WOW, UHH, FENIX, I DON'T THINK YOU'VE MET JOHANN YET, HAVE YOU?
SERVING YOUR FELLOW MAN IS NOT MEANT TO BE A PARTY, I DON'T BELIEVE.
IT REQUIRES SACRIFICE. DO YOU KNOW HOW MANY YEARS I'VE LIVED INSIDE THIS BAG?
DEVON HERE, AND DR. CORRIGAN, THEY'RE UNABLE TO MAINTAIN ANY SORT OF INTIMATE RELATION-SHIPS.
WELL, THAT'S NOT TOTALLY ACCUR--
AND THAT "OLD LADY HASN'T WALKED FOR OVER A CENTURY, BU SHE DIDN'T COMPLAIN YOU ABOUT THAT, DID SHE?

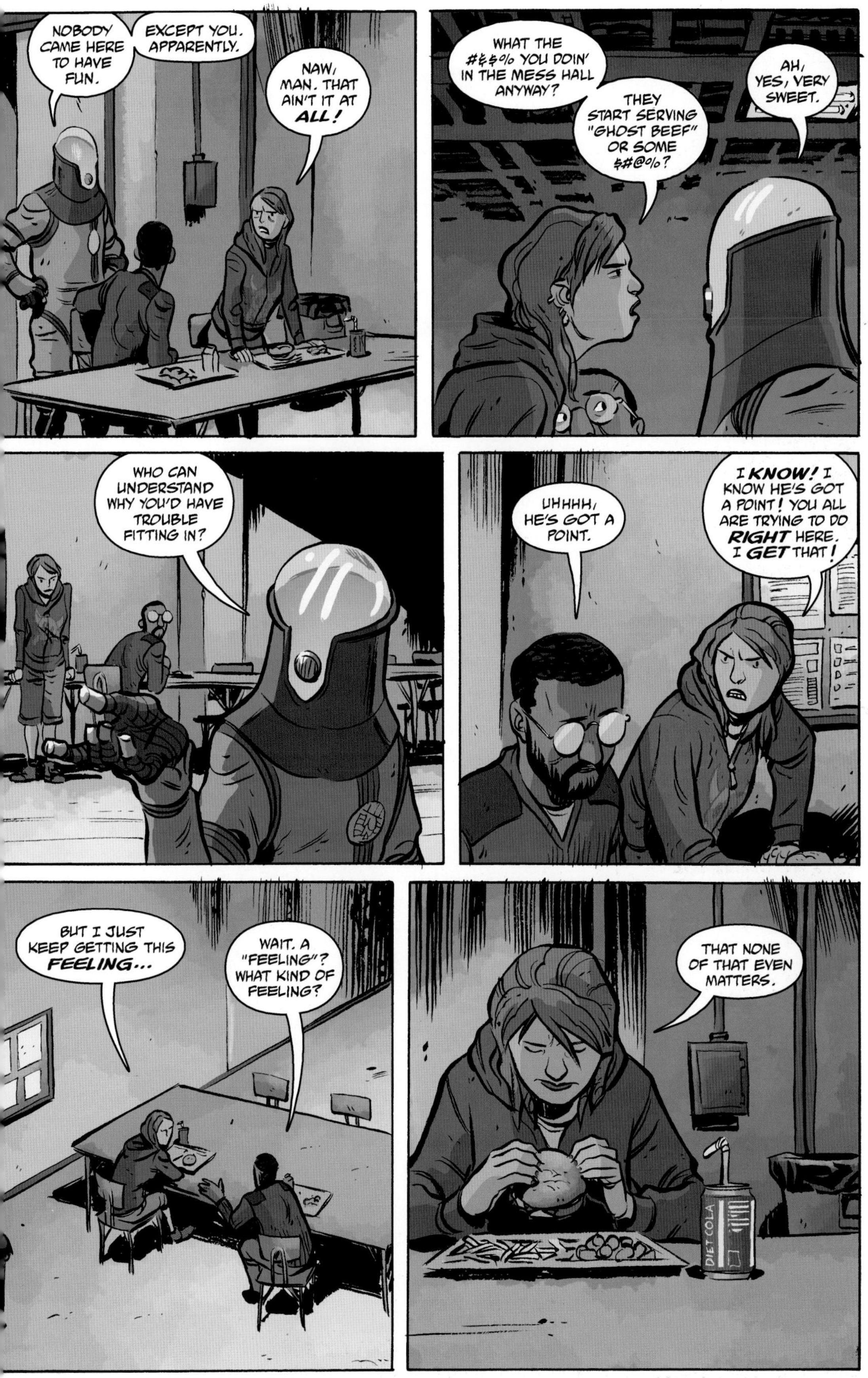
NOBODY CAME HERE TO HAVE FUN.
EXCEPT YOU. APPARENTLY.
NAW, MAN. THAT AIN'T IT AT ALL!
WHAT THE #&$% YOU DOIN' IN THE MESS HALL ANYWAY?
THEY START SERVING "GHOST BEEF" OR SOME $#@%?
AH, YES, VERY SWEET.
WHO CAN UNDERSTAND WHY YOU'D HAVE TROUBLE FITTING IN?
UHHHH, HE'S GOT A POINT.
I KNOW! I KNOW HE'S GOT A POINT! YOU ALL ARE TRYING TO DO RIGHT HERE. I GET THAT!
BUT I JUST KEEP GETTING THIS FEELING...
WAIT. A "FEELING"? WHAT KIND OF FEELING?
THAT NONE OF THAT EVEN MATTERS.
DIET COLA

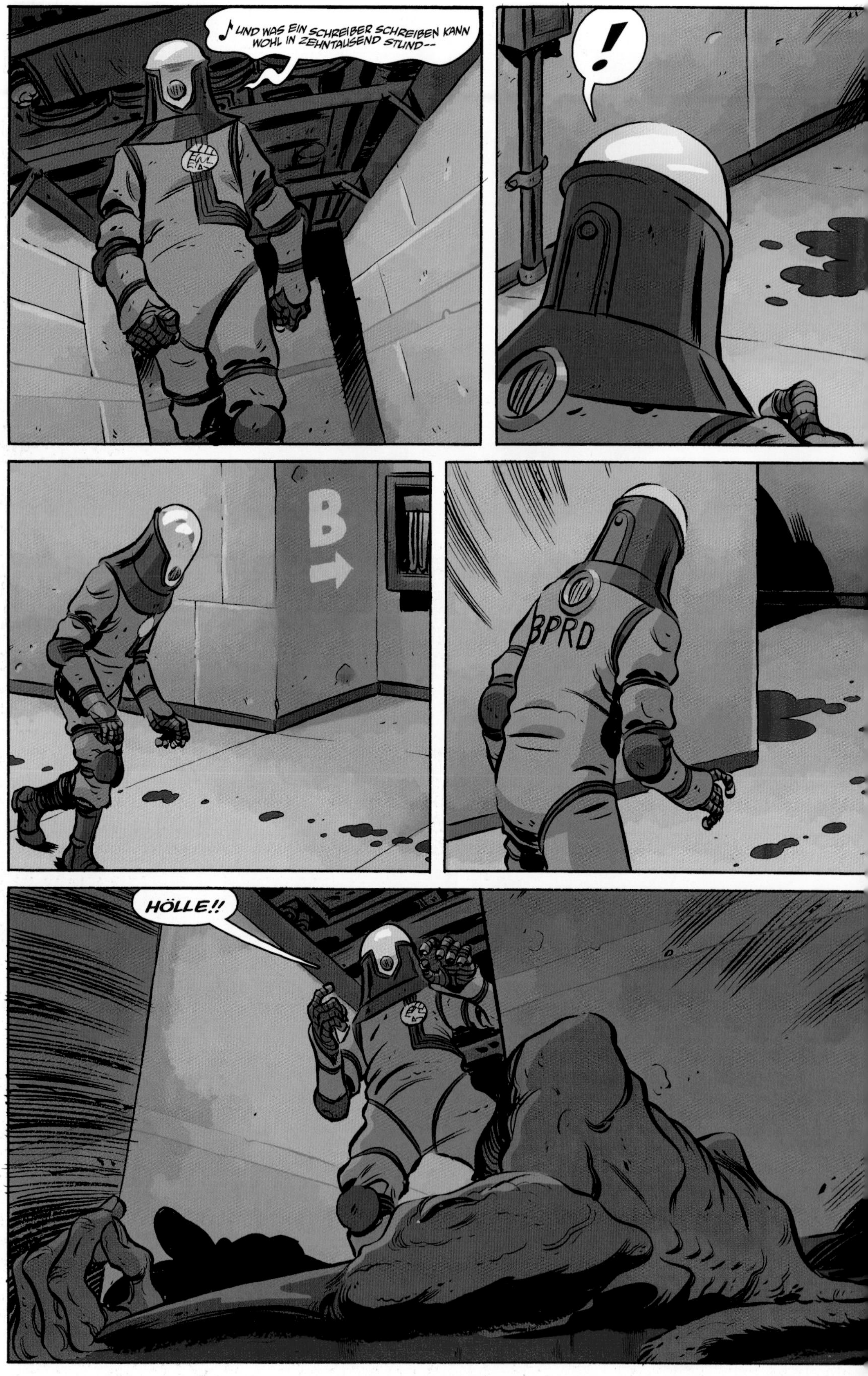
♪ UND WAS EIN SCHREIBER SCHREIBEN KANN WOHL IN ZEHNTAUSEND STUND--
!
B
BPRD
HÖLLE!!

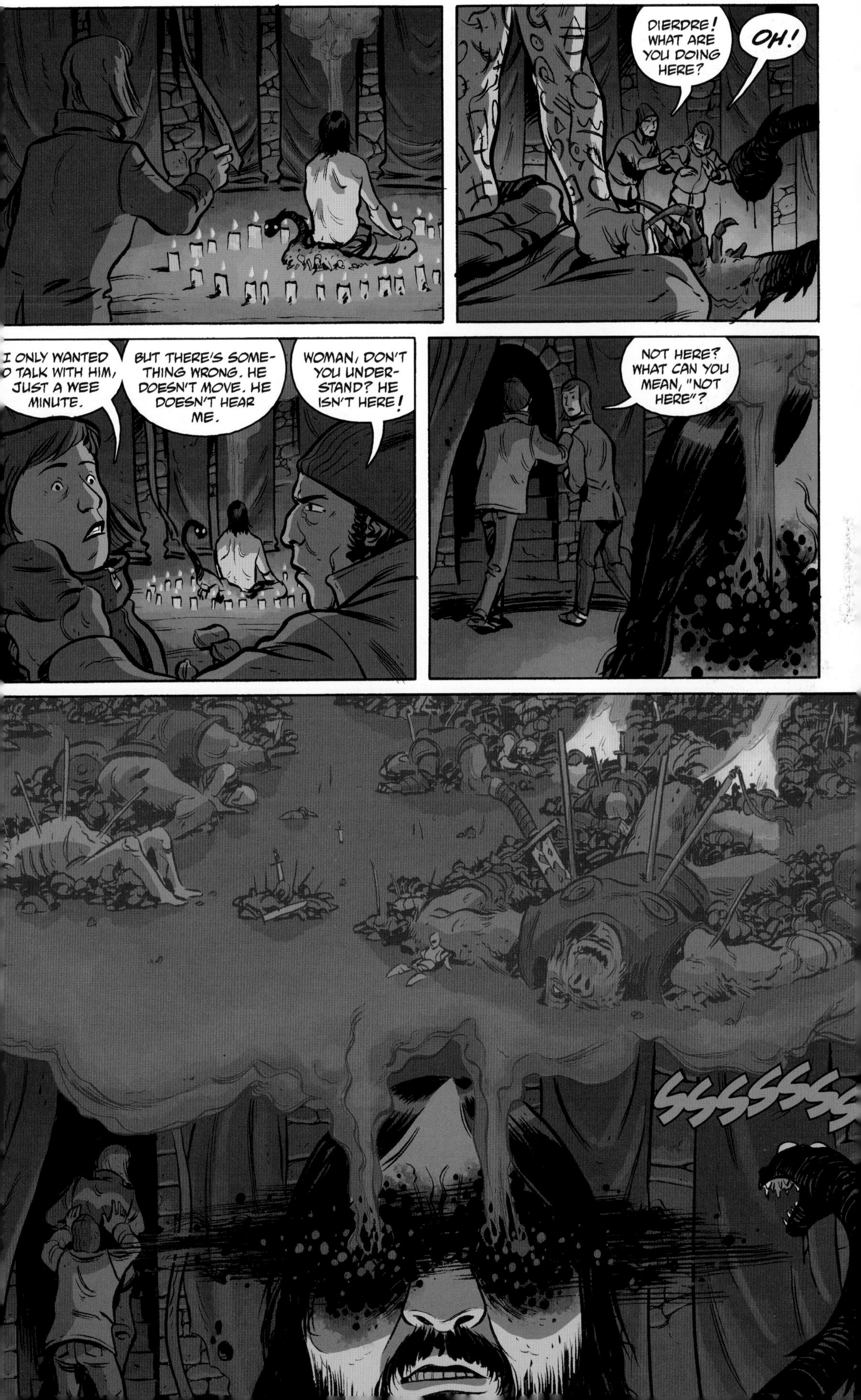
DIERDRE! WHAT ARE YOU DOING HERE?
OH!
I ONLY WANTED TO TALK WITH HIM, JUST A WEE MINUTE.
BUT THERE'S SOMETHING WRONG. HE DOESN'T MOVE. HE DOESN'T HEAR ME.
WOMAN, DON'T YOU UNDERSTAND? HE ISN'T HERE!
NOT HERE? WHAT CAN YOU MEAN, "NOT HERE"?
SSSSSSS

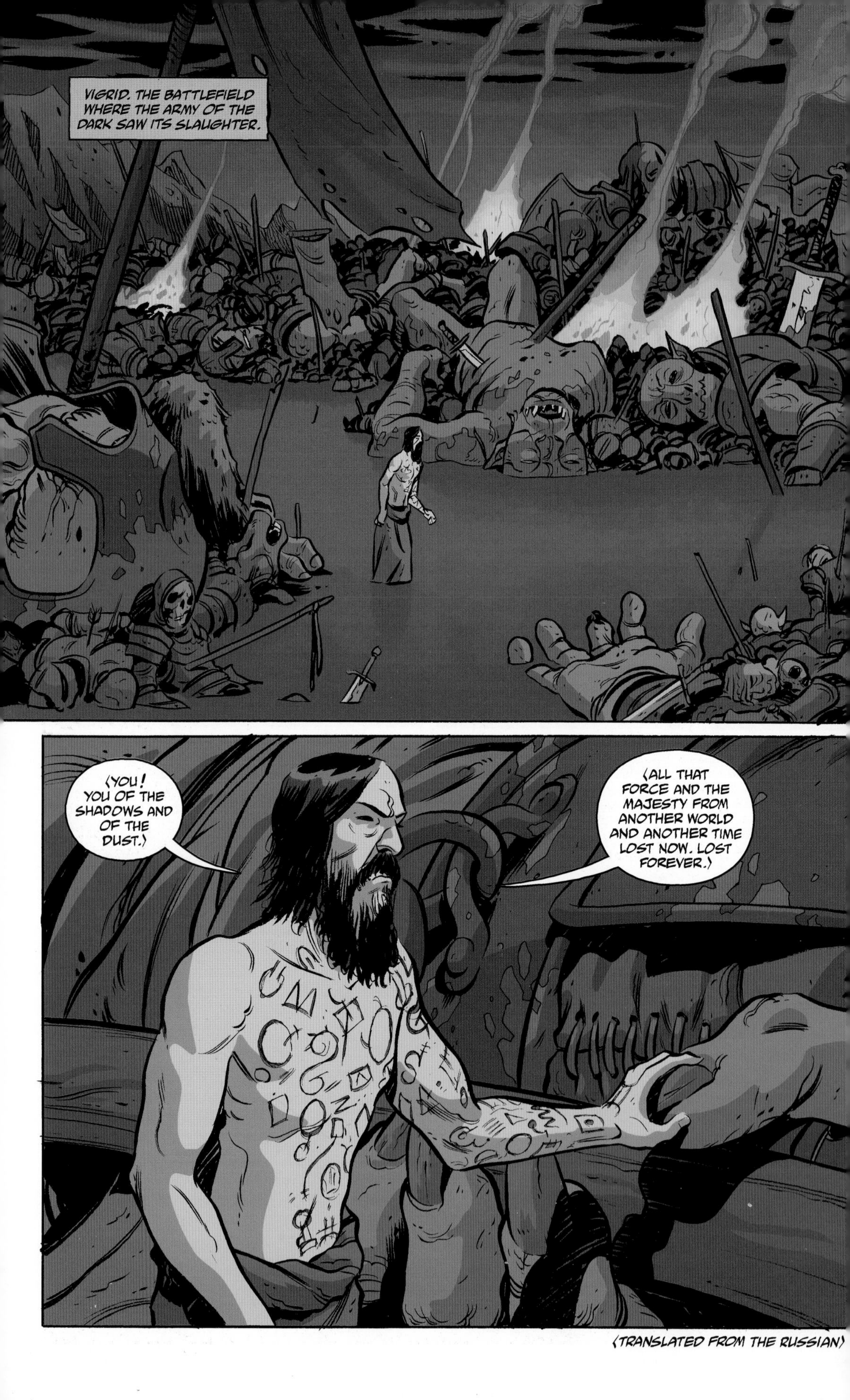
VIGRID. THE BATTLEFIELD WHERE THE ARMY OF THE DARK SAW ITS SLAUGHTER.
‹YOU! YOU OF THE SHADOWS AND OF THE DUST.›
‹ALL THAT FORCE AND THE MAJESTY FROM ANOTHER WORLD AND ANOTHER TIME LOST NOW. LOST FOREVER.›

‹TRANSLATED FROM THE RUSSIAN›

(BUT PERHAPS NOT **REALLY** FOREVER.)

(PERHAPS NOT FOR ALL OF YOU.)

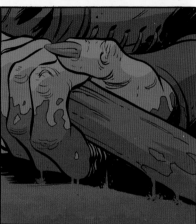

B.U.N. IS PERFECT, BLOOD GASES ARE ALL NORMAL. 84 SYSTOLIC, 47 DIASTOLIC, HEMATOCRIT AT 57%. BILIRUBIN, ALT, ASP--

THE ONSLAUGHT OF DATA IS UNNECESSARY. PREPARE THE BODY FOR TRANSFER.

OXYGEN 2

WAIT. THIS E.E.G. READING. SHOULD IT BE THAT HIGH?

IT'S NOTHING. WE EXPECT OCCASIONAL ANOMALOUS READINGS, USUALLY FROM AUTONOMIC ACTIVITY.

TUNK

OXYGEN 2

VAS!?

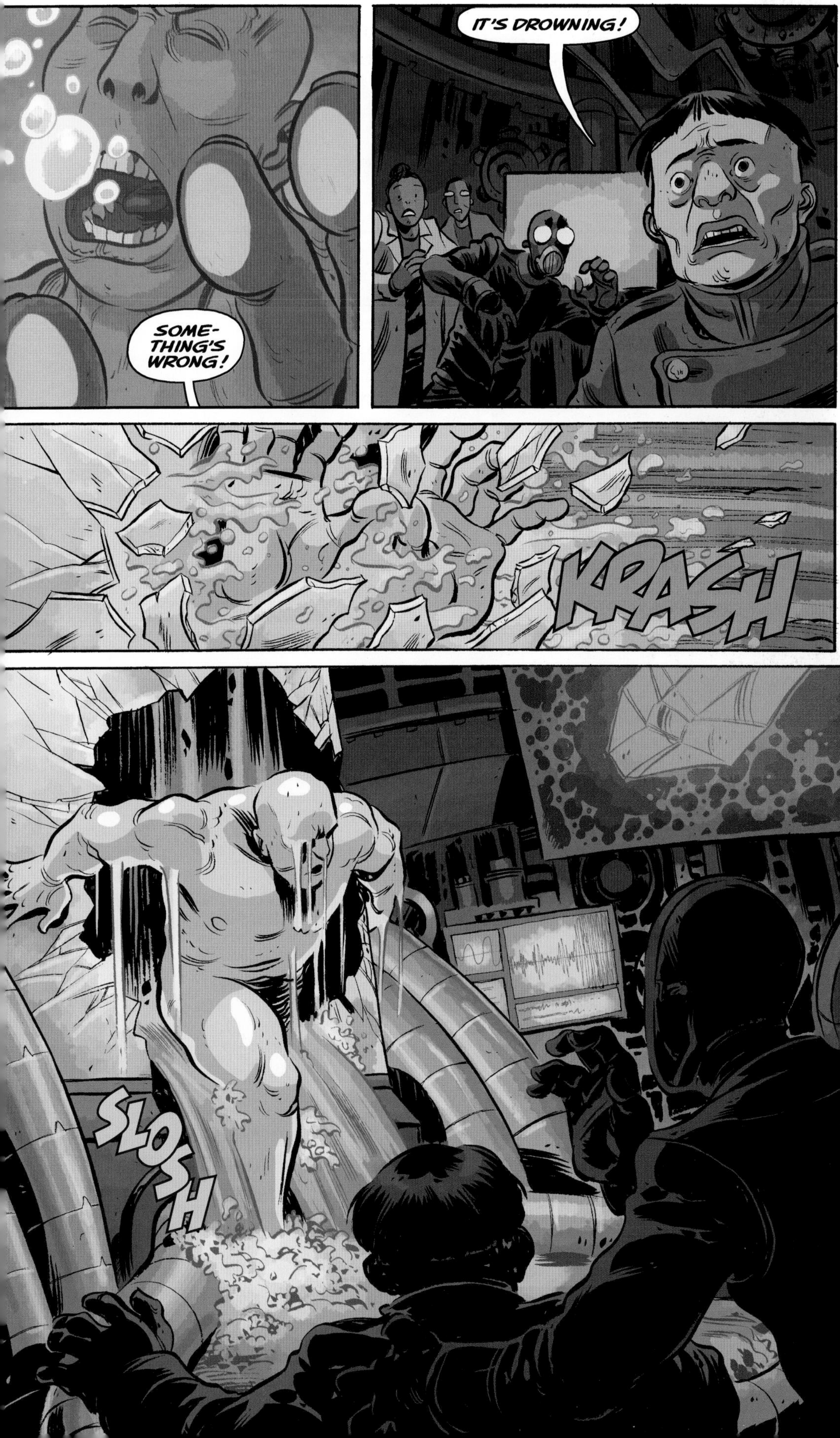
SOME-
THING'S
WRONG!
IT'S DROWNING!
KRASH
SLOSH

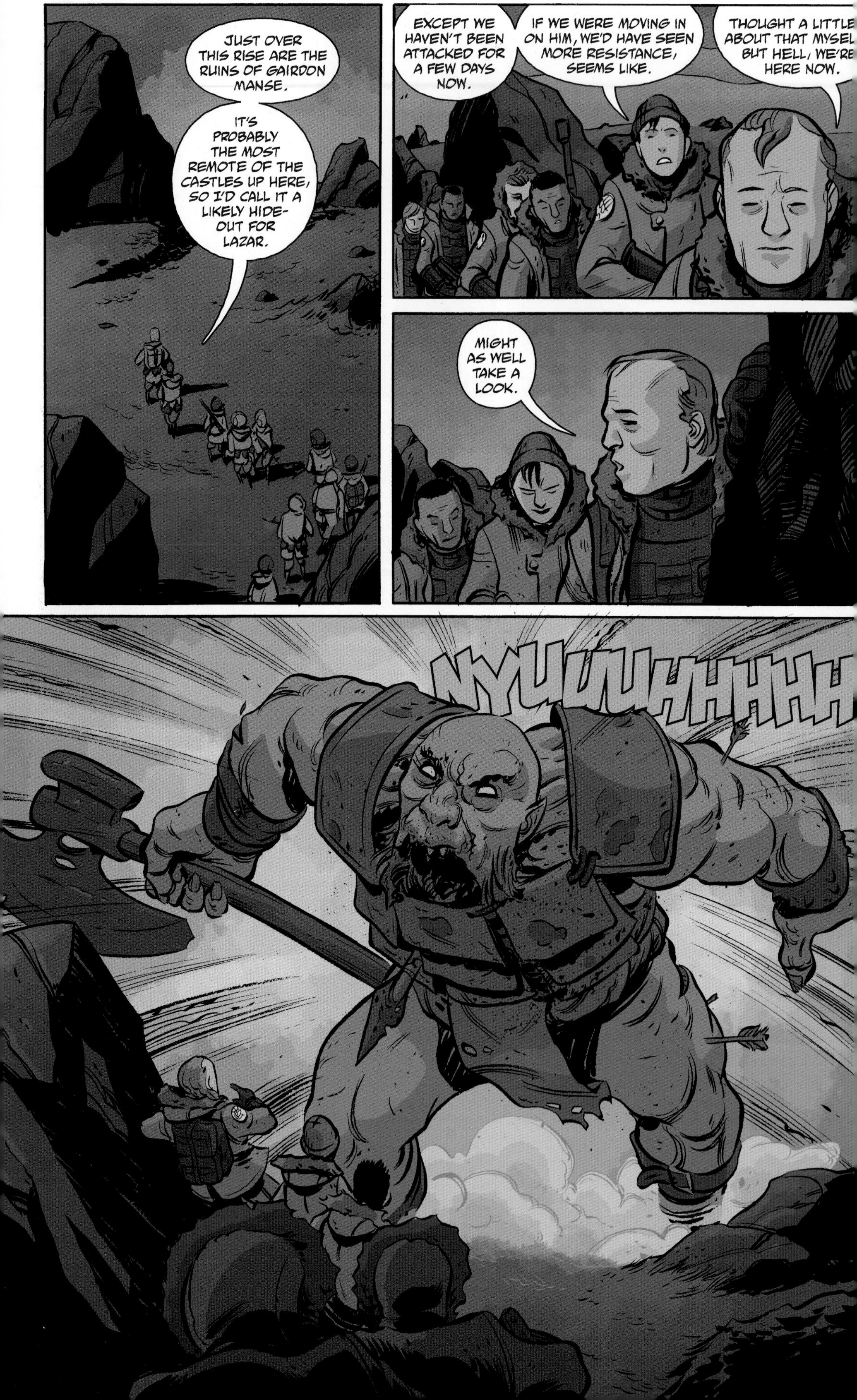
JUST OVER THIS RISE ARE THE RUINS OF GAIRDON MANSE.
IT'S PROBABLY THE MOST REMOTE OF THE CASTLES UP HERE, SO I'D CALL IT A LIKELY HIDE-OUT FOR LAZAR.
EXCEPT WE HAVEN'T BEEN ATTACKED FOR A FEW DAYS NOW.
IF WE WERE MOVING IN ON HIM, WE'D HAVE SEEN MORE RESISTANCE, SEEMS LIKE.
THOUGHT A LITTLE ABOUT THAT MYSEL BUT HELL, WE'RE HERE NOW.
MIGHT AS WELL TAKE A LOOK.
NYUUUHHHHH

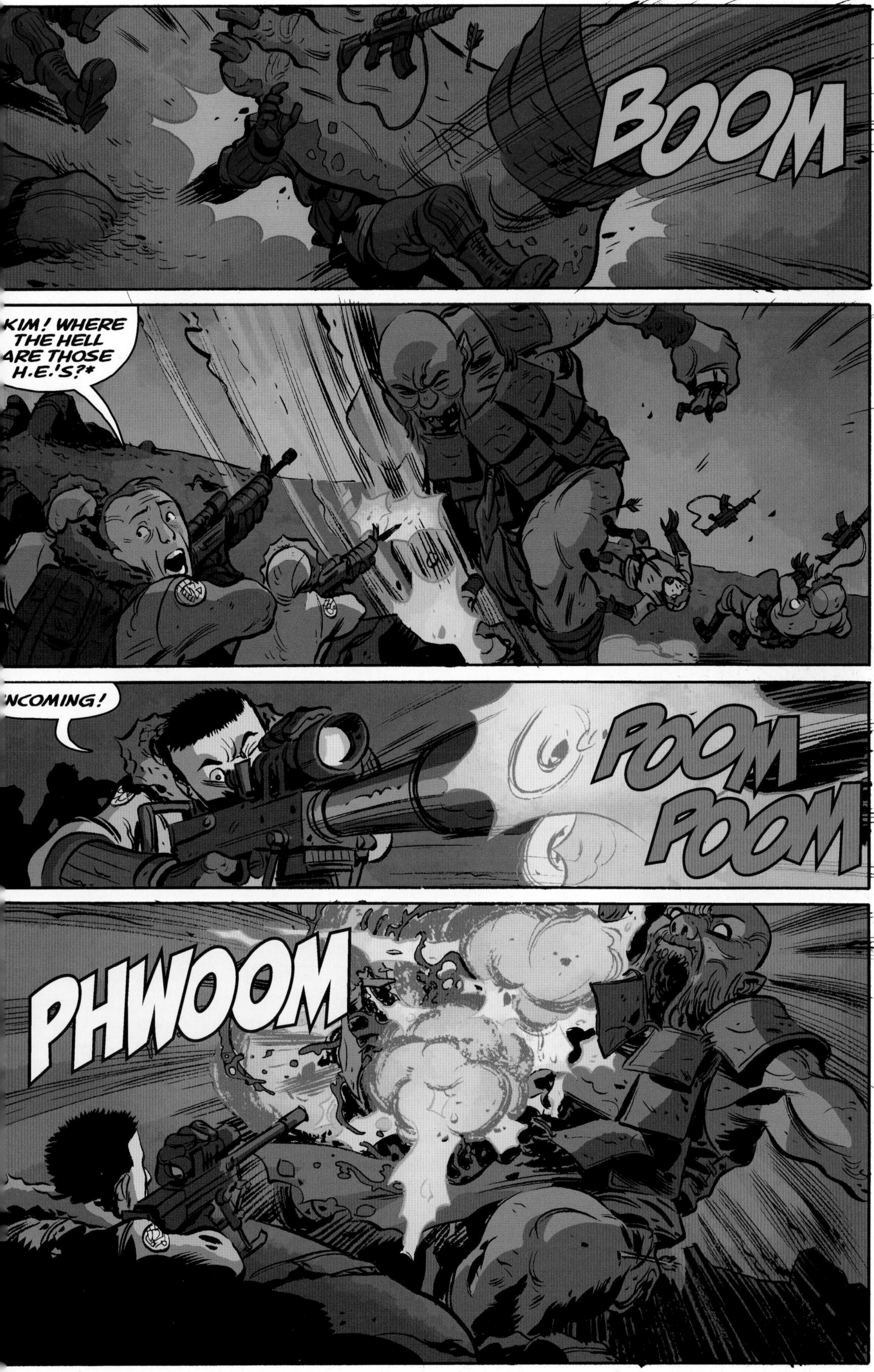
BOOM
KIM! WHERE THE HELL ARE THOSE H.E.'S?*
INCOMING!
POOM
POOM
PHWOOM

*HIGH EXPLOSIVE ROUNDS

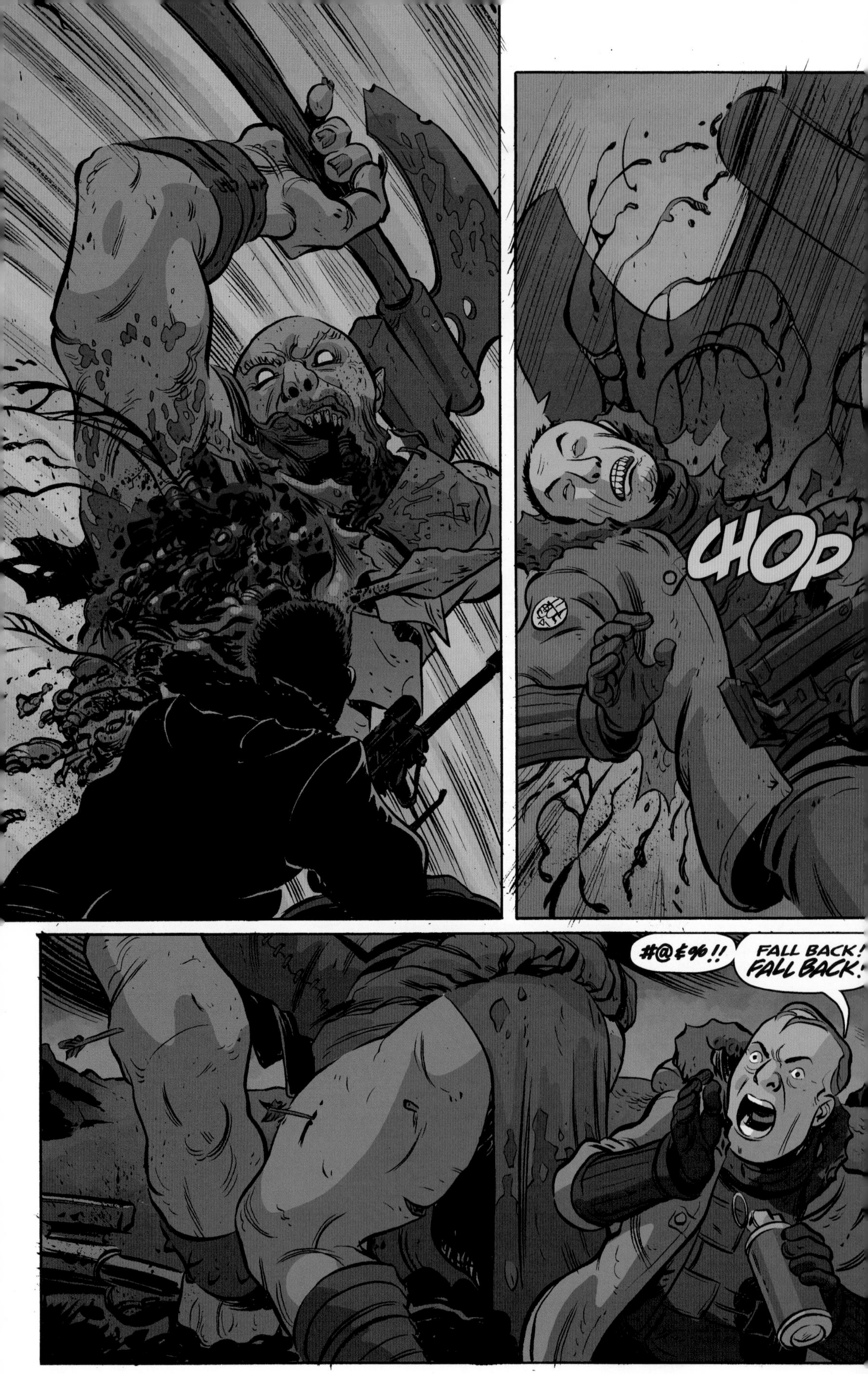
CHOP
#@£%!!
FALL BACK!
FALL BACK!

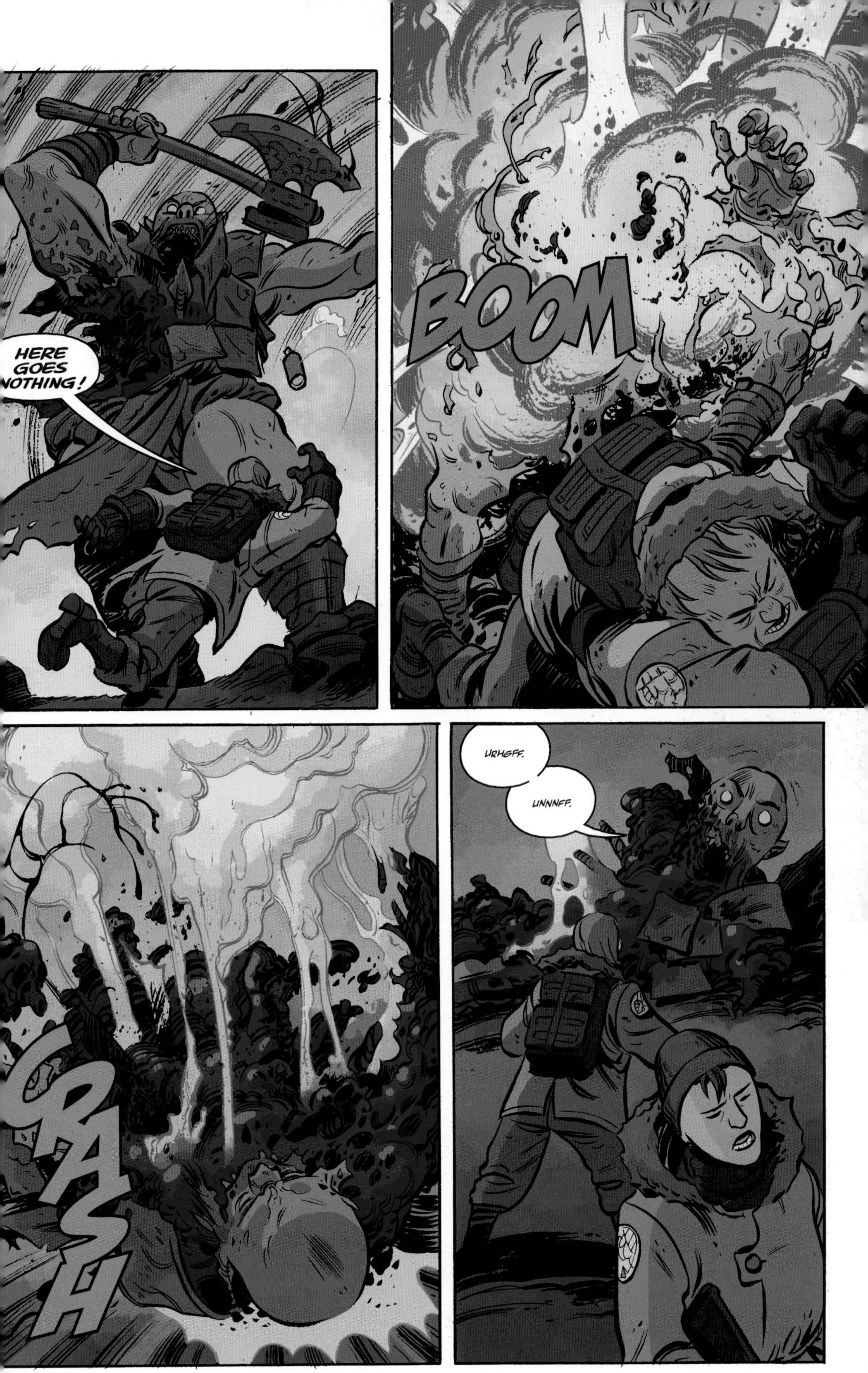
HERE GOES NOTHING!
BOOM
CRASH
URHGFF.
UNNNFF.

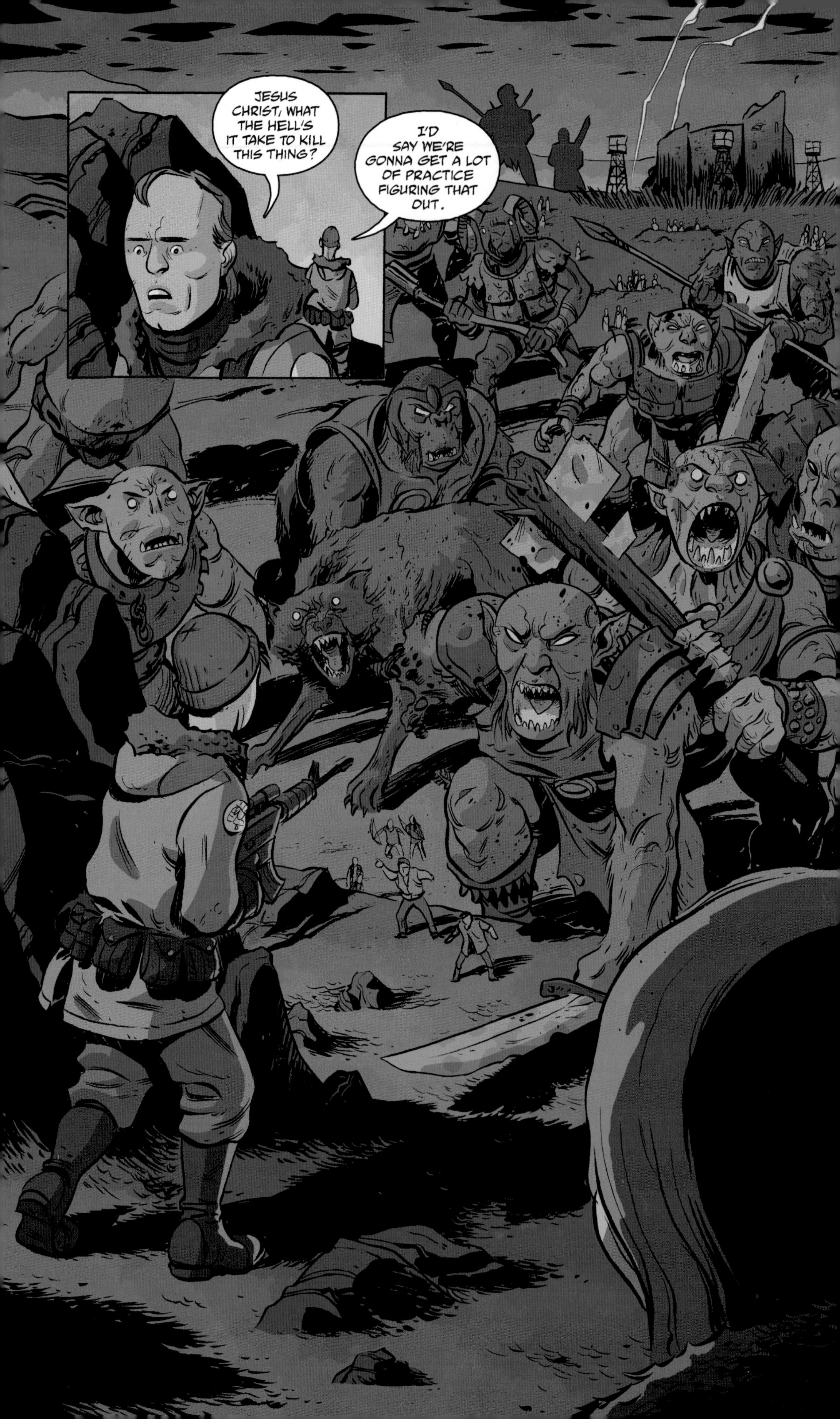
JESUS CHRIST, WHAT THE HELL'S IT TAKE TO KILL THIS THING?
I'D SAY WE'RE GONNA GET A LOT OF PRACTICE FIGURING THAT OUT.

# THE RETURN OF THE MASTER CHAPTER FOUR

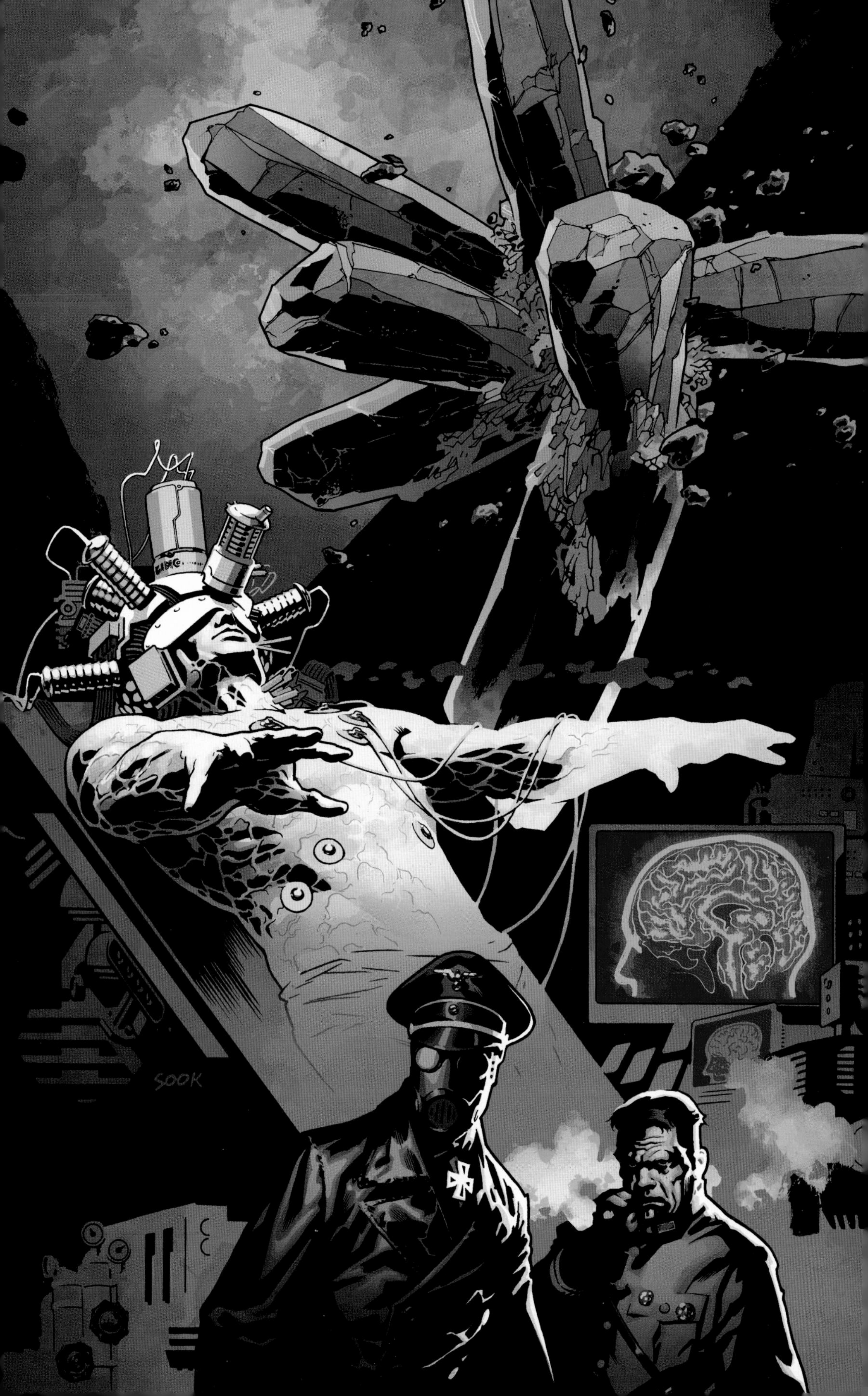
SOOK

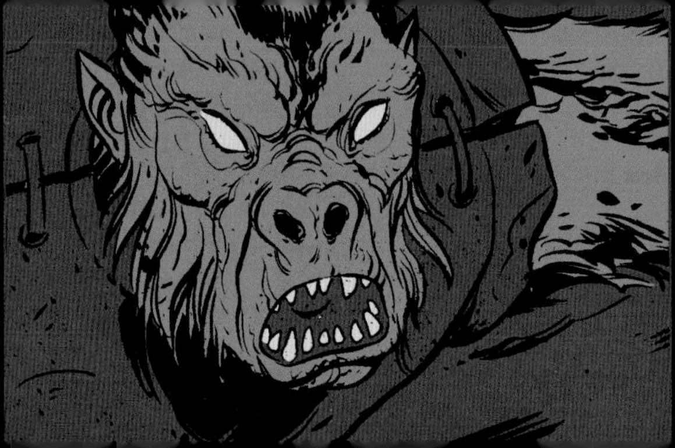

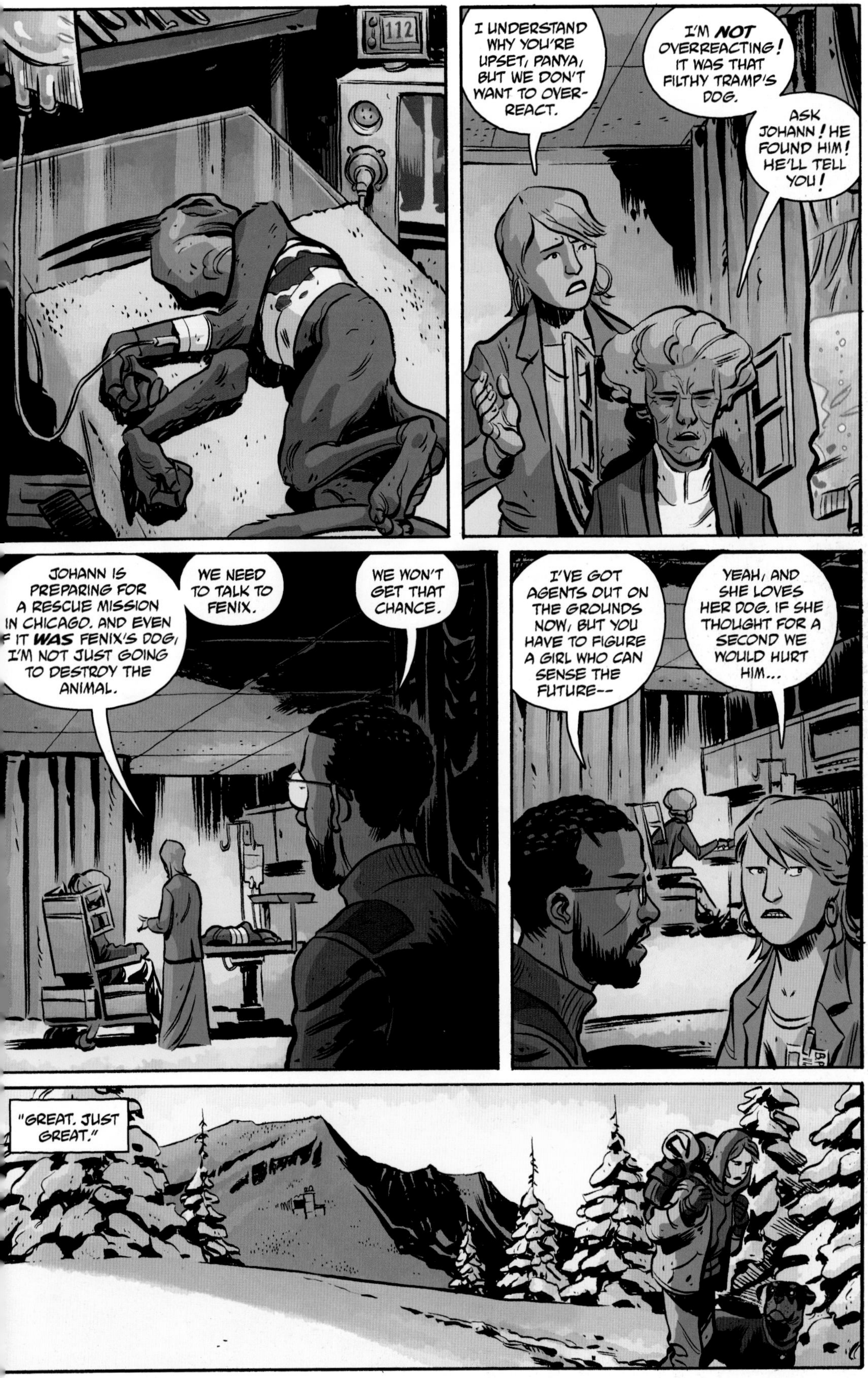
112
I UNDERSTAND WHY YOU'RE UPSET, PANYA, BUT WE DON'T WANT TO OVER-REACT.
I'M NOT OVERREACTING! IT WAS THAT FILTHY TRAMP'S DOG.
ASK JOHANN! HE FOUND HIM! HE'LL TELL YOU!
JOHANN IS PREPARING FOR A RESCUE MISSION IN CHICAGO. AND EVEN IF IT WAS FENIX'S DOG, I'M NOT JUST GOING TO DESTROY THE ANIMAL.
WE NEED TO TALK TO FENIX.
WE WON'T GET THAT CHANCE.
I'VE GOT AGENTS OUT ON THE GROUNDS NOW, BUT YOU HAVE TO FIGURE A GIRL WHO CAN SENSE THE FUTURE--
YEAH, AND SHE LOVES HER DOG. IF SHE THOUGHT FOR A SECOND WE WOULD HURT HIM...
"GREAT. JUST GREAT."

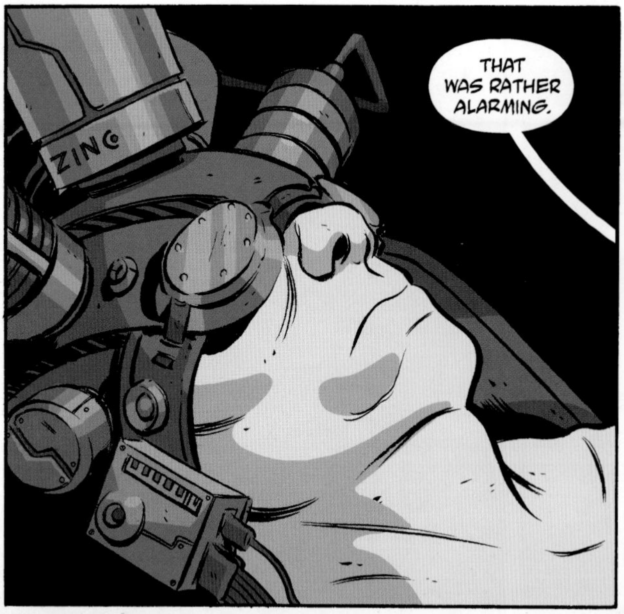
THAT WAS RATHER ALARMING.

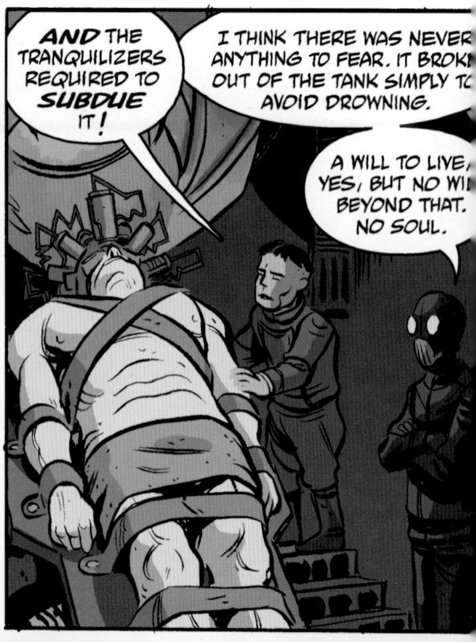
AND THE TRANQUILIZERS REQUIRED TO SUBDUE IT!
I THINK THERE WAS NEVER ANYTHING TO FEAR. IT BROKE OUT OF THE TANK SIMPLY TO AVOID DROWNING.
A WILL TO LIVE, YES, BUT NO WI BEYOND THAT. NO SOUL.

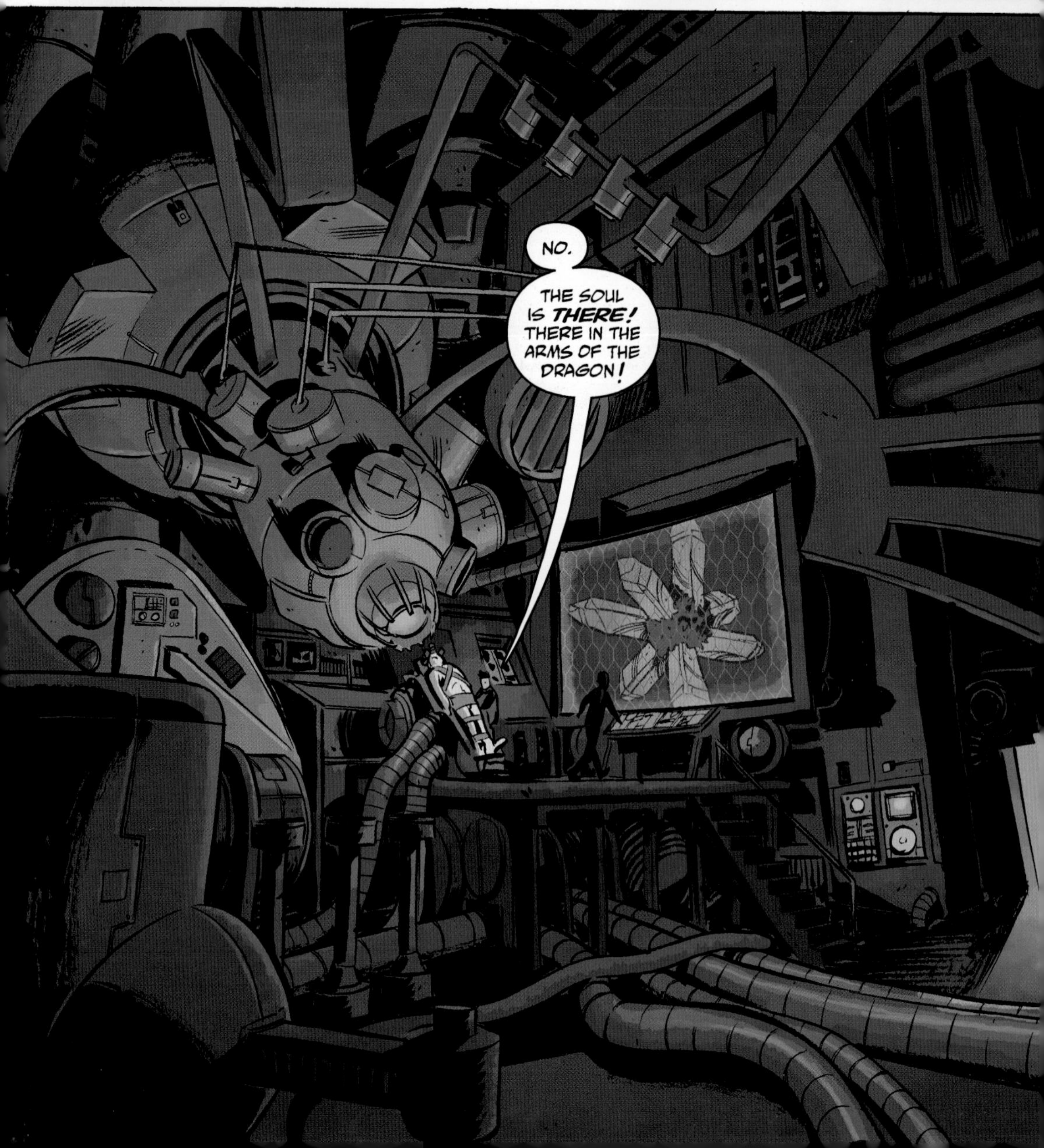
NO.
THE SOUL IS THERE! THERE IN THE ARMS OF THE DRAGON!

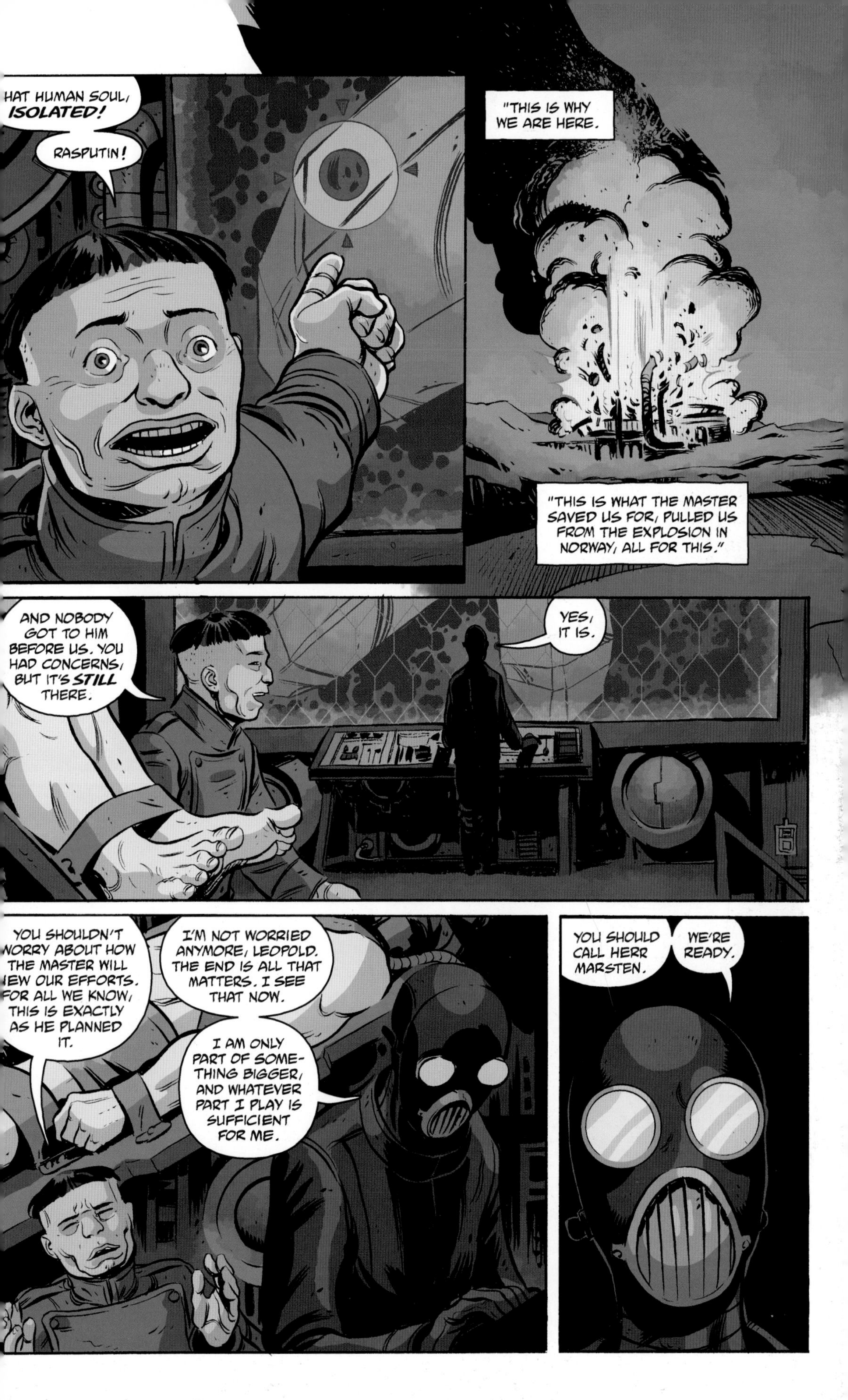
HAT HUMAN SOUL, ISOLATED!
RASPUTIN!
"THIS IS WHY WE ARE HERE.
"THIS IS WHAT THE MASTER SAVED US FOR, PULLED US FROM THE EXPLOSION IN NORWAY, ALL FOR THIS."
AND NOBODY GOT TO HIM BEFORE US. YOU HAD CONCERNS, BUT IT'S STILL THERE.
YES, IT IS.
YOU SHOULDN'T WORRY ABOUT HOW THE MASTER WILL IEW OUR EFFORTS. FOR ALL WE KNOW, THIS IS EXACTLY AS HE PLANNED IT.
I'M NOT WORRIED ANYMORE, LEOPOLD. THE END IS ALL THAT MATTERS. I SEE THAT NOW.
I AM ONLY PART OF SOMETHING BIGGER, AND WHATEVER PART I PLAY IS SUFFICIENT FOR ME.
YOU SHOULD CALL HERR MARSTEN.
WE'RE READY.

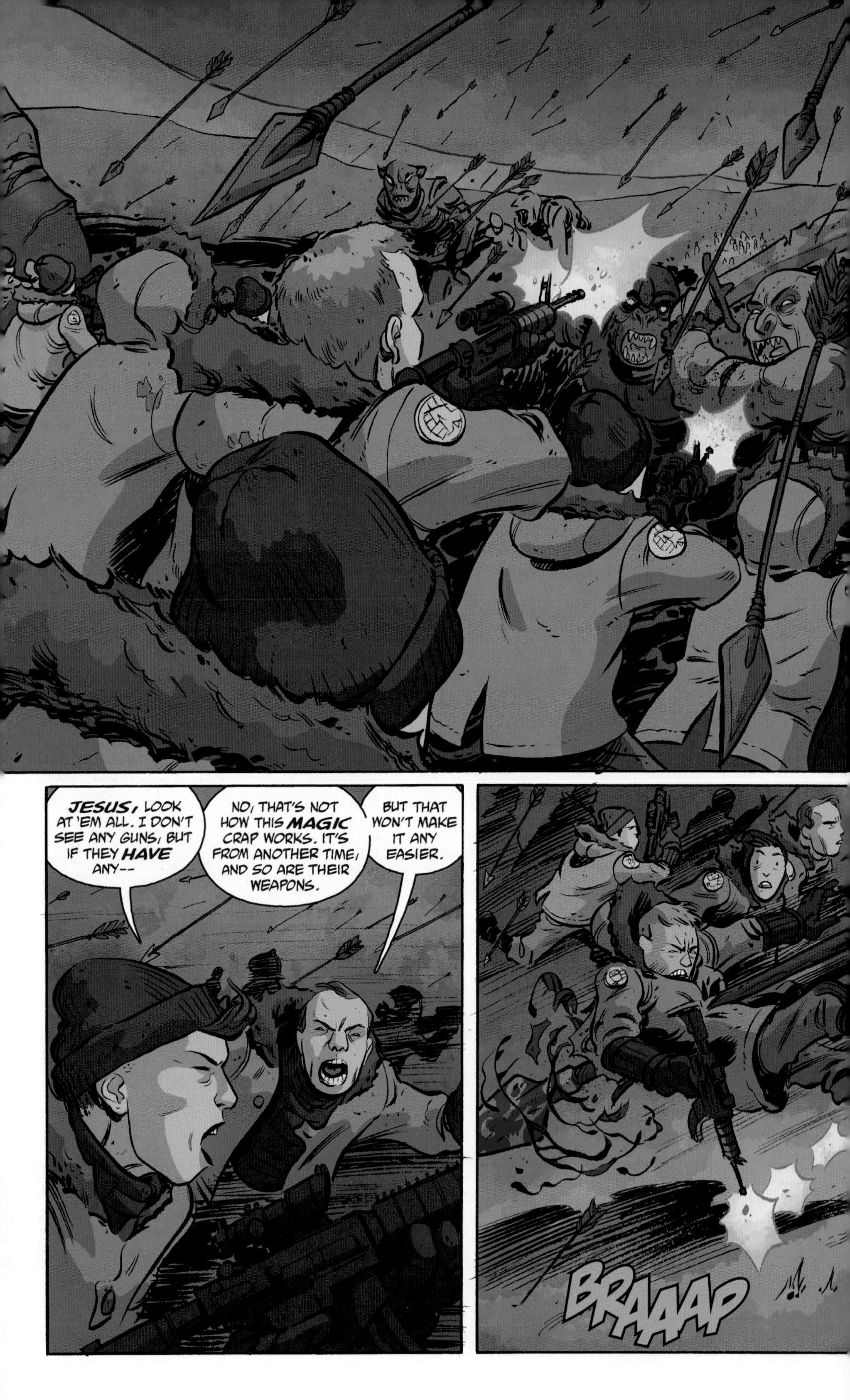
JESUS, LOOK AT 'EM ALL. I DON'T SEE ANY GUNS, BUT IF THEY HAVE ANY--
NO, THAT'S NOT HOW THIS MAGIC CRAP WORKS. IT'S FROM ANOTHER TIME, AND SO ARE THEIR WEAPONS.
BUT THAT WON'T MAKE IT ANY EASIER.
BRAAAP

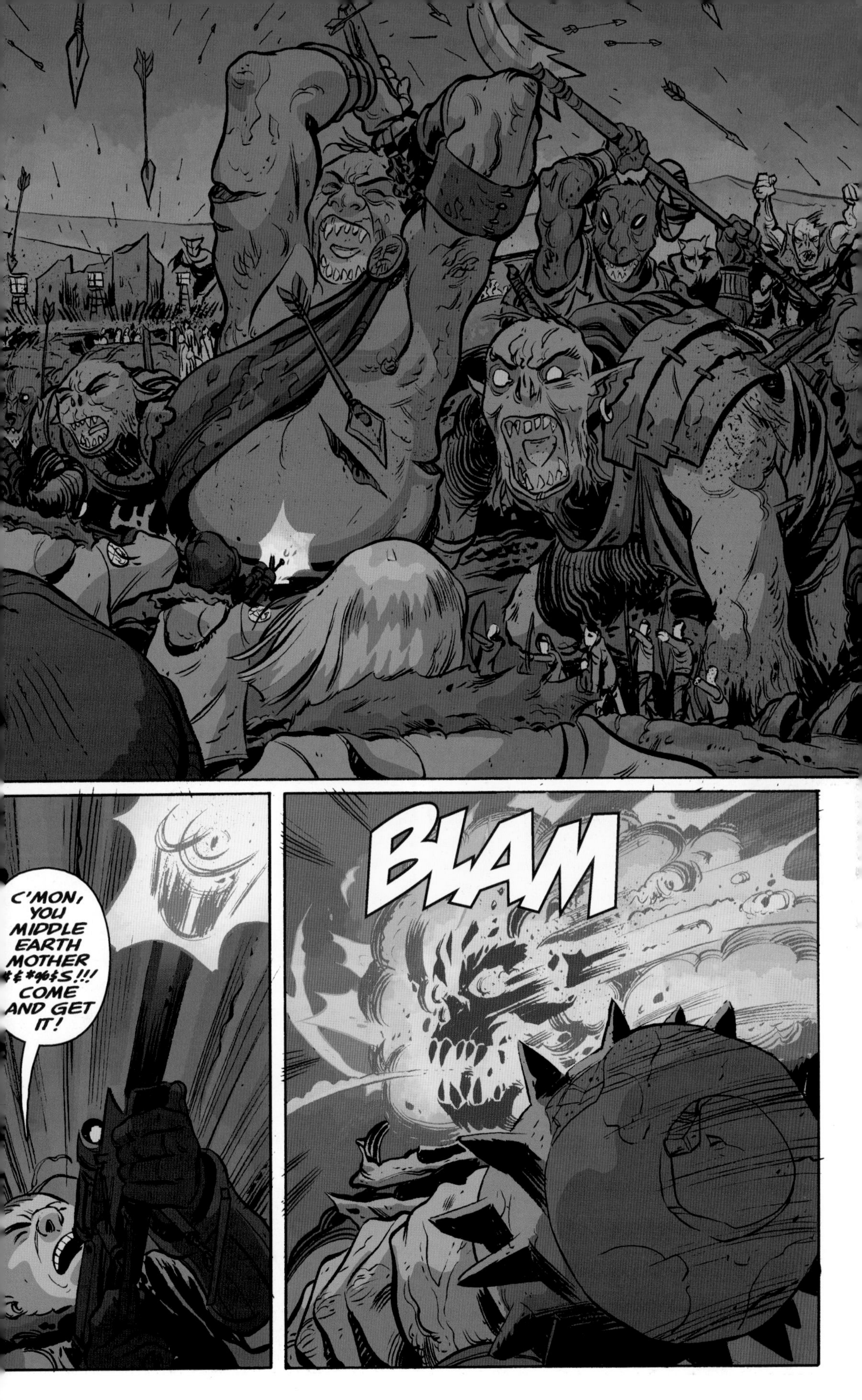
C'MON, YOU MIDDLE EARTH MOTHER #&*%$S!!! COME AND GET IT!
BLAM

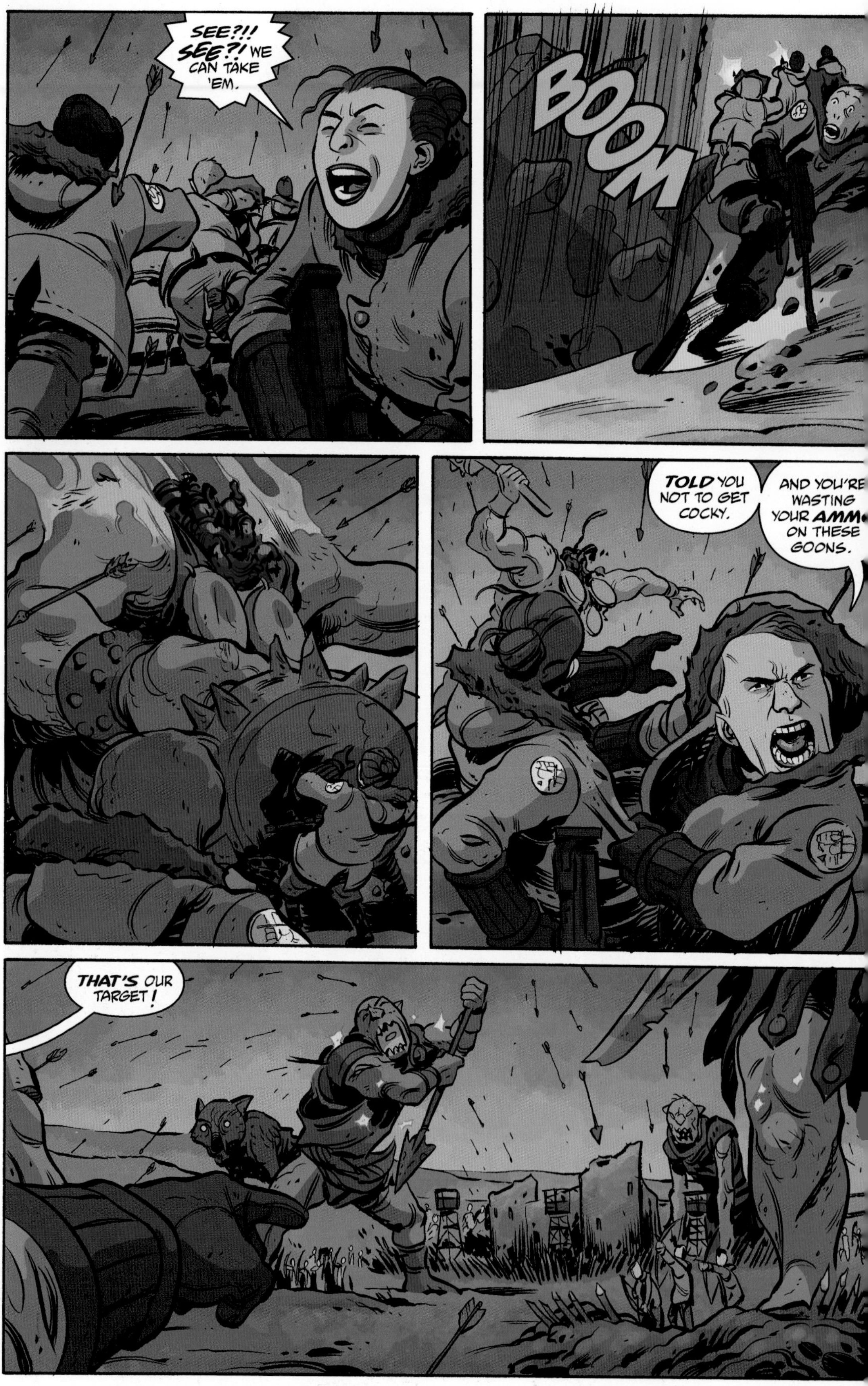
SEE?!! SEE?! WE CAN TAKE 'EM.
BOOM
TOLD YOU NOT TO GET COCKY.
AND YOU'RE WASTING YOUR AMM ON THESE GOONS.
THAT'S OUR TARGET!

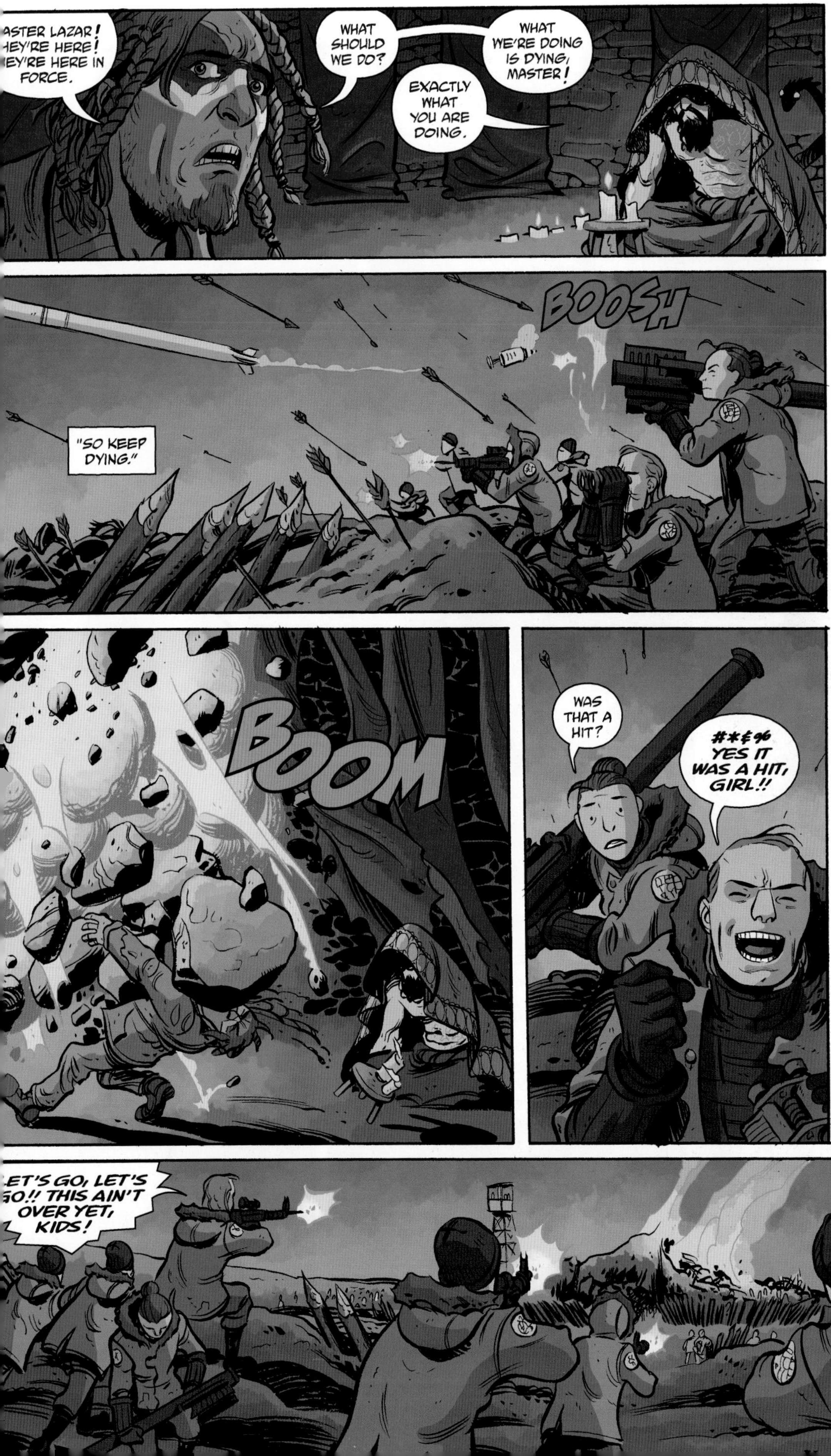
ASTER LAZAR! HEY'RE HERE! HEY'RE HERE IN FORCE.
WHAT SHOULD WE DO?
WHAT WE'RE DOING IS DYING, MASTER!
EXACTLY WHAT YOU ARE DOING.
BOOSH
"SO KEEP DYING."
BOOM
WAS THAT A HIT?
#*&% YES IT WAS A HIT, GIRL!!
LET'S GO, LET'S GO!! THIS AIN'T OVER YET, KIDS!

ABE, I SWEAR TO GOD I WISH YOU WERE HERE...

EXCUSE ME, KATHERINE?

OH, HI, JOHANN.

THOUGHT YOU'D LEFT.

WE'RE WAITING ON CLEARANCE FROM DENVER. THE TEXAS VOLCANO TOSSED UP MORE ASH THIS MORNING.

HOLD ON. "KATHERINE"?

YOU HAVEN'T CALLED ME THAT IN YEARS.

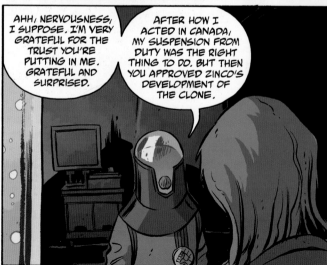

AHH, NERVOUSNESS, I SUPPOSE. I'M VERY GRATEFUL FOR THE TRUST YOU'RE PUTTING IN ME. GRATEFUL AND SURPRISED.

AFTER HOW I ACTED IN CANADA, MY SUSPENSION FROM DUTY WAS THE RIGHT THING TO DO. BUT THEN YOU APPROVED ZINCO'S DEVELOPMENT OF THE CLONE.

AND NOW, ONLY A WEEK LATER, YOU ARE SENDING ME OUT AGAIN. THAT MEANS A GREAT DEAL TO ME.

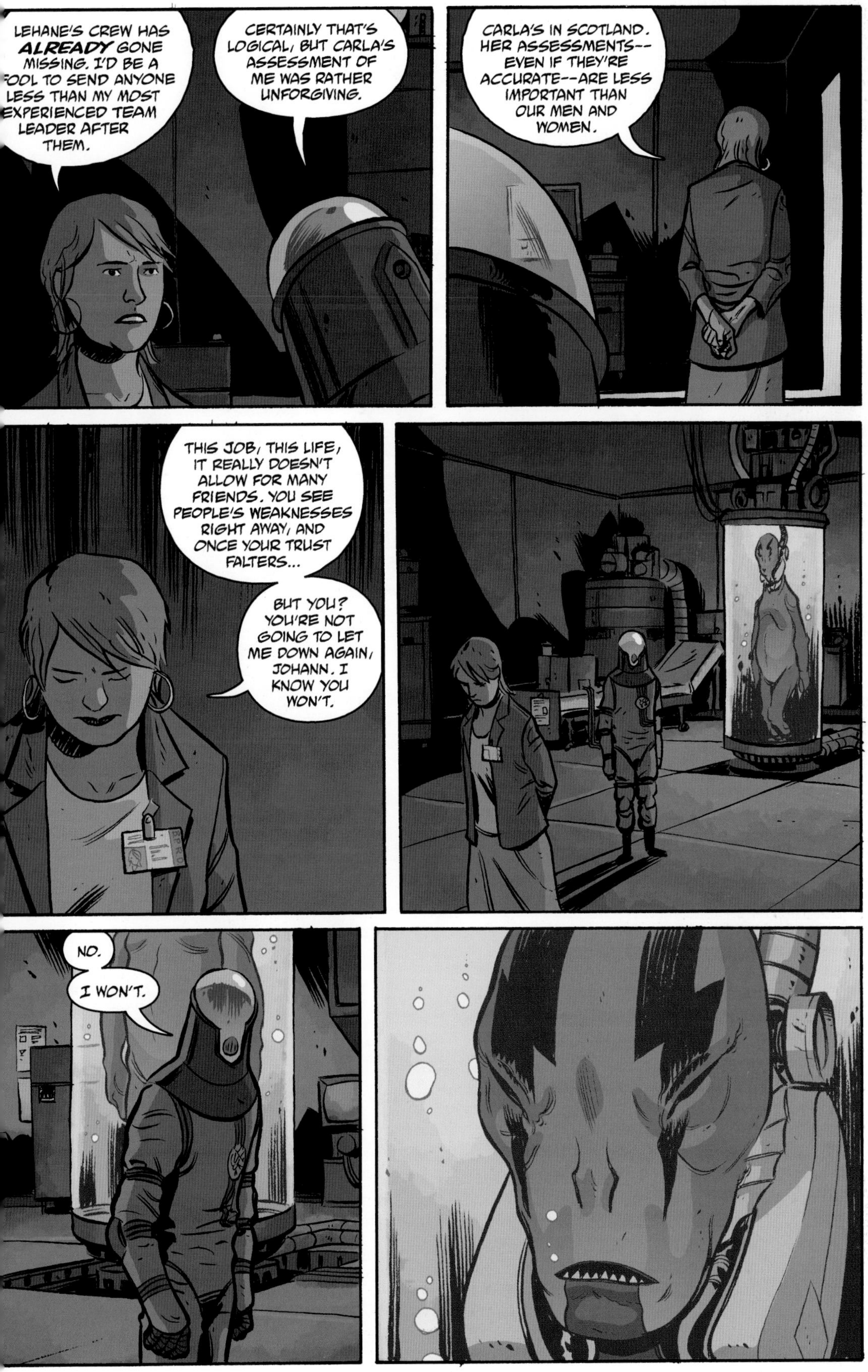
LEHANE'S CREW HAS ALREADY GONE MISSING. I'D BE A FOOL TO SEND ANYONE LESS THAN MY MOST EXPERIENCED TEAM LEADER AFTER THEM.
CERTAINLY THAT'S LOGICAL, BUT CARLA'S ASSESSMENT OF ME WAS RATHER UNFORGIVING.
CARLA'S IN SCOTLAND. HER ASSESSMENTS--EVEN IF THEY'RE ACCURATE--ARE LESS IMPORTANT THAN OUR MEN AND WOMEN.
THIS JOB, THIS LIFE, IT REALLY DOESN'T ALLOW FOR MANY FRIENDS. YOU SEE PEOPLE'S WEAKNESSES RIGHT AWAY, AND ONCE YOUR TRUST FALTERS...
BUT YOU? YOU'RE NOT GOING TO LET ME DOWN AGAIN, JOHANN. I KNOW YOU WON'T.
NO.
I WON'T.

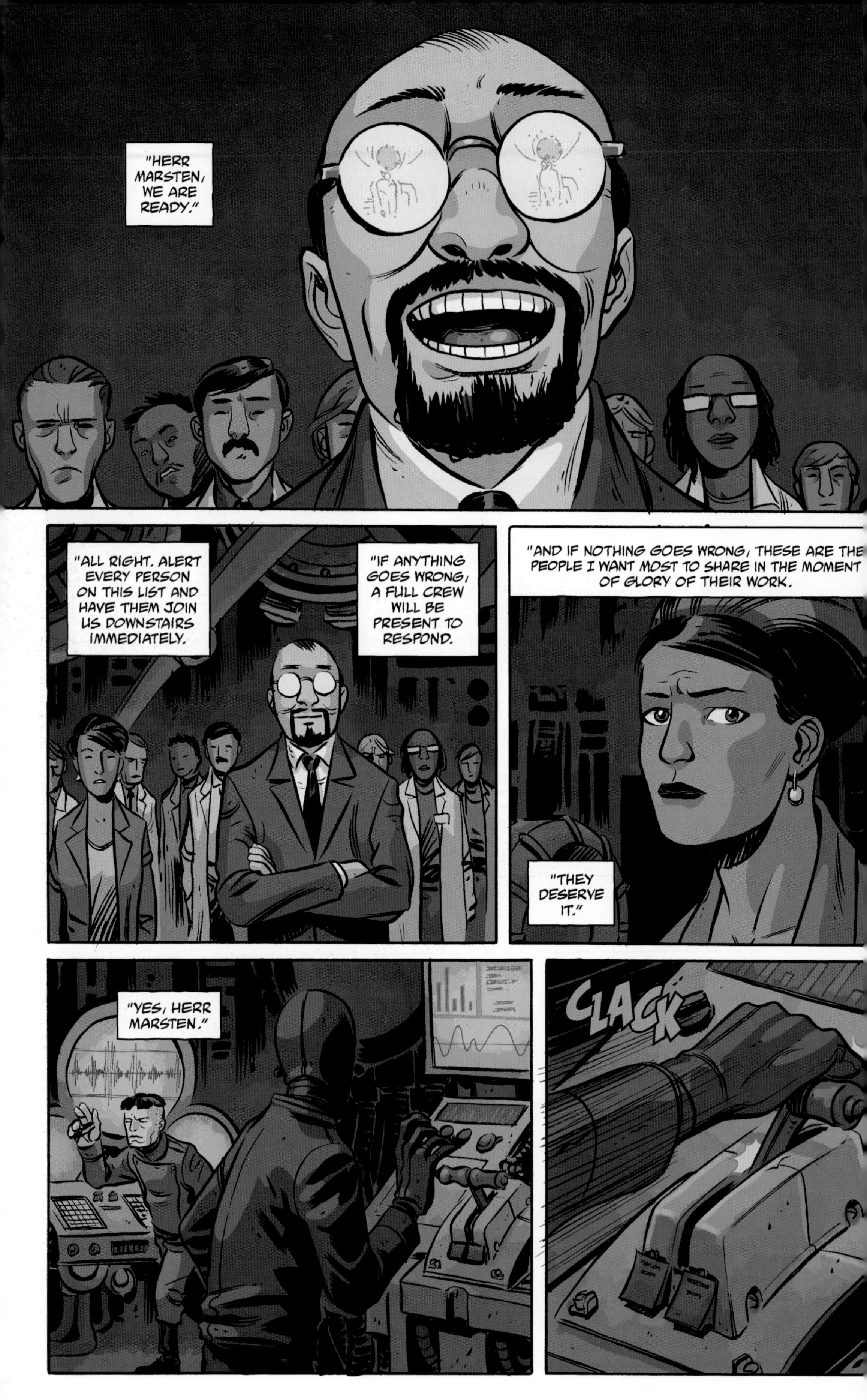
"HERR MARSTEN, WE ARE READY."
"ALL RIGHT. ALERT EVERY PERSON ON THIS LIST AND HAVE THEM JOIN US DOWNSTAIRS IMMEDIATELY.
"IF ANYTHING GOES WRONG, A FULL CREW WILL BE PRESENT TO RESPOND.
"AND IF NOTHING GOES WRONG, THESE ARE THE PEOPLE I WANT MOST TO SHARE IN THE MOMENT OF GLORY OF THEIR WORK.
"THEY DESERVE IT."
"YES, HERR MARSTEN."
CLACK

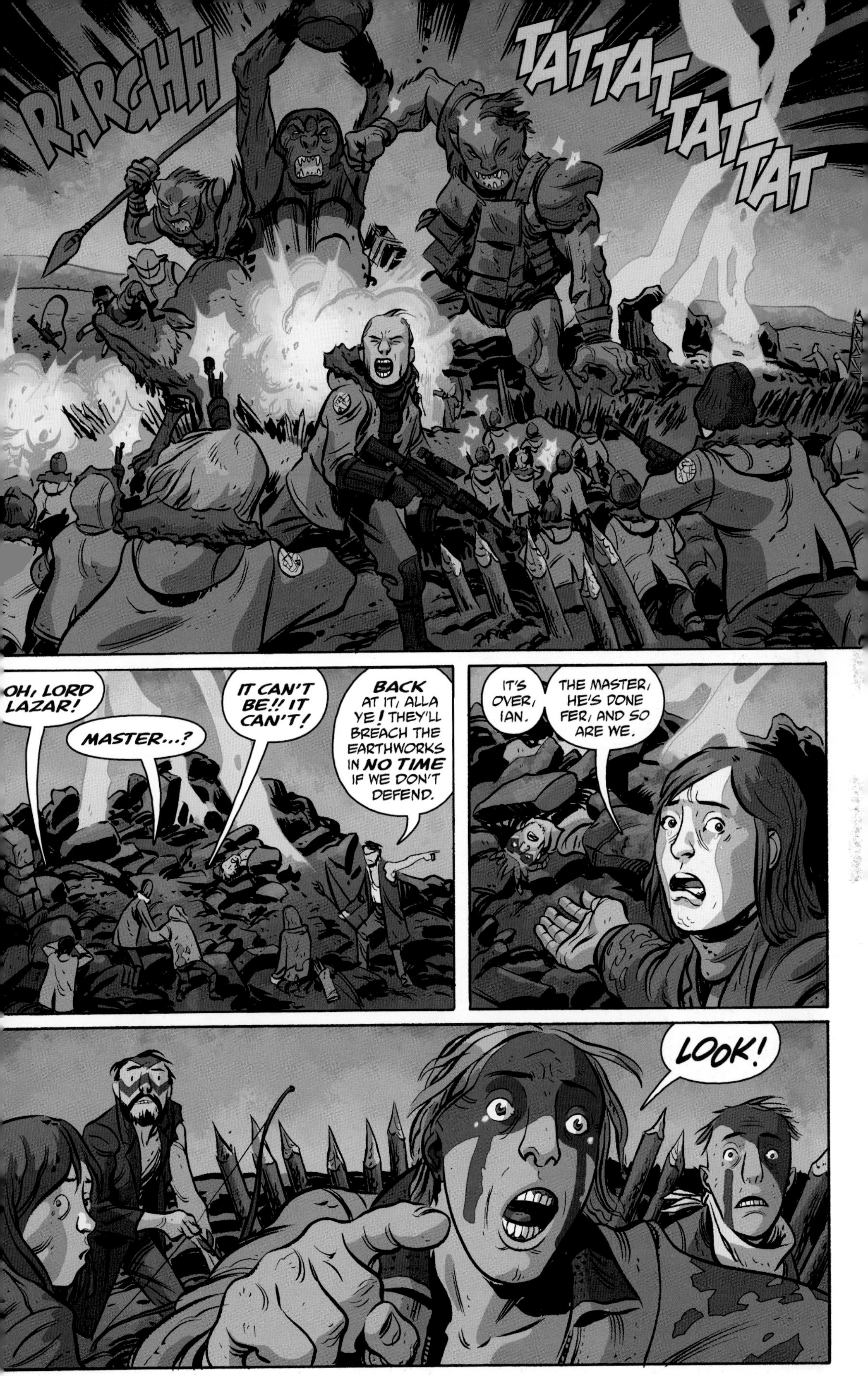
RARGHH
TATTAT TATTAT TAT
OH, LORD LAZAR!
MASTER...?
IT CAN'T BE!! IT CAN'T!
BACK AT IT, ALLA YE! THEY'LL BREACH THE EARTHWORKS IN NO TIME IF WE DON'T DEFEND.
IT'S OVER, IAN.
THE MASTER, HE'S DONE FER, AND SO ARE WE.
LOOK!

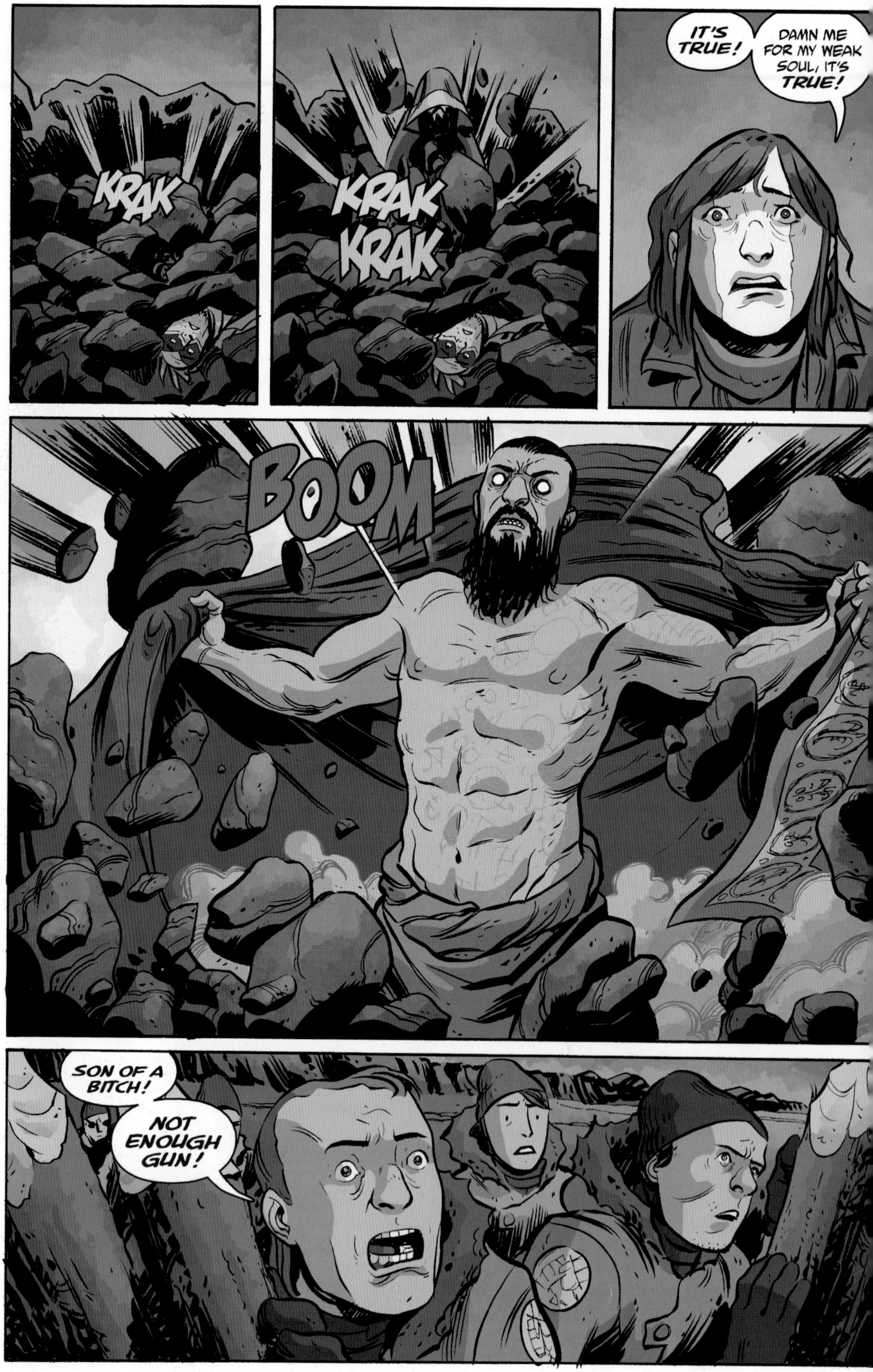
KRAK
KRAK
KRAK
IT'S TRUE!
DAMN ME FOR MY WEAK SOUL, IT'S TRUE!
BOOM
SON OF A BITCH!
NOT ENOUGH GUN!

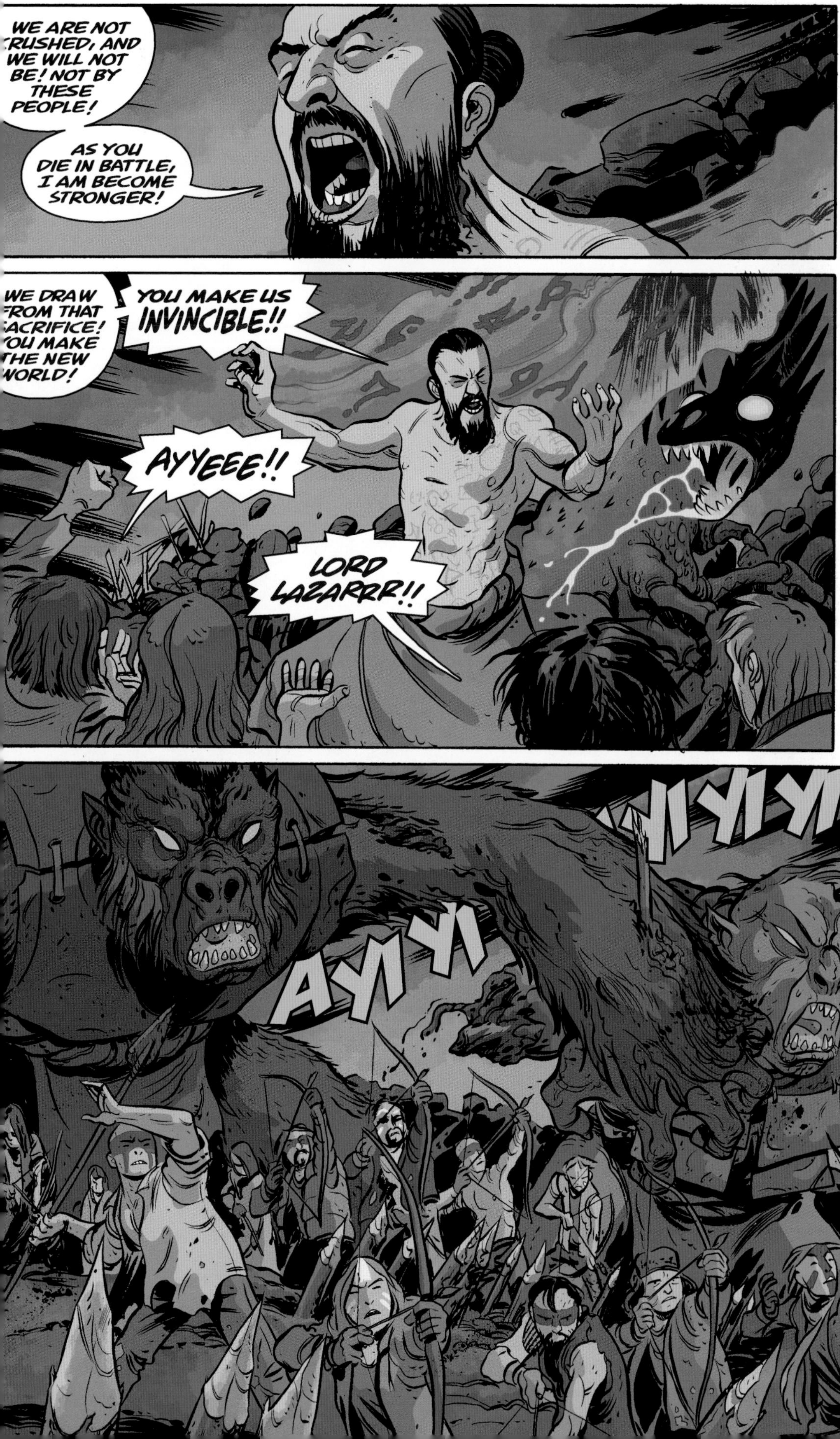
WE ARE NOT CRUSHED, AND WE WILL NOT BE! NOT BY THESE PEOPLE!
AS YOU DIE IN BATTLE, I AM BECOME STRONGER!
WE DRAW FROM THAT SACRIFICE! YOU MAKE THE NEW WORLD!
YOU MAKE US INVINCIBLE!!
AYYEEE!!
LORD LAZARRR!!
AYIYI
YIYIYIYI

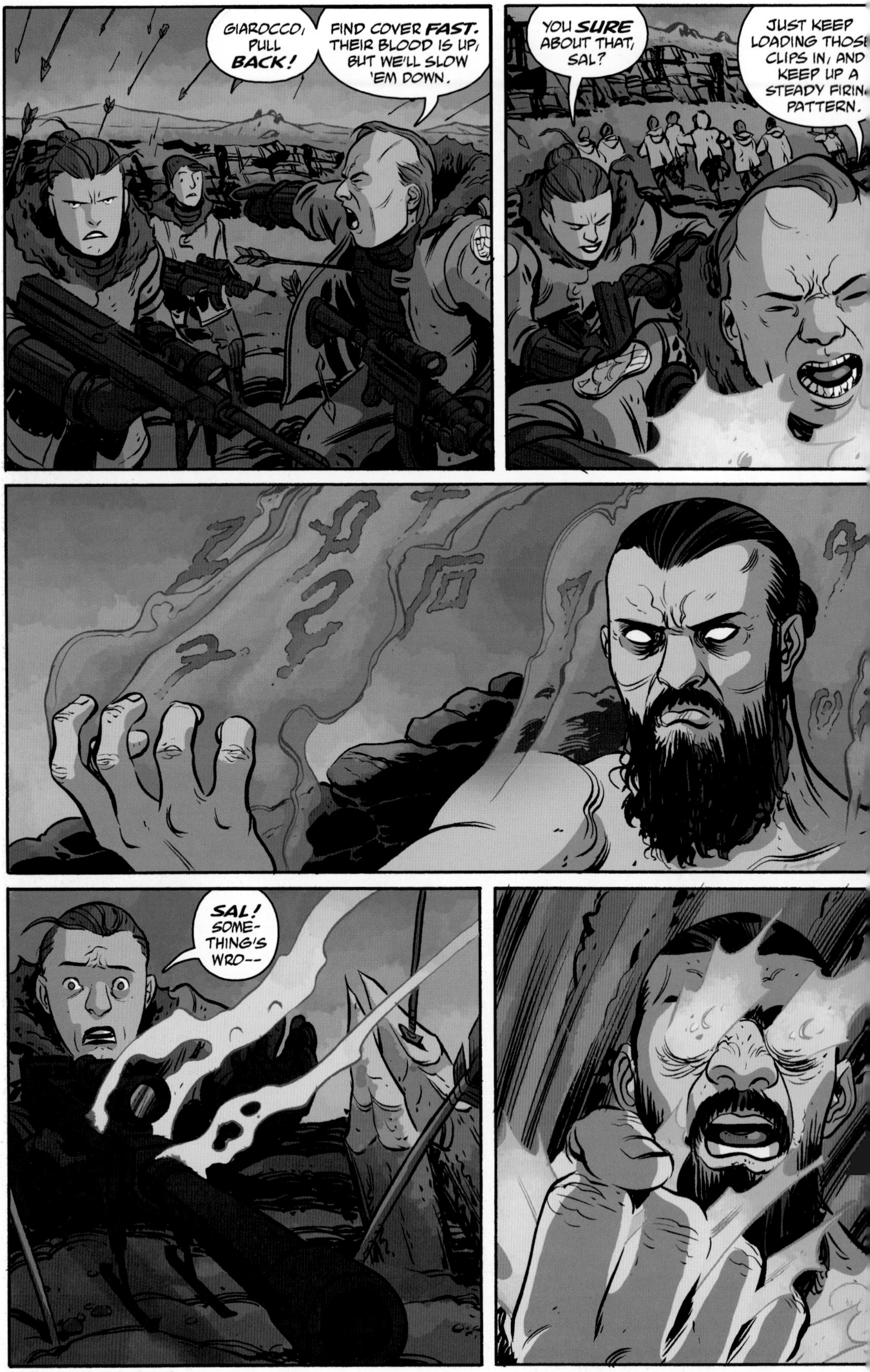
GIAROCCO, PULL BACK!
FIND COVER FAST. THEIR BLOOD IS UP, BUT WE'LL SLOW 'EM DOWN.
YOU SURE ABOUT THAT, SAL?
JUST KEEP LOADING THOSE CLIPS IN, AND KEEP UP A STEADY FIRING PATTERN.
SAL! SOME-THING'S WRO--

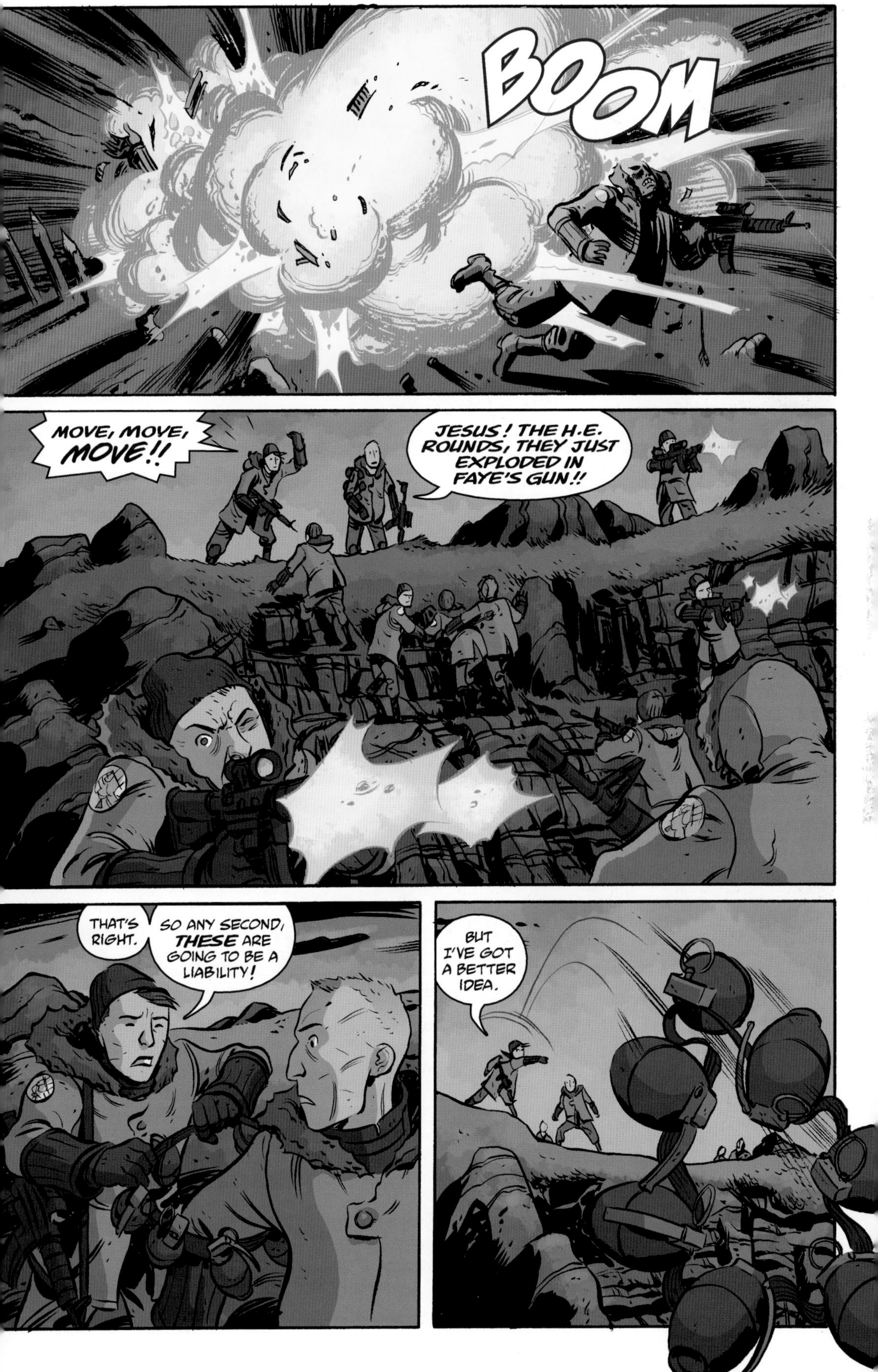
BOOM
MOVE, MOVE, MOVE!!
JESUS! THE H.E. ROUNDS, THEY JUST EXPLODED IN FAYE'S GUN!!
THAT'S RIGHT.
SO ANY SECOND, THESE ARE GOING TO BE A LIABILITY!
BUT I'VE GOT A BETTER IDEA.

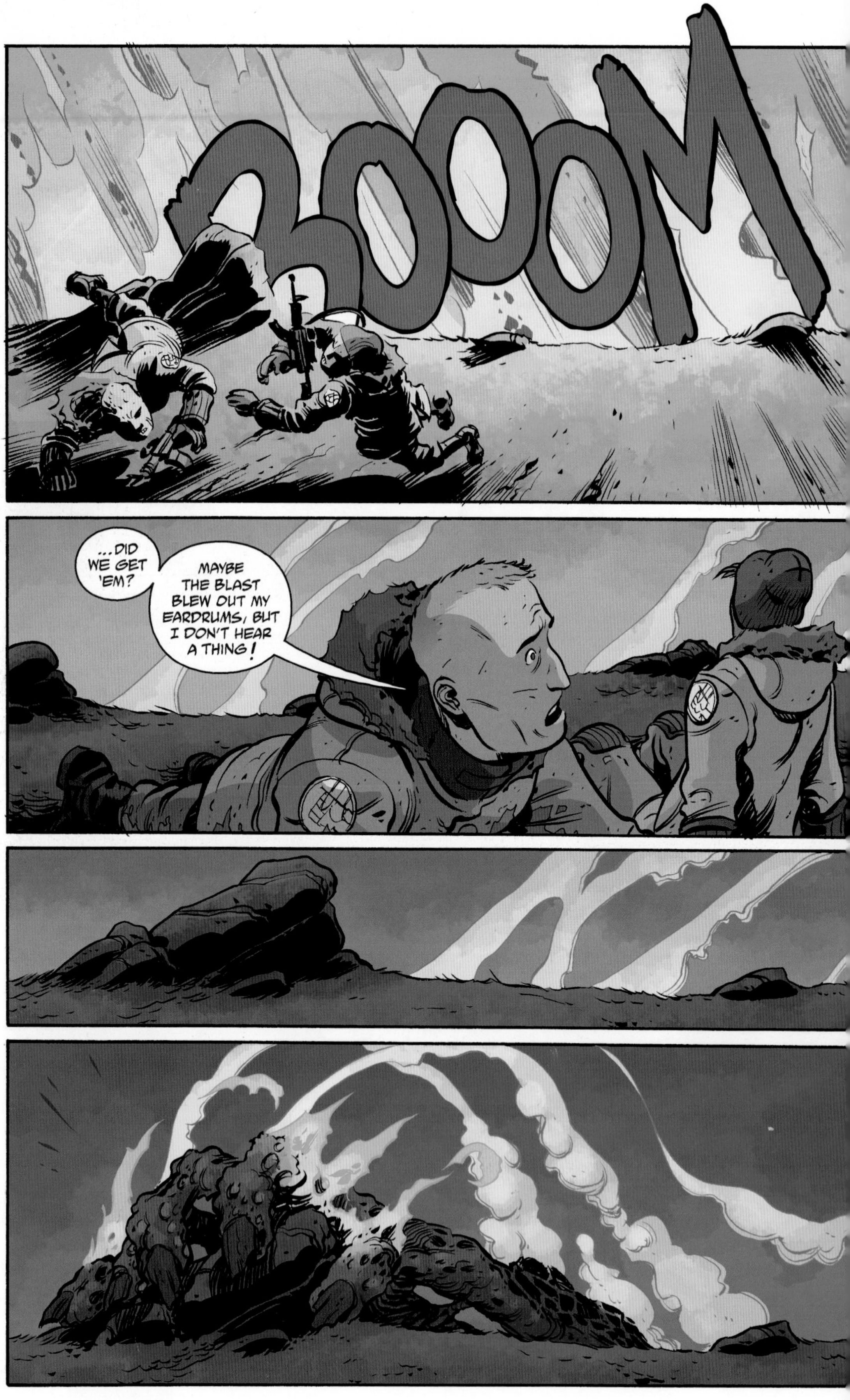
BOOOM
...DID WE GET 'EM?
MAYBE THE BLAST BLEW OUT MY EARDRUMS, BUT I DON'T HEAR A THING!

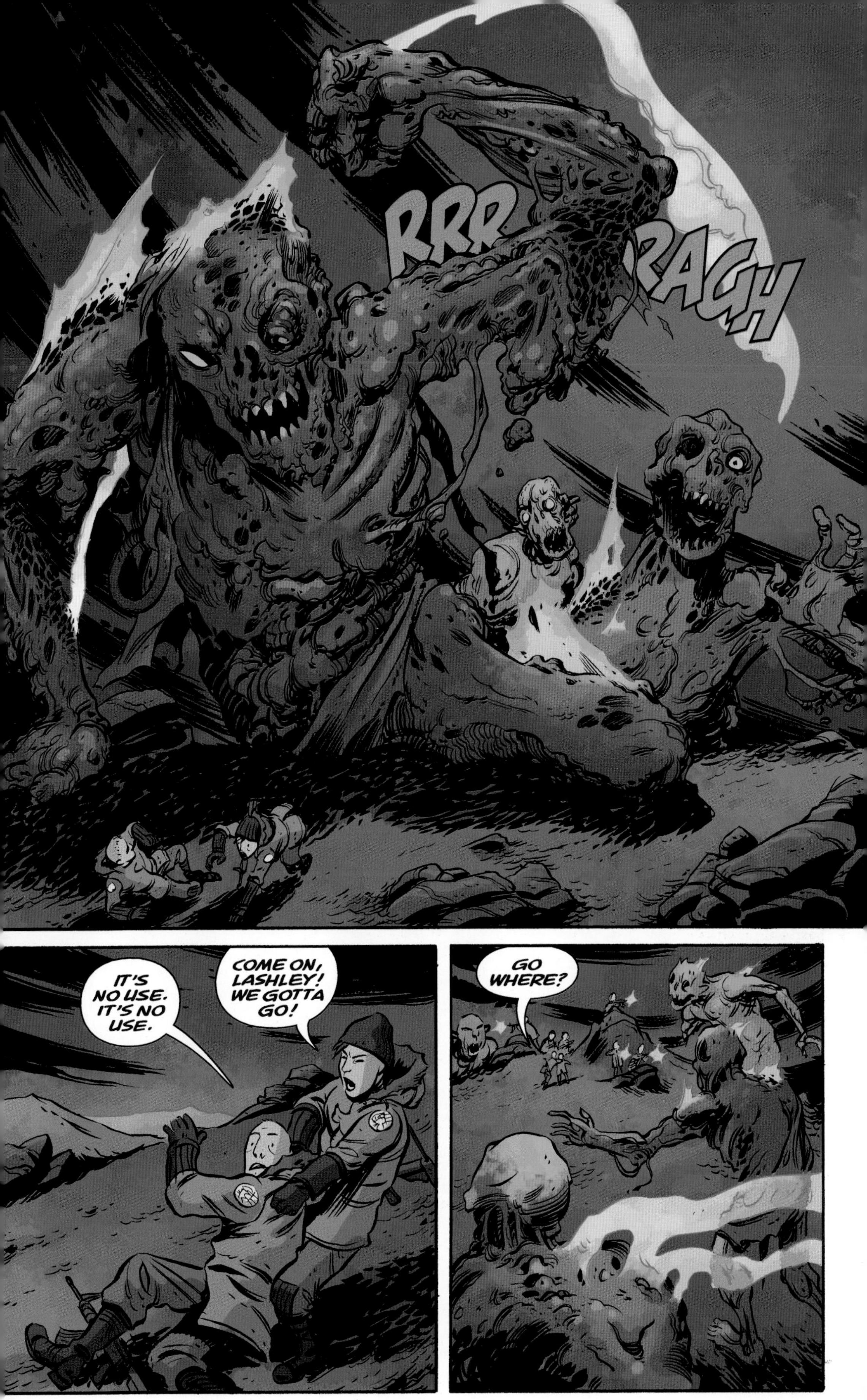
RRRRAGH
IT'S NO USE. IT'S NO USE.
COME ON, LASHLEY! WE GOTTA GO!
GO WHERE?

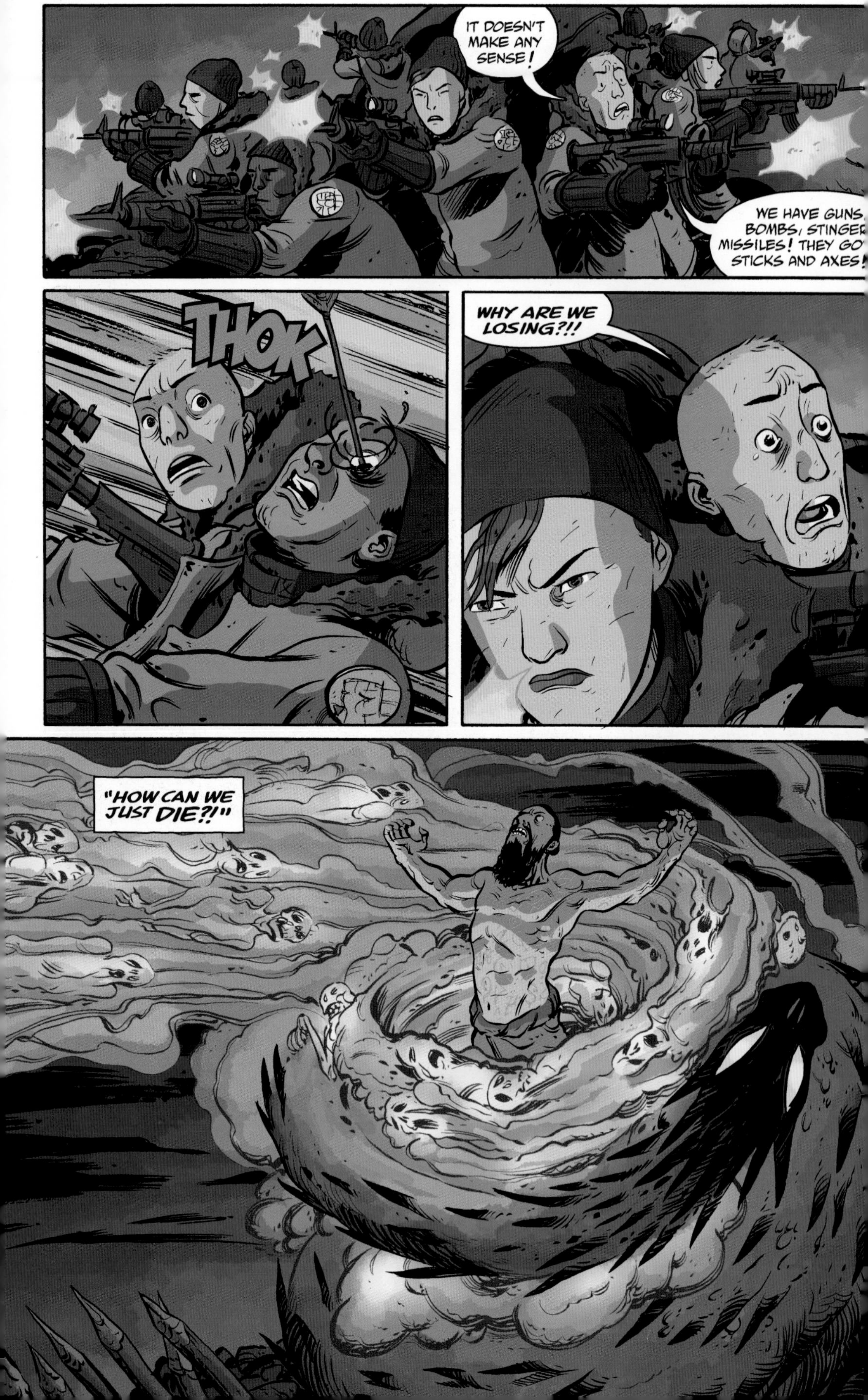
IT DOESN'T MAKE ANY SENSE!
WE HAVE GUNS, BOMBS, STINGER MISSILES! THEY GOT STICKS AND AXES!
THOK
WHY ARE WE LOSING?!!
"HOW CAN WE JUST DIE?!"

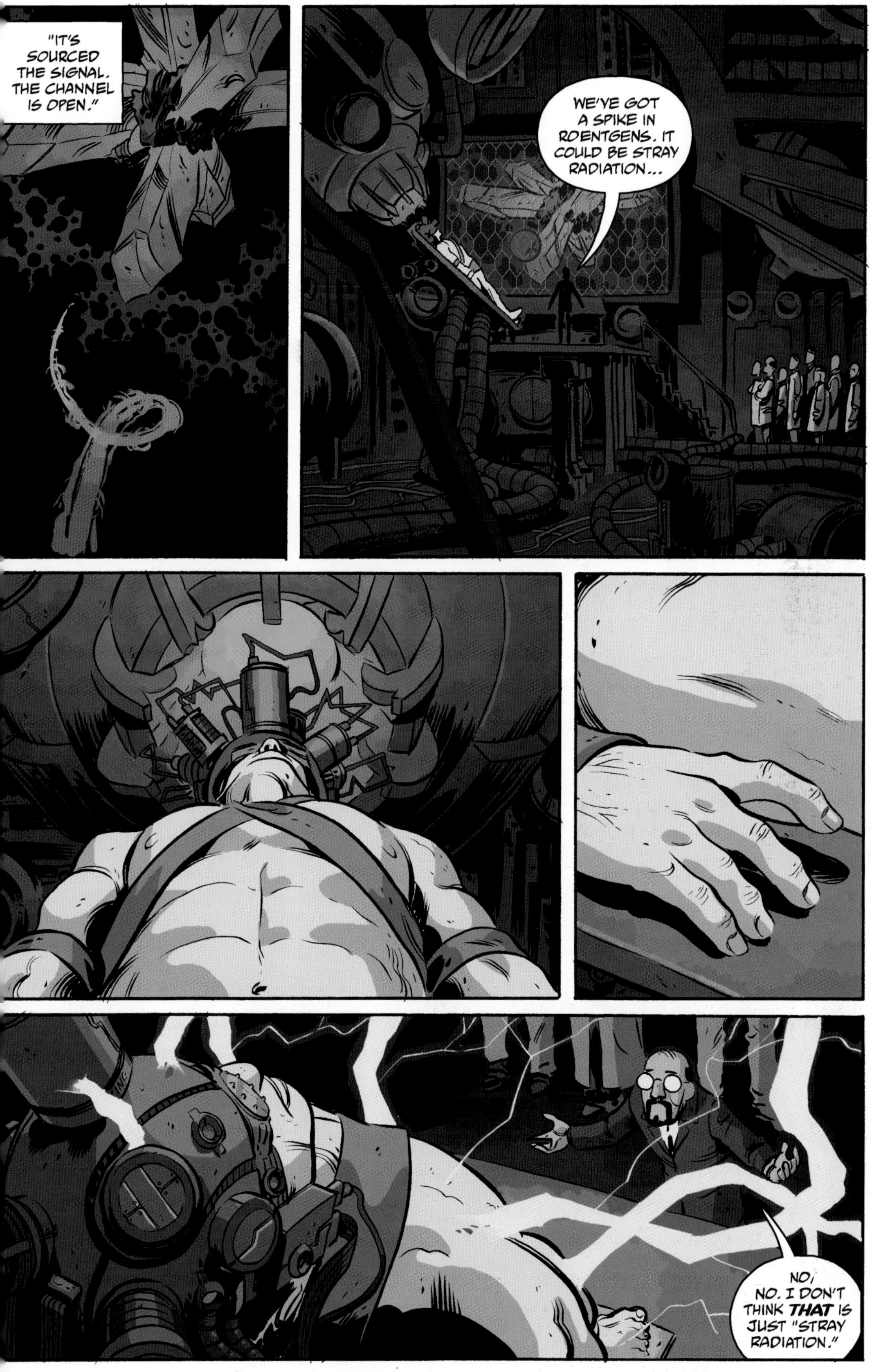
"IT'S SOURCED THE SIGNAL. THE CHANNEL IS OPEN."
WE'VE GOT A SPIKE IN ROENTGENS. IT COULD BE STRAY RADIATION...
NO, NO. I DON'T THINK **THAT** IS JUST "STRAY RADIATION."

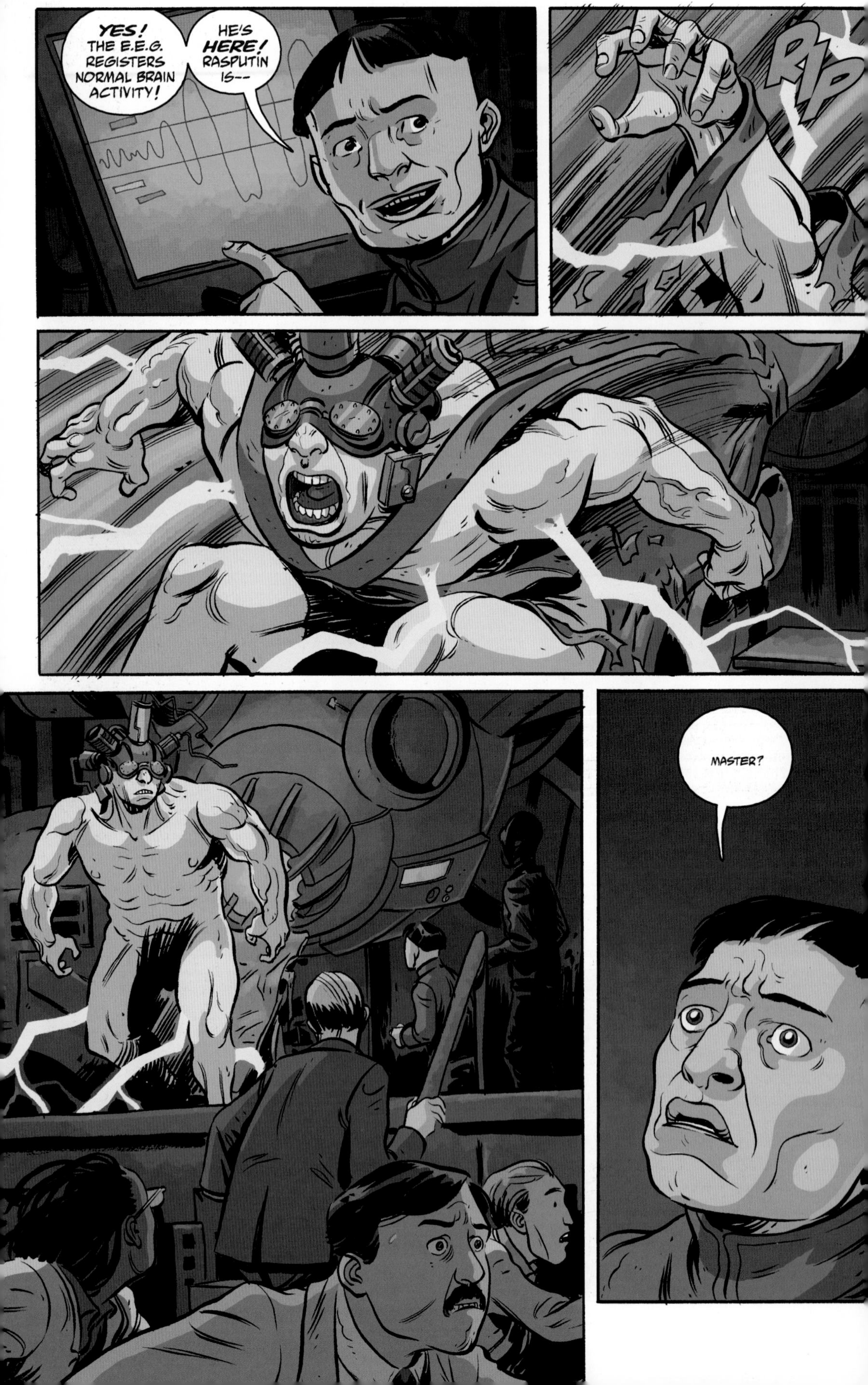
YES! THE E.E.G. REGISTERS NORMAL BRAIN ACTIVITY!
HE'S HERE! RASPUTIN IS--
RIP
MASTER?

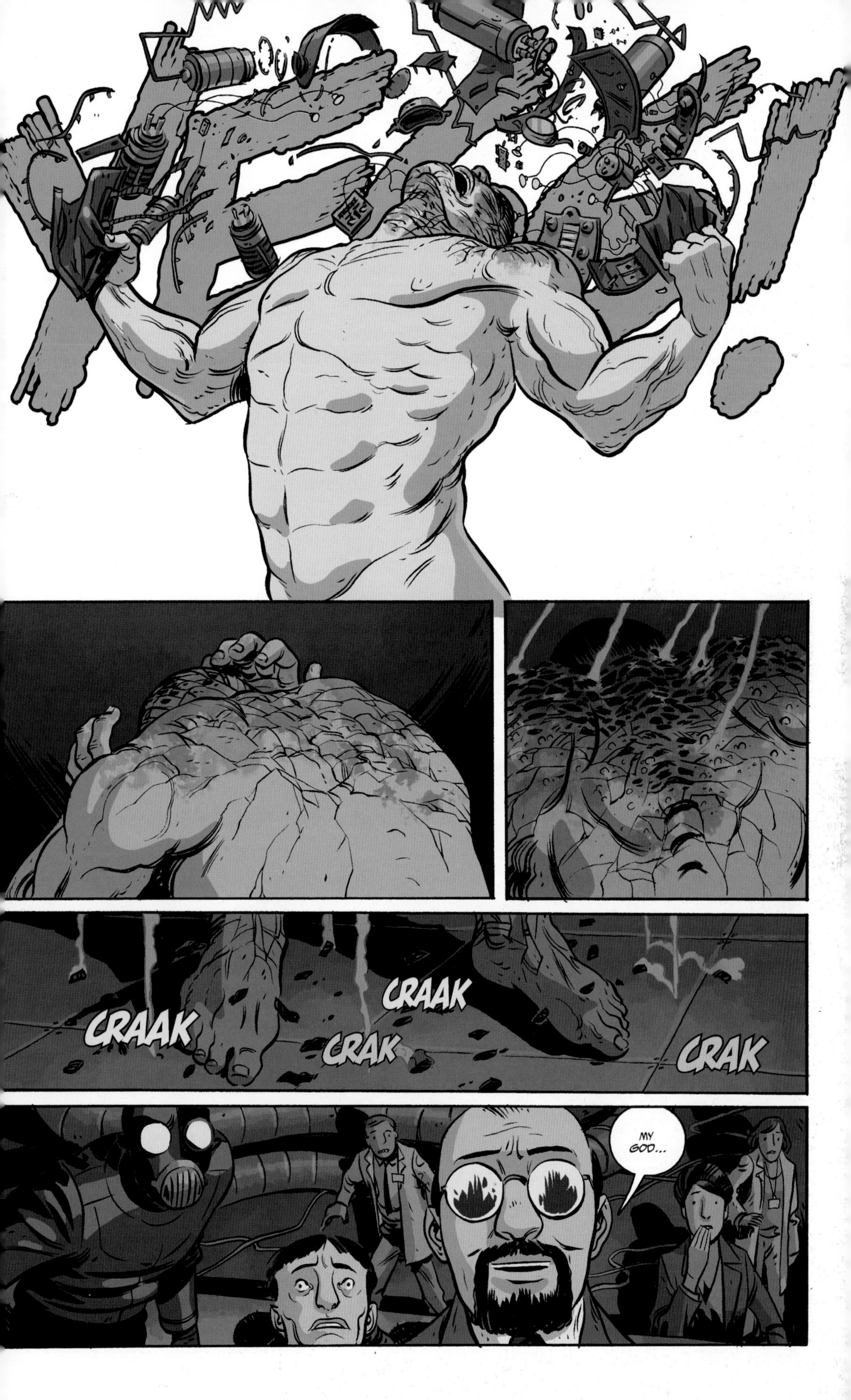
CRAAK
CRAAK
CRAK
CRAK
MY GOD...

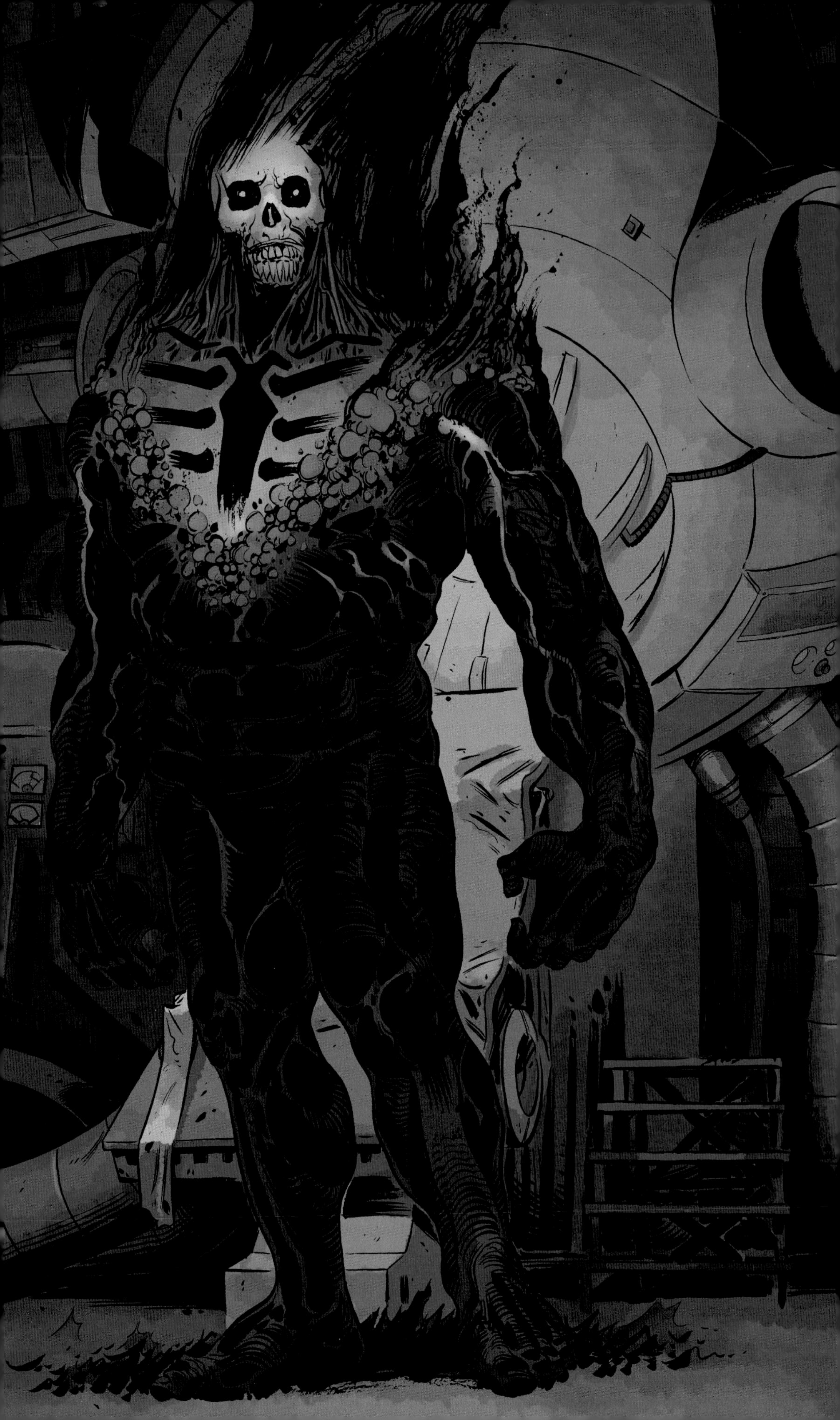

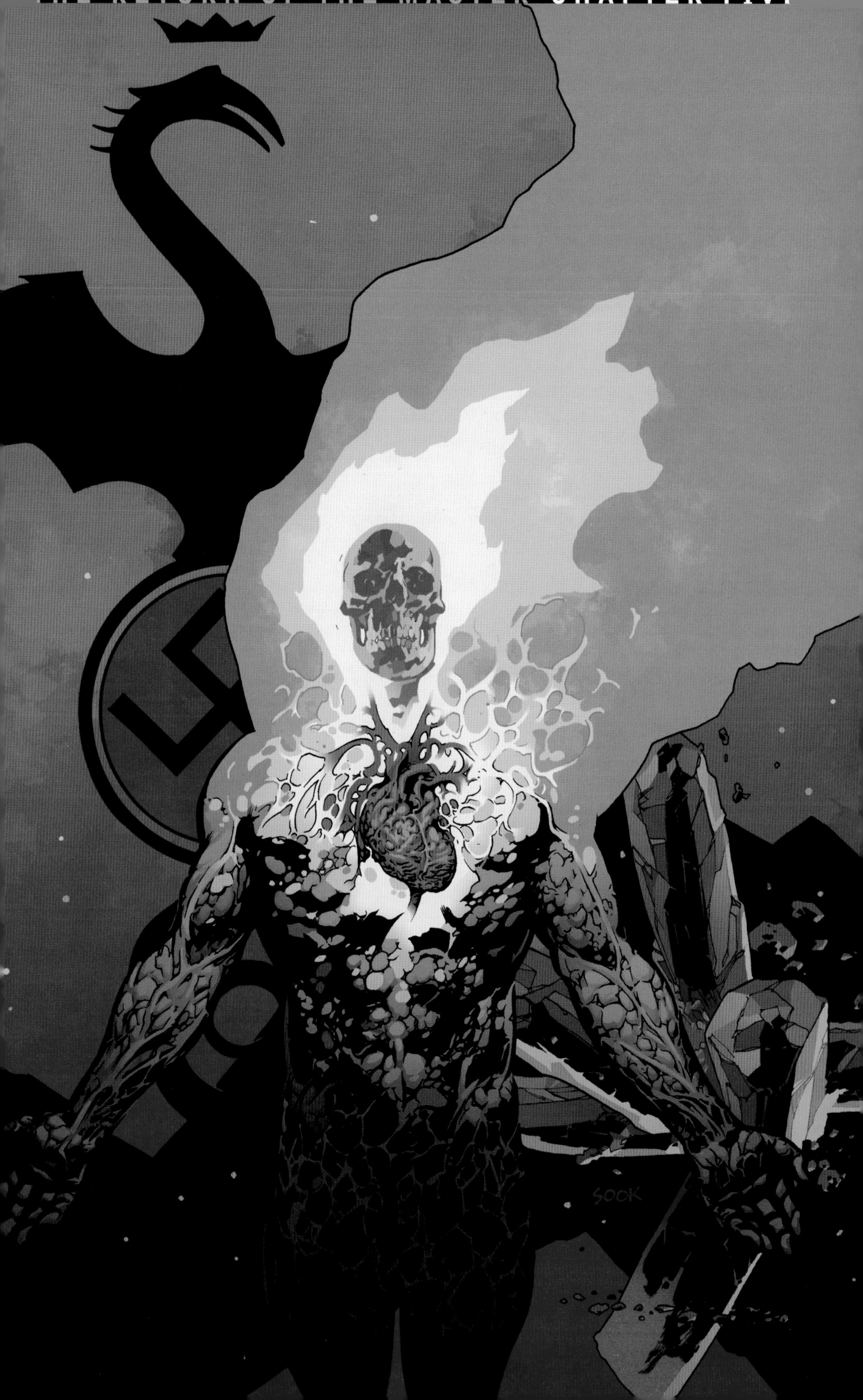
SOOK

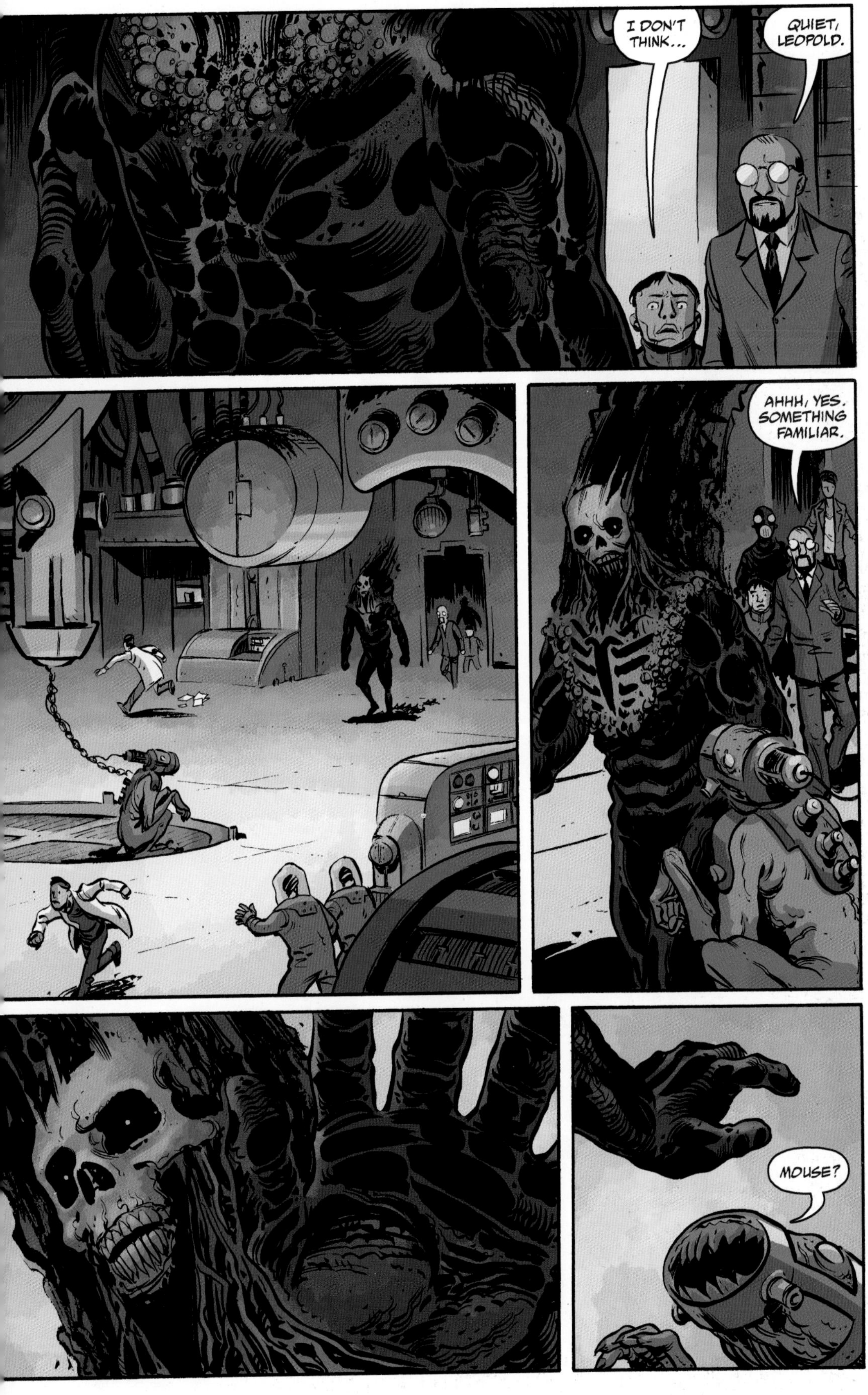
I DON'T THINK...
QUIET, LEOPOLD.
AHHH, YES. SOMETHING FAMILIAR.
MOUSE?

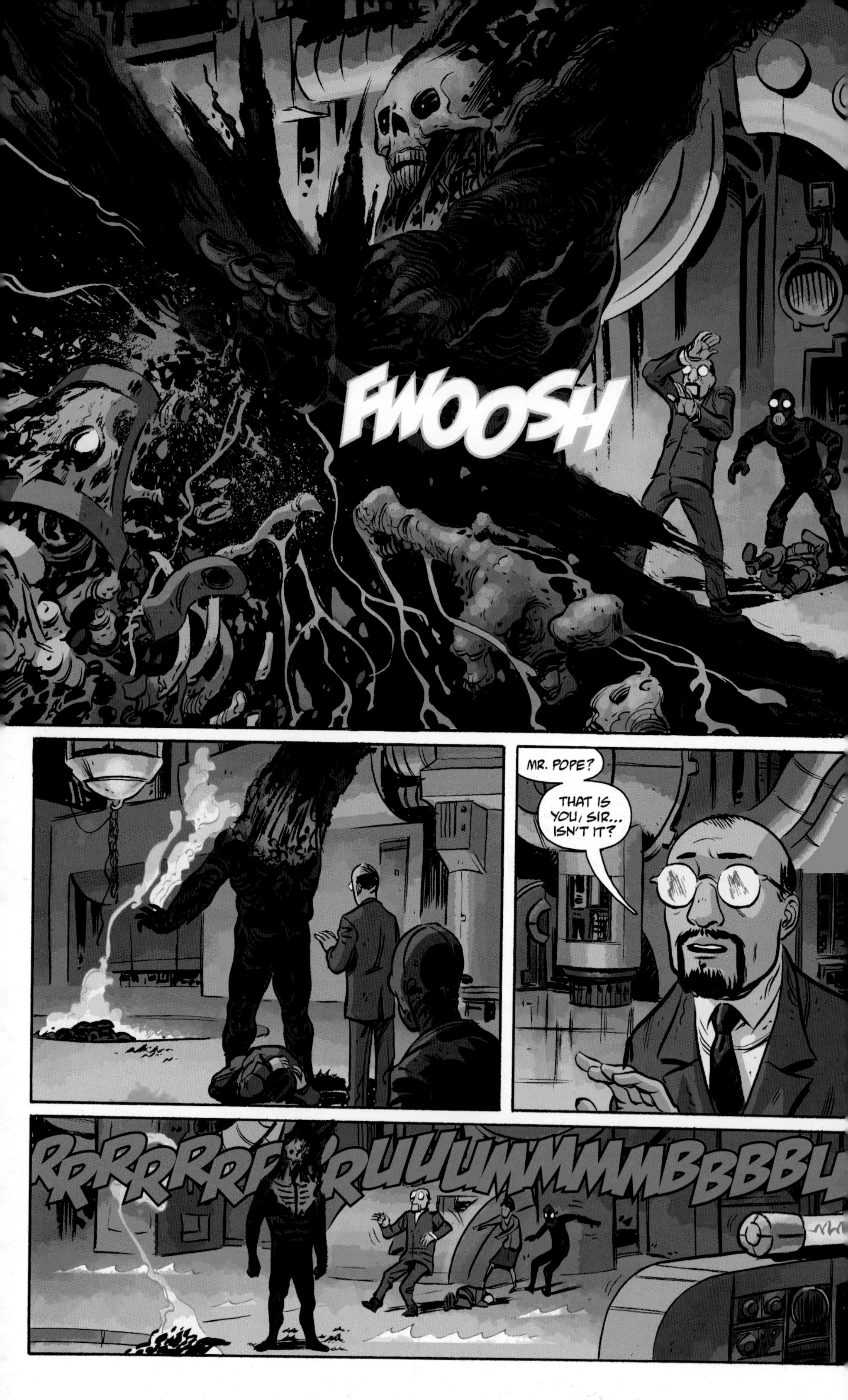
FWOOSH
MR. POPE?
THAT IS YOU, SIR... ISN'T IT?
RRRRRRRRRUUUMMMMBBBBL

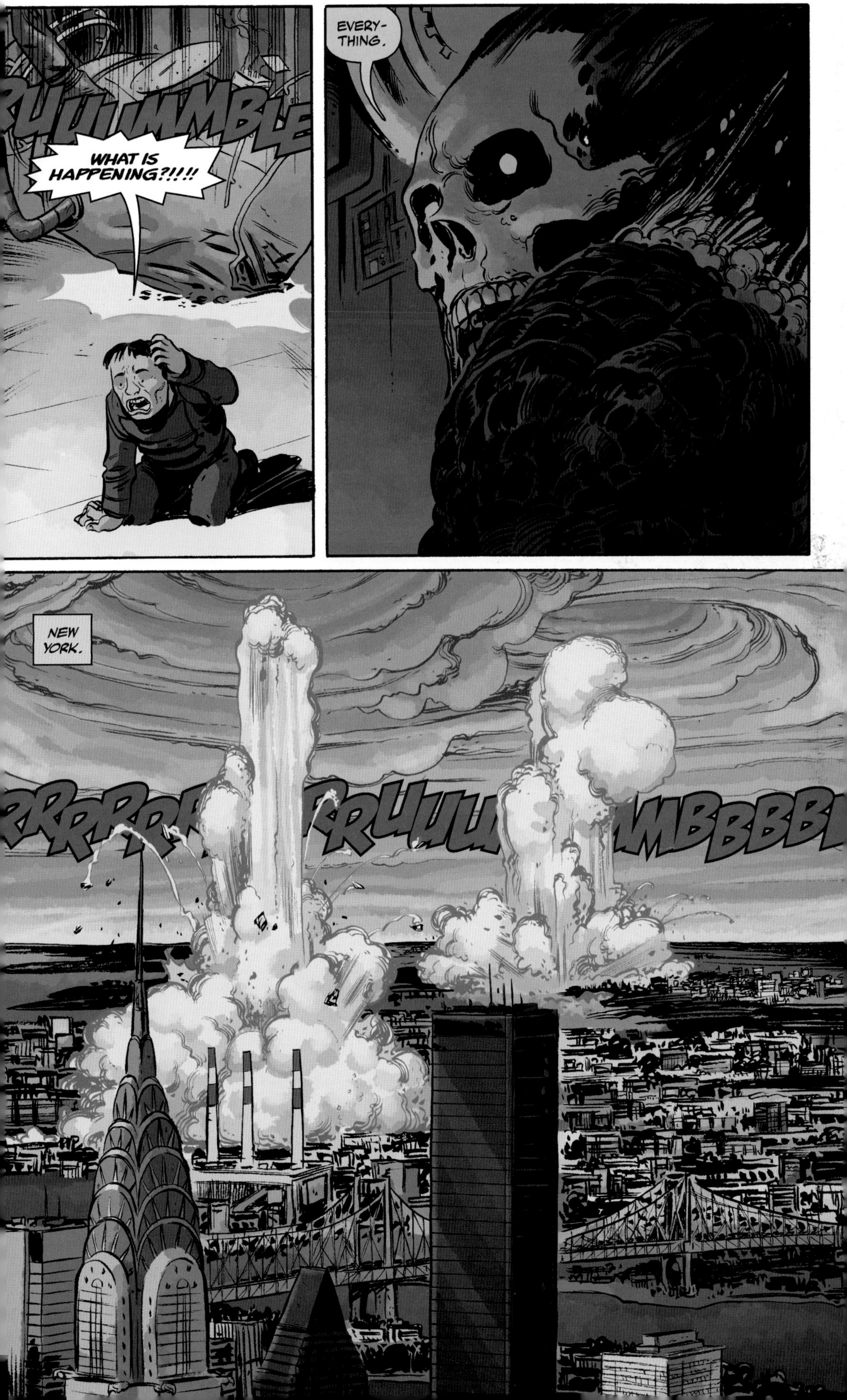
RUUUMMBLE
WHAT IS HAPPENING?!!!!
EVERY-THING.
NEW YORK.
RRRRRRRRUUUUMBBBB

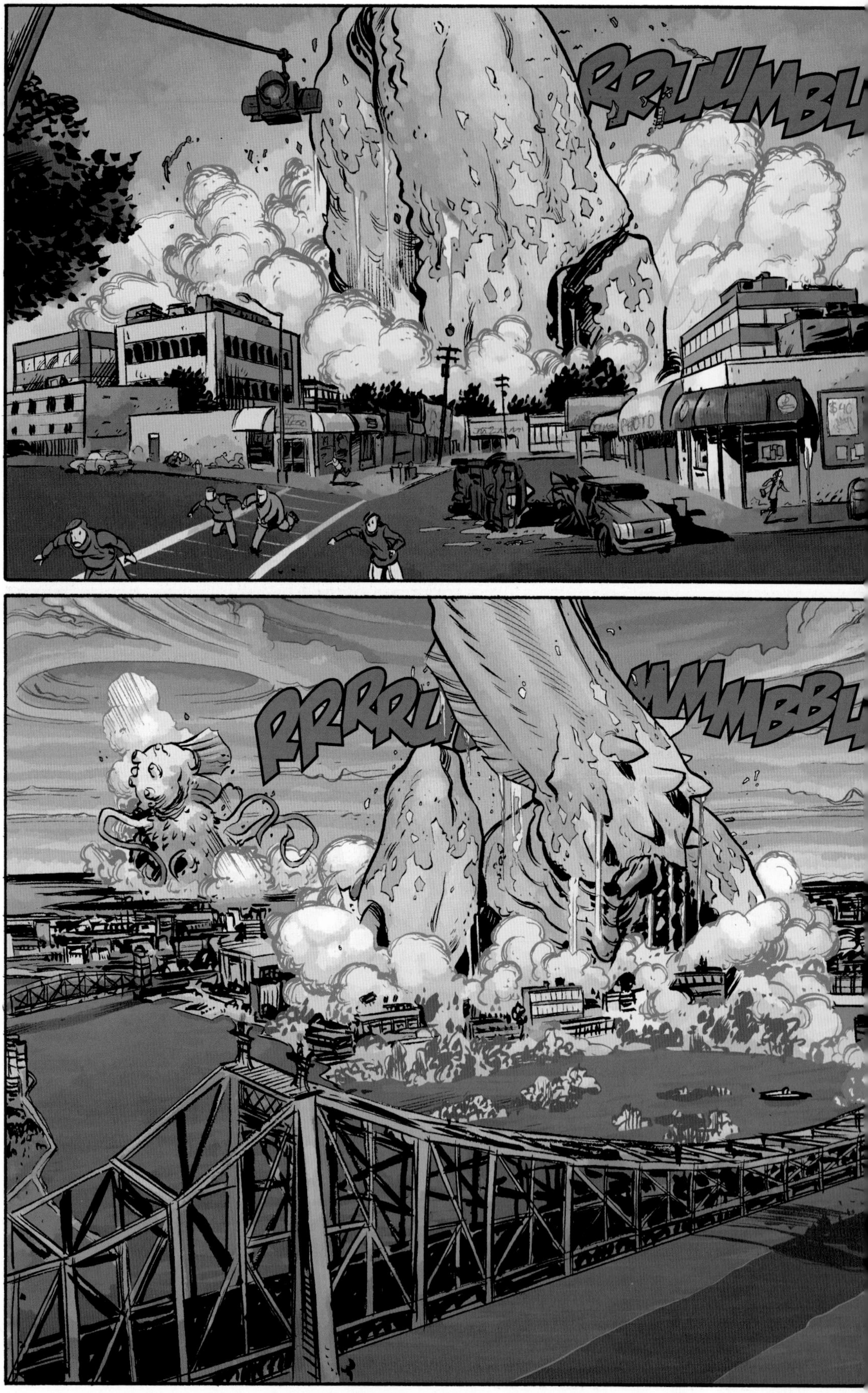
RRUUMBL
PHOTO
$40
RRRRU
MMMBBL

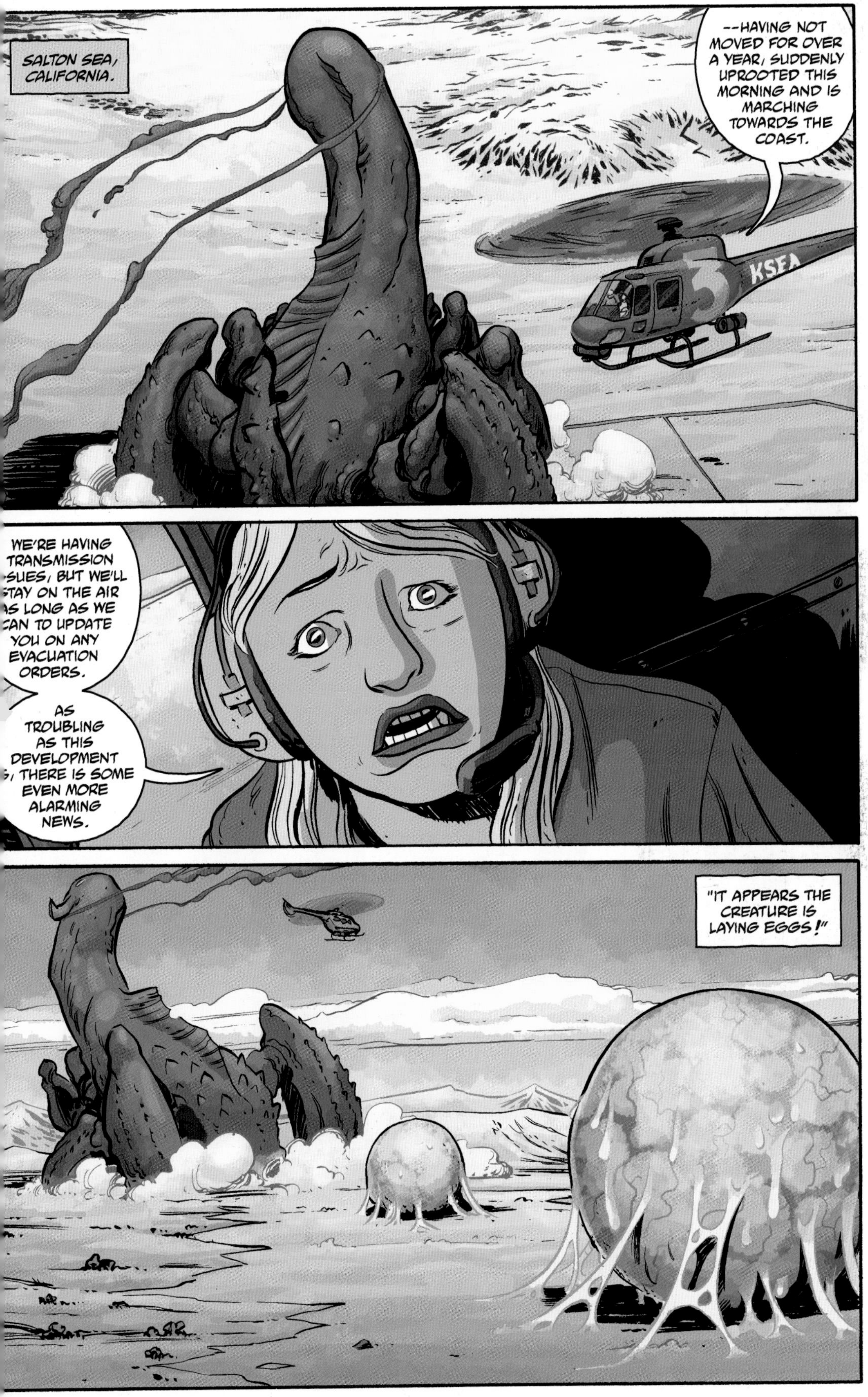
SALTON SEA, CALIFORNIA.
--HAVING NOT MOVED FOR OVER A YEAR, SUDDENLY UPROOTED THIS MORNING AND IS MARCHING TOWARDS THE COAST.
KSEA
WE'RE HAVING TRANSMISSION ISSUES, BUT WE'LL STAY ON THE AIR AS LONG AS WE CAN TO UPDATE YOU ON ANY EVACUATION ORDERS.
AS TROUBLING AS THIS DEVELOPMENT IS, THERE IS SOME EVEN MORE ALARMING NEWS.
"IT APPEARS THE CREATURE IS LAYING EGGS!"

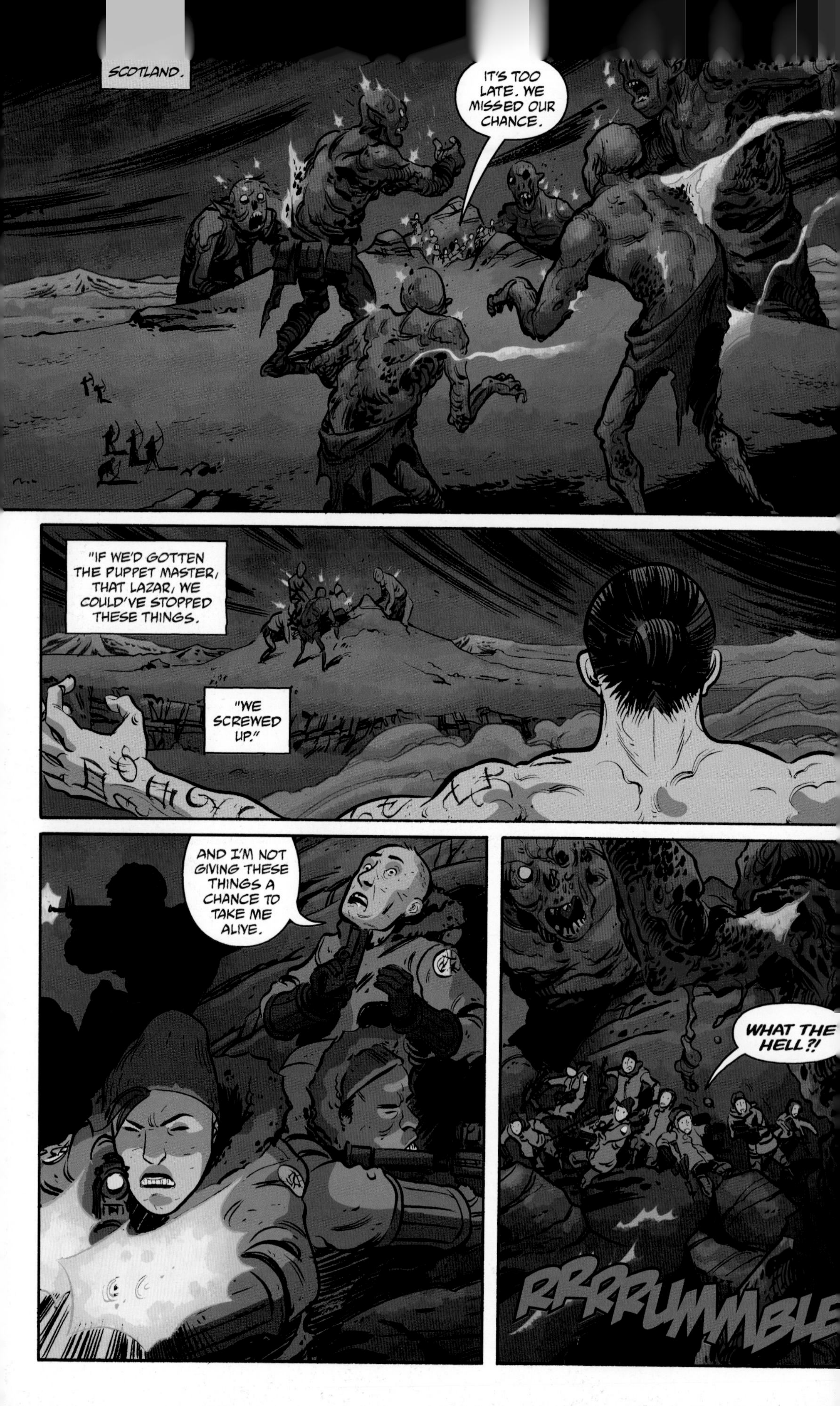
SCOTLAND.
IT'S TOO LATE. WE MISSED OUR CHANCE.
"IF WE'D GOTTEN THE PUPPET MASTER, THAT LAZAR, WE COULD'VE STOPPED THESE THINGS.
"WE SCREWED UP."
AND I'M NOT GIVING THESE THINGS A CHANCE TO TAKE ME ALIVE.
WHAT THE HELL?!
RRRRUMMBLE

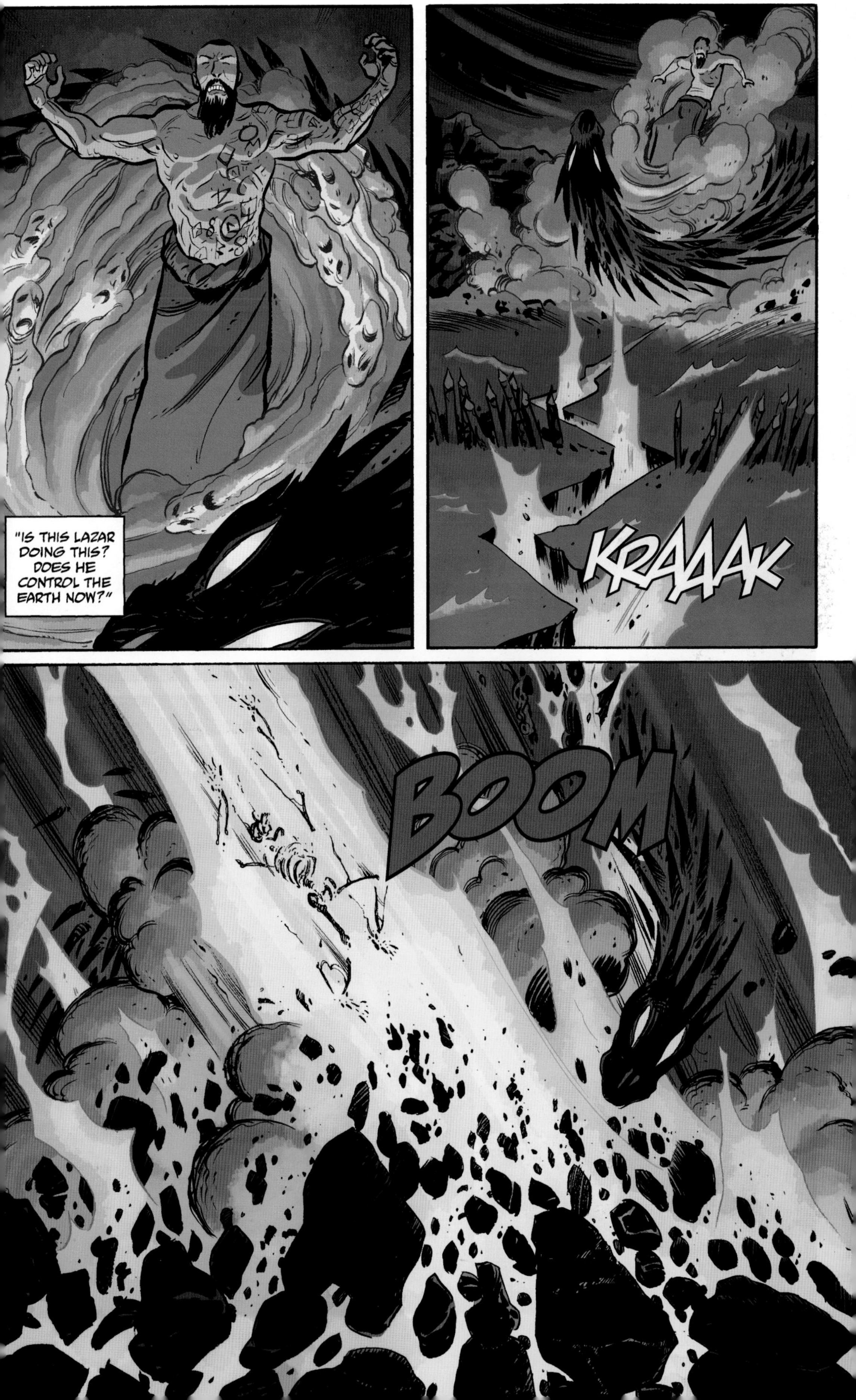

"IS THIS LAZAR DOING THIS? DOES HE CONTROL THE EARTH NOW?"
KRAAAK
BOOM

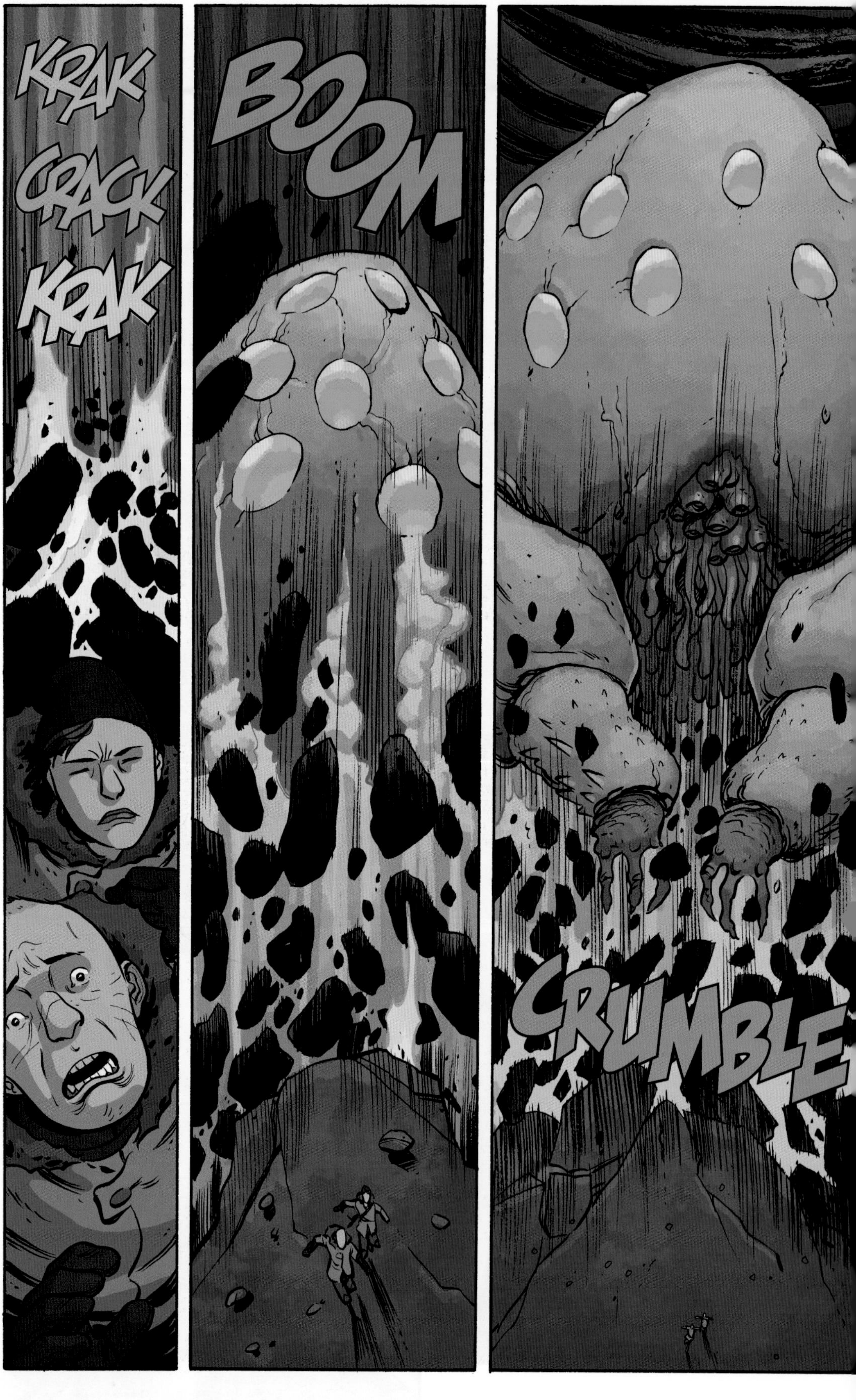
KRAK
CRACK
KRAK
BOOM
CRUMBLE

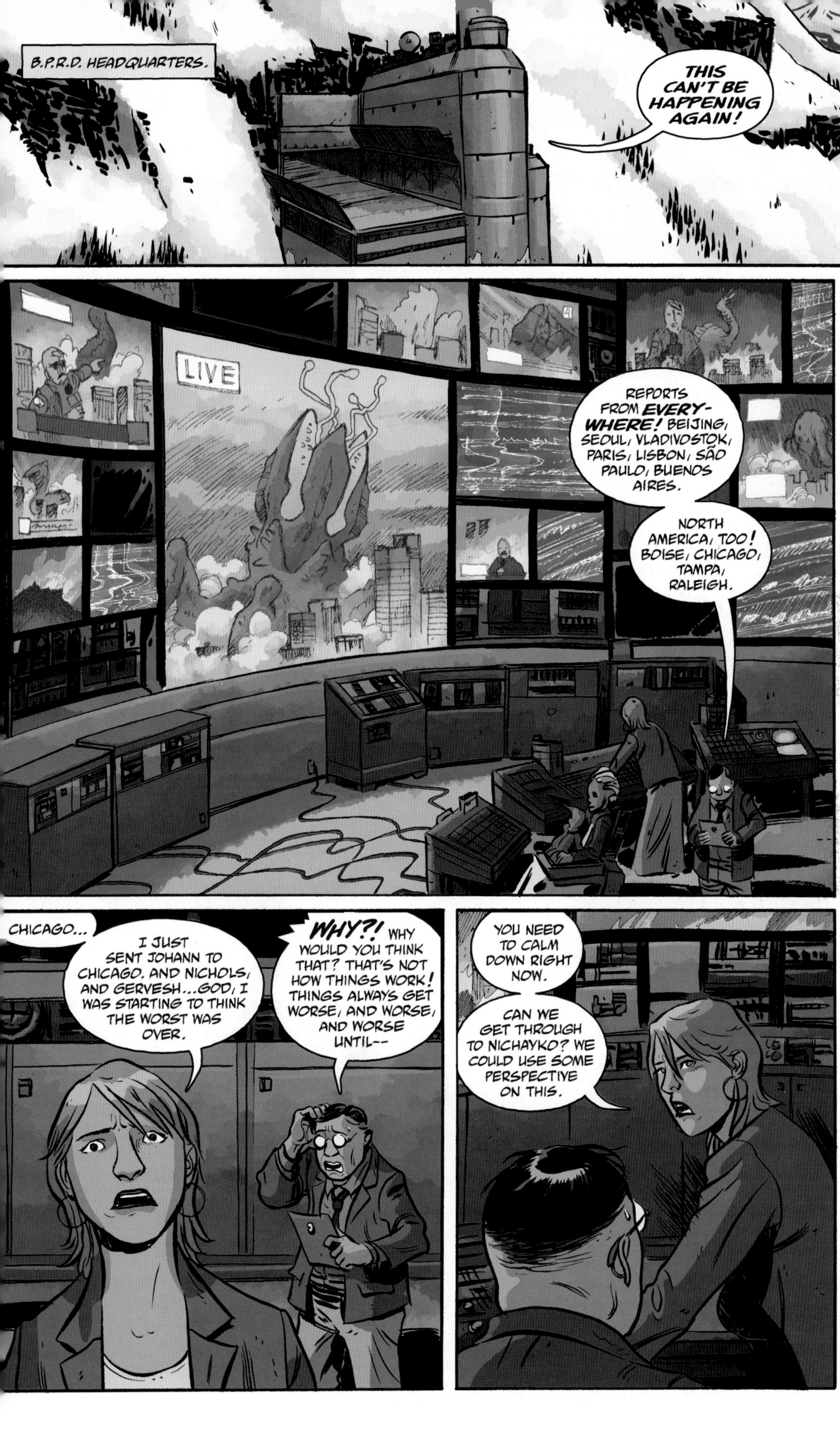
B.P.R.D. HEADQUARTERS.
THIS CAN'T BE HAPPENING AGAIN!
LIVE
REPORTS FROM EVERY-WHERE! BEIJING, SEOUL, VLADIVOSTOK, PARIS, LISBON, SÃO PAULO, BUENOS AIRES.
NORTH AMERICA, TOO! BOISE, CHICAGO, TAMPA, RALEIGH.
CHICAGO...
I JUST SENT JOHANN TO CHICAGO. AND NICHOLS, AND GERVESH...GOD, I WAS STARTING TO THINK THE WORST WAS OVER.
WHY?! WHY WOULD YOU THINK THAT? THAT'S NOT HOW THINGS WORK! THINGS ALWAYS GET WORSE, AND WORSE, AND WORSE UNTIL--
YOU NEED TO CALM DOWN RIGHT NOW.
CAN WE GET THROUGH TO NICHAYKO? WE COULD USE SOME PERSPECTIVE ON THIS.

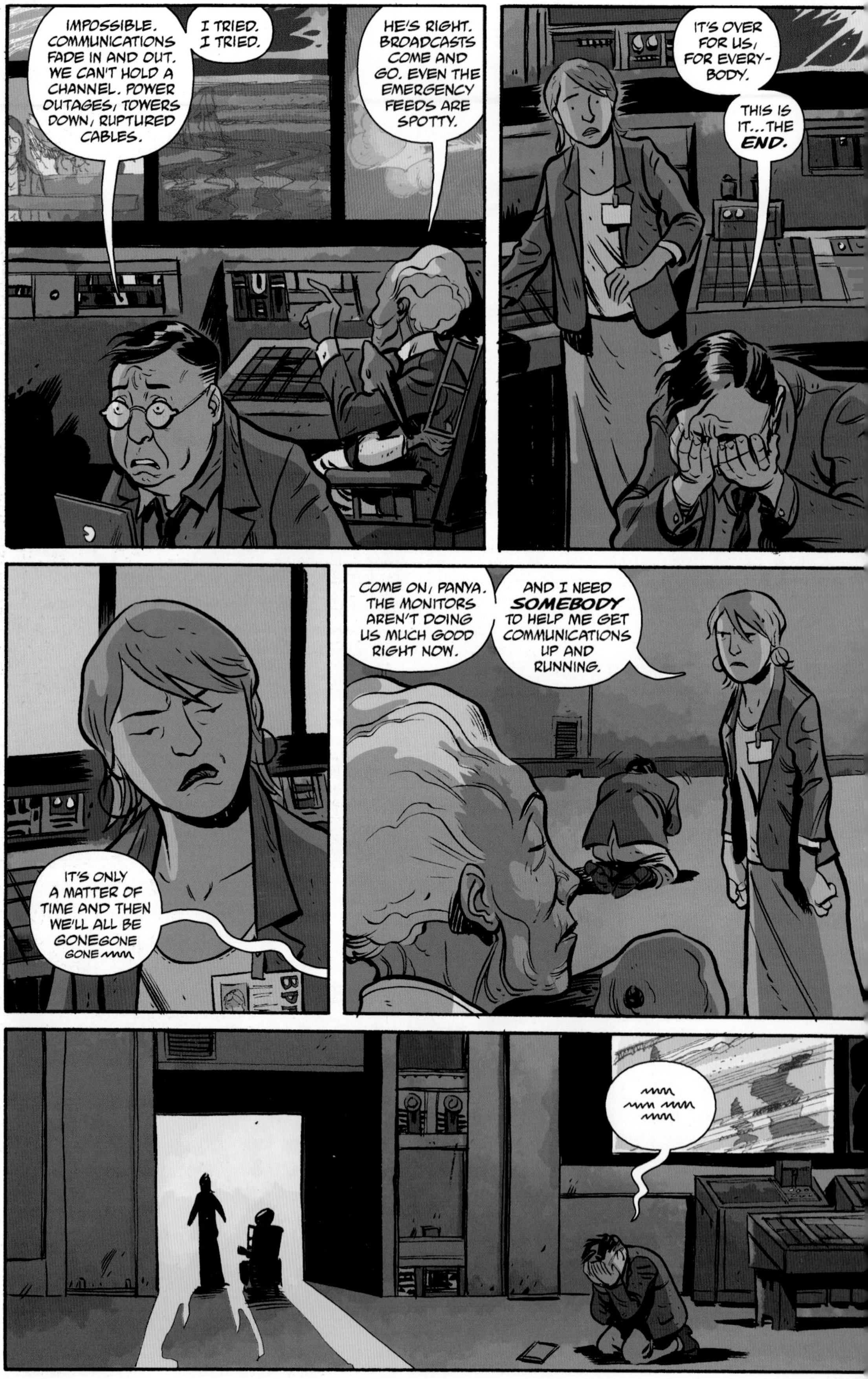
IMPOSSIBLE. COMMUNICATIONS FADE IN AND OUT. WE CAN'T HOLD A CHANNEL. POWER OUTAGES, TOWERS DOWN, RUPTURED CABLES.
I TRIED. I TRIED.
HE'S RIGHT. BROADCASTS COME AND GO. EVEN THE EMERGENCY FEEDS ARE SPOTTY.
IT'S OVER FOR US, FOR EVERY-BODY.
THIS IS IT... THE **END.**
IT'S ONLY A MATTER OF TIME AND THEN WE'LL ALL BE GONEGONE GONE
COME ON, PANYA. THE MONITORS AREN'T DOING US MUCH GOOD RIGHT NOW.
AND I NEED **SOMEBODY** TO HELP ME GET COMMUNICATIONS UP AND RUNNING.

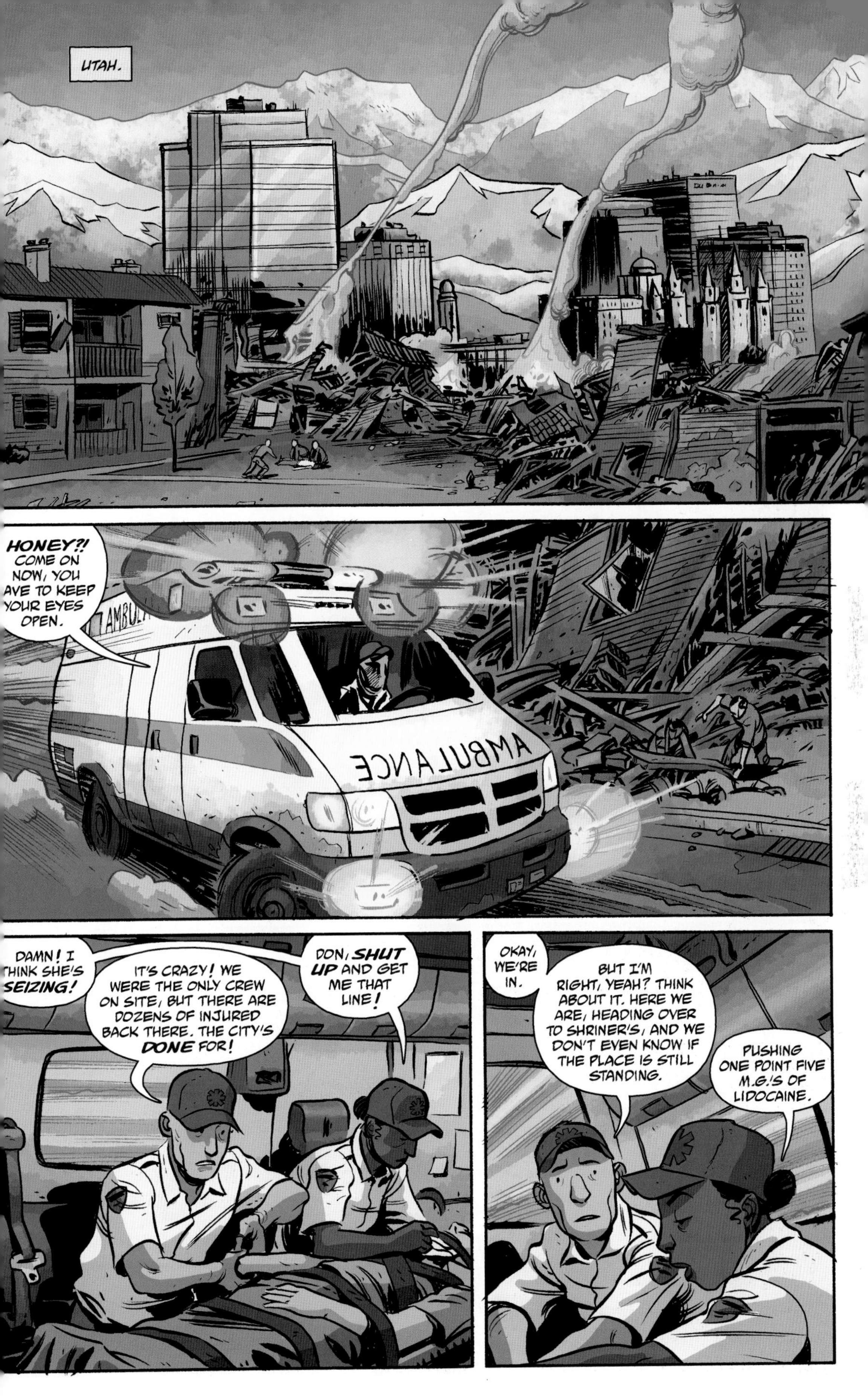
UTAH.
HONEY?! COME ON NOW, YOU AVE TO KEEP YOUR EYES OPEN.
AMBULANCE
DAMN! I THINK SHE'S SEIZING!
IT'S CRAZY! WE WERE THE ONLY CREW ON SITE, BUT THERE ARE DOZENS OF INJURED BACK THERE. THE CITY'S DONE FOR!
DON, SHUT UP AND GET ME THAT LINE!
OKAY, WE'RE IN.
BUT I'M RIGHT, YEAH? THINK ABOUT IT. HERE WE ARE, HEADING OVER TO SHRINER'S, AND WE DON'T EVEN KNOW IF THE PLACE IS STILL STANDING.
PUSHING ONE POINT FIVE M.G.'S OF LIDOCAINE.

AND IF SHRINER'S IS COLLAPSED, WE FIND ANOTHER HOSPITAL, OKAY?

LOOK, DON, IF YOU DON'T LIKE TOUGH SITUATIONS, WHY THE HELL'D YOU EVER BECOME AN E.M.T.?

TO HELP PEOPLE, *THAT'S* WHY! I WANTED TO HELP PEOPLE.

BUT RIGHT NOW I FEEL HELPLES. I SEE THE WHOL CITY--HELL, THE WORLD-- CRUMBLING. I MEAN, THAT WASN'T IN M' TRAINING.

*YOU* FEEL HELPLESS!

SO THE WORLD'S COLLAPSING. WE GOT A GIRL RIGHT *HERE* IN THE RIG WHO'S TOUCH AND GO, BUT *YOU*--

UHHHHH...

AH, THAT'S WHAT WE WANT.

OKAY, MISS, DO YOU KNOW WHERE YOU ARE? CAN YOU TELL ME YOUR NAME? CAN YOU DO THAT?

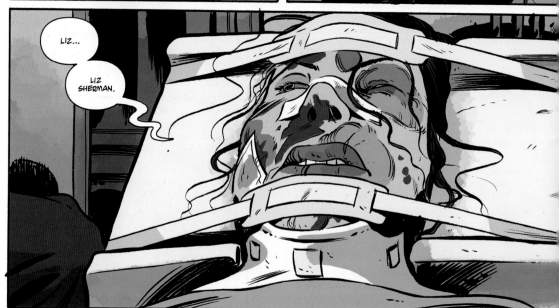

LIZ...

LIZ SHERMAN.

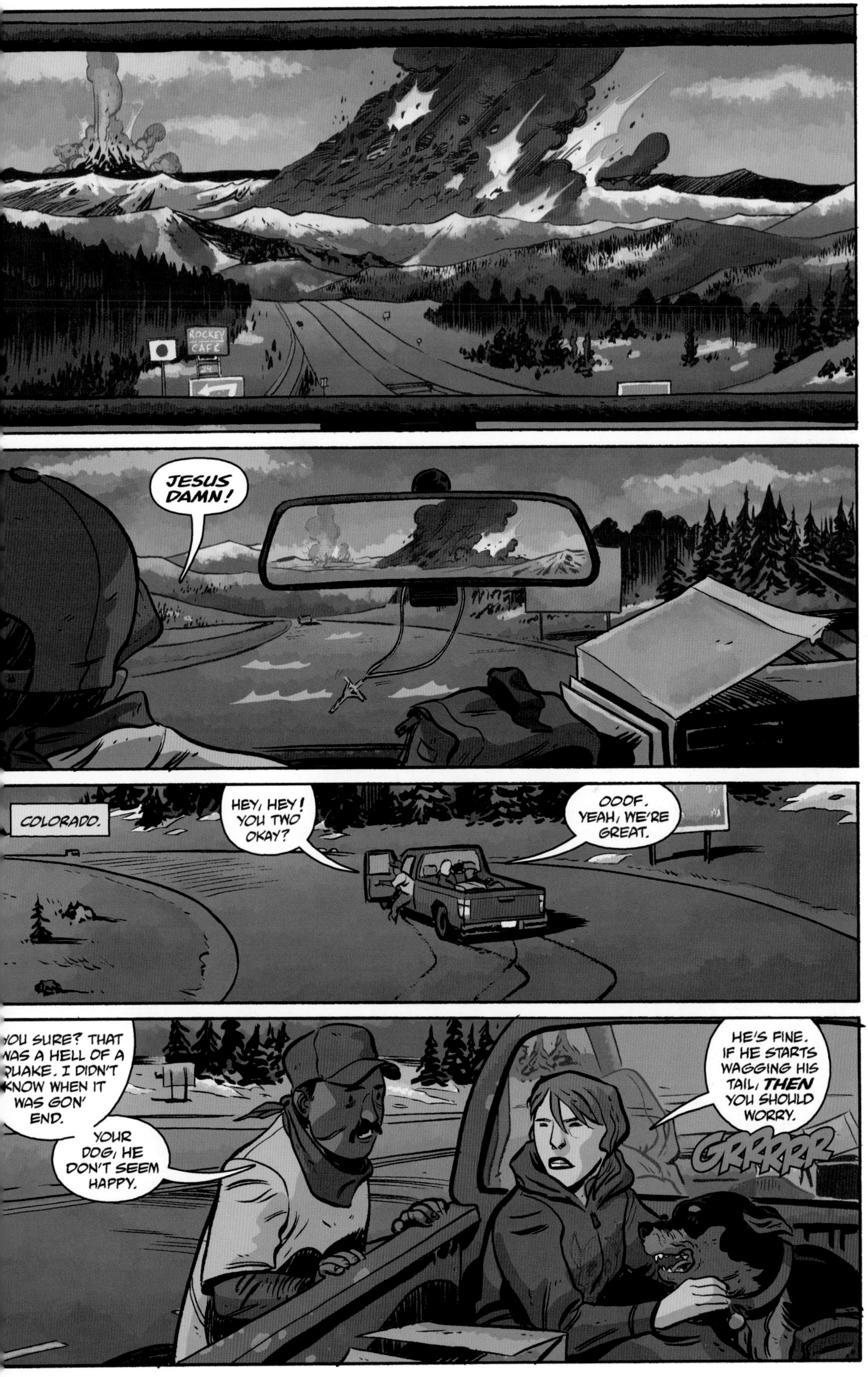
ROCKEY CAFÉ
JESUS DAMN!
COLORADO.
HEY, HEY! YOU TWO OKAY?
OOOF. YEAH, WE'RE GREAT.
YOU SURE? THAT WAS A HELL OF A QUAKE. I DIDN'T KNOW WHEN IT WAS GON' END.
YOUR DOG, HE DON'T SEEM HAPPY.
HE'S FINE. IF HE STARTS WAGGING HIS TAIL, **THEN** YOU SHOULD WORRY.
GRRRRR

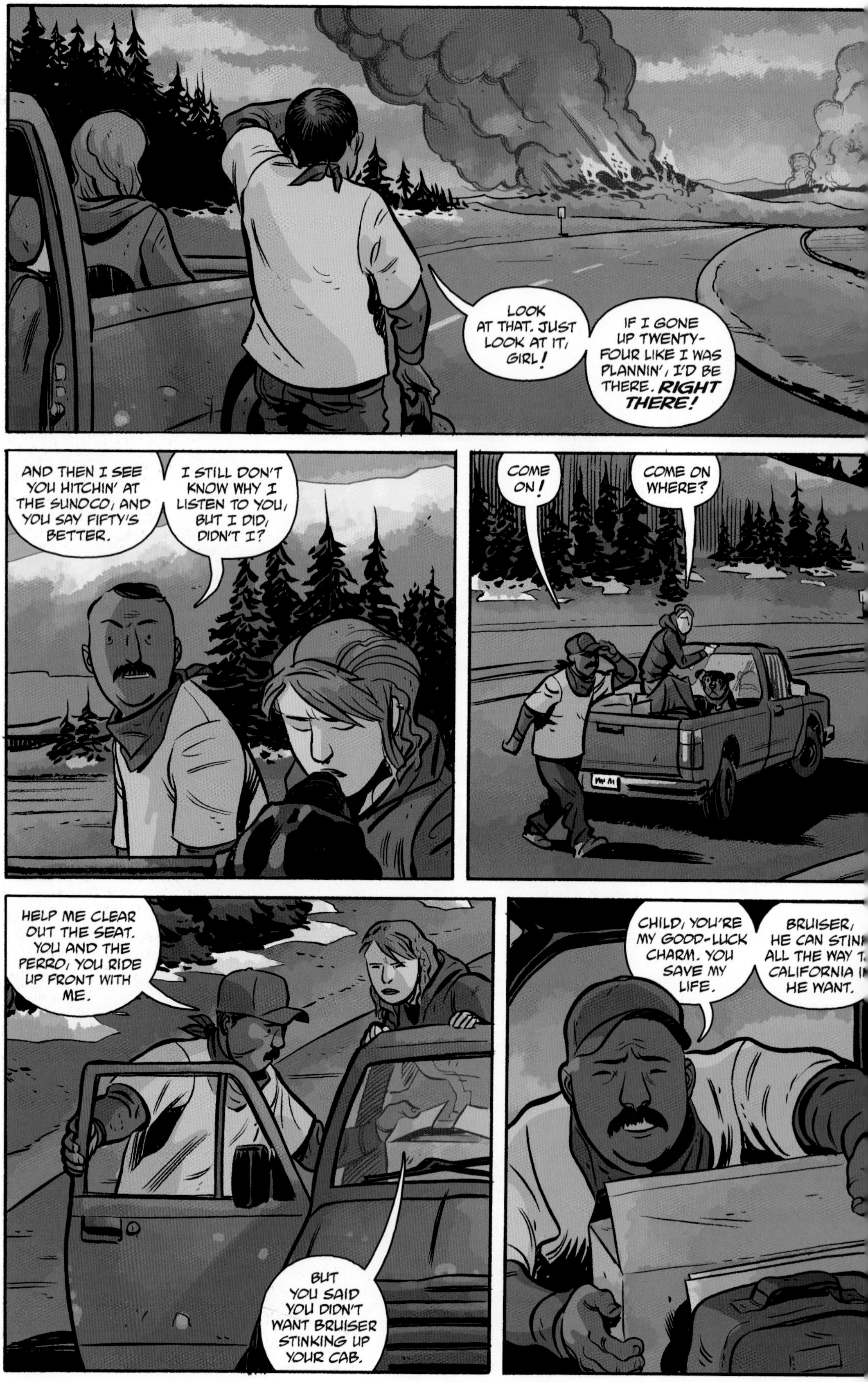
LOOK AT THAT. JUST LOOK AT IT, GIRL!
IF I GONE UP TWENTY-FOUR LIKE I WAS PLANNIN', I'D BE THERE. RIGHT THERE!
AND THEN I SEE YOU HITCHIN' AT THE SUNOCO, AND YOU SAY FIFTY'S BETTER.
I STILL DON'T KNOW WHY I LISTEN TO YOU, BUT I DID, DIDN'T I?
COME ON!
COME ON WHERE?
HELP ME CLEAR OUT THE SEAT. YOU AND THE PERRO, YOU RIDE UP FRONT WITH ME.
BUT YOU SAID YOU DIDN'T WANT BRUISER STINKING UP YOUR CAB.
CHILD, YOU'RE MY GOOD-LUCK CHARM. YOU SAVE MY LIFE.
BRUISER, HE CAN STIN ALL THE WAY T CALIFORNIA I HE WANT.

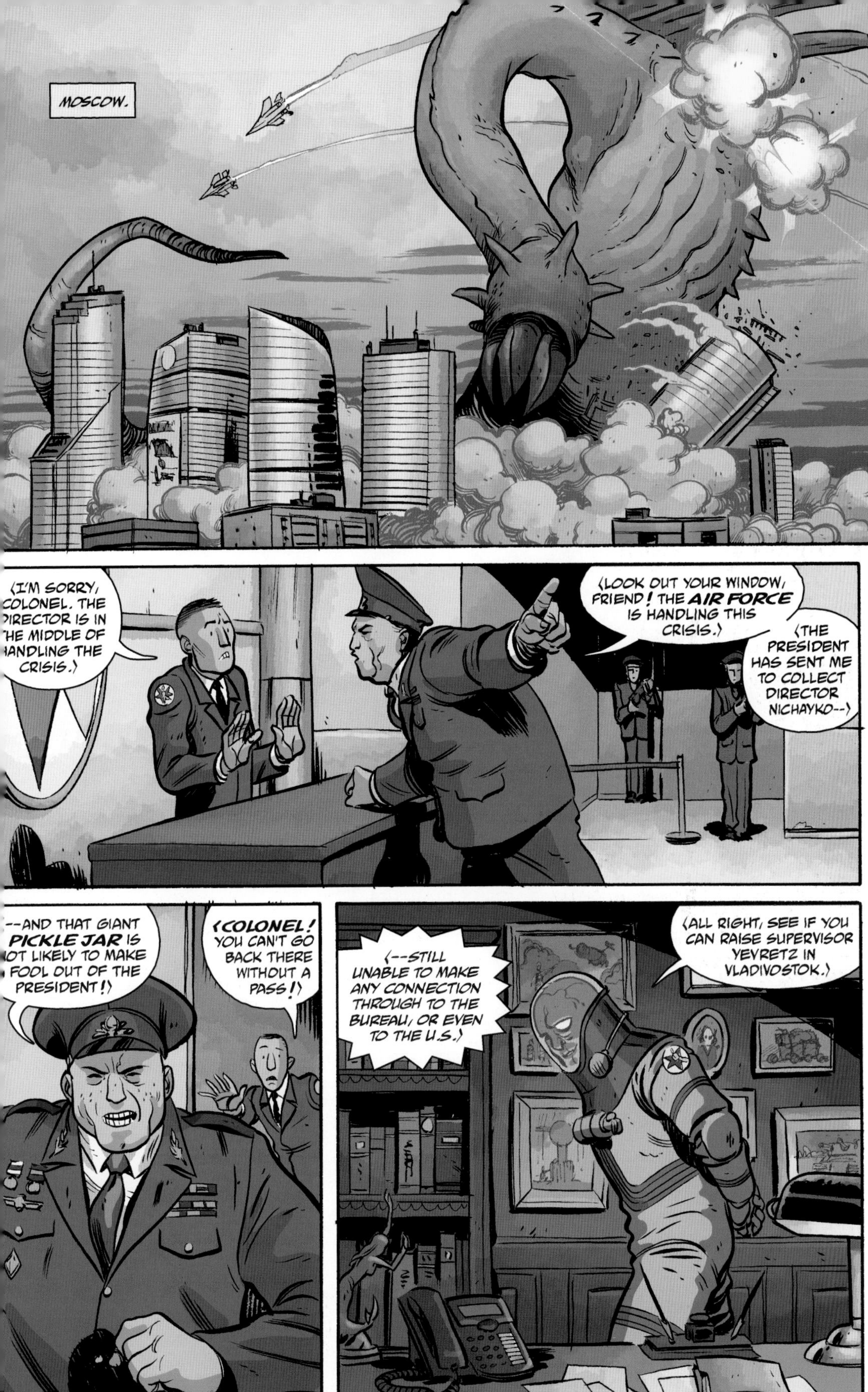
MOSCOW.
⟨I'M SORRY, COLONEL. THE DIRECTOR IS IN THE MIDDLE OF HANDLING THE CRISIS.⟩
⟨LOOK OUT YOUR WINDOW, FRIEND! THE AIR FORCE IS HANDLING THIS CRISIS.⟩
⟨THE PRESIDENT HAS SENT ME TO COLLECT DIRECTOR NICHAYKO--⟩
--AND THAT GIANT PICKLE JAR IS NOT LIKELY TO MAKE A FOOL OUT OF THE PRESIDENT!⟩
⟨COLONEL! YOU CAN'T GO BACK THERE WITHOUT A PASS!⟩
⟨--STILL UNABLE TO MAKE ANY CONNECTION THROUGH TO THE BUREAU, OR EVEN TO THE U.S.⟩
⟨ALL RIGHT, SEE IF YOU CAN RAISE SUPERVISOR YEVRETZ IN VLADIVOSTOK.⟩
TRANSLATED FROM THE RUSSIAN⟩

⟨AND GET THE LAST TRANSMITTED COORDINATES ON THE SCOTLAND MISSION. WE SHOULD HAVE THOSE--⟩

⟨SCOTLAND?!! THAT'S NOT YOUR COUNTRY, DIRECTOR!⟩

⟨COLONEL STARSHIY, YOU WERE TOLD TO WAIT IN THE LOBBY.⟩

⟨DON'T MAKE ME LAUGH, NICHAYKO! THE PRESIDENT WILL SEE YOU NOW.⟩

⟨MY CAR IS WAITING OUTSIDE.⟩

⟨I UNDERSTAND THAT YOU SEE MOSCOW UNDER ATTACK, BUT THIS IS AN INTERNATIONAL CRISIS. MY RESPONSIBILITIES AND COMMITMENTS EXPAND BEYOND YOUR VISION.⟩

⟨THE S.S.S. IS A RUSSIAN AGENCY AND RUSSIA'S LEADER REQUIRES YOUR PRESENCE.⟩

⟨AND IF YOU THINK WON'T DRA YOU--⟩

WHAK

BAM

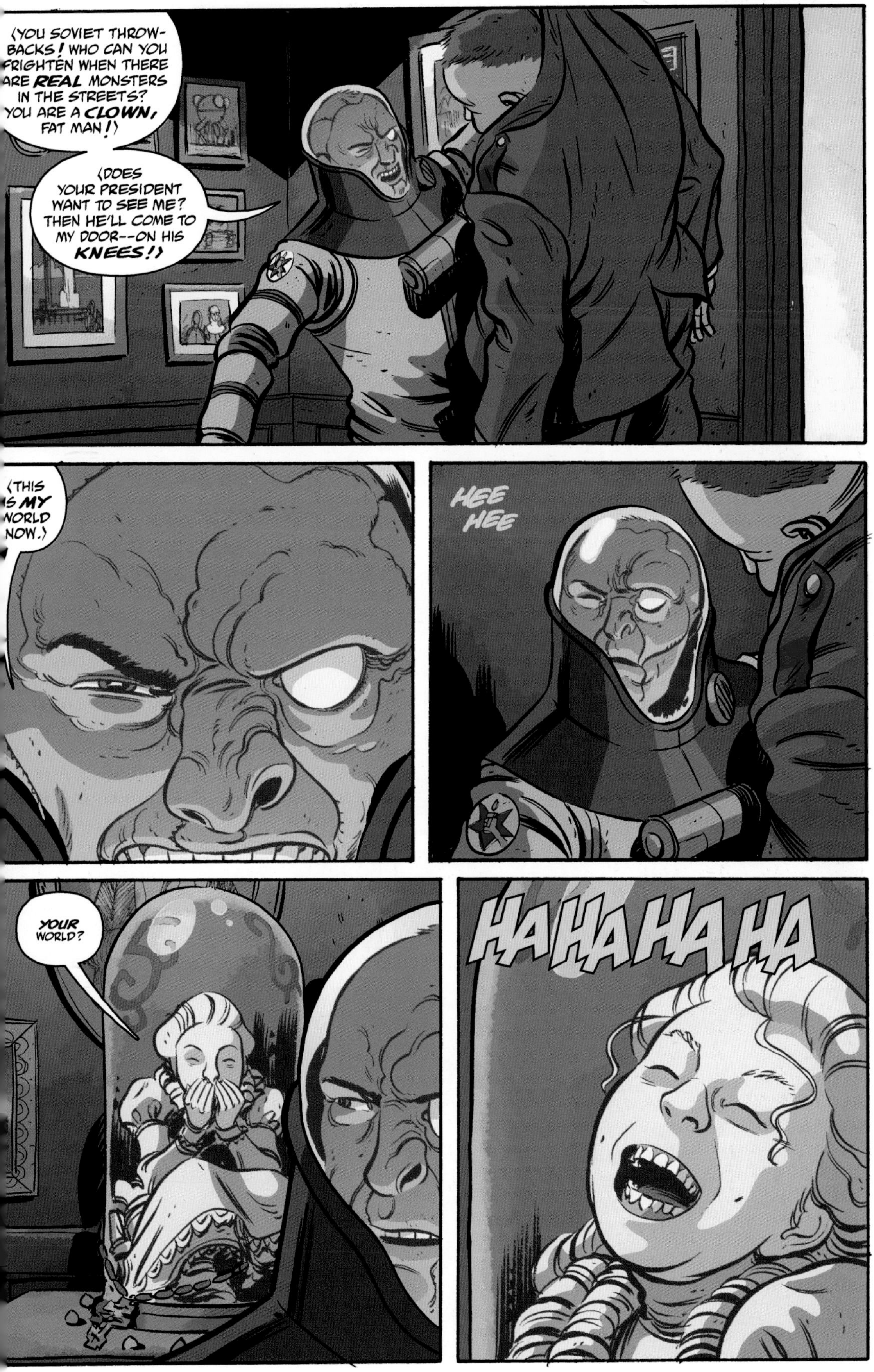
⟨YOU SOVIET THROW-BACKS! WHO CAN YOU FRIGHTEN WHEN THERE ARE REAL MONSTERS IN THE STREETS? YOU ARE A CLOWN, FAT MAN!⟩
⟨DOES YOUR PRESIDENT WANT TO SEE ME? THEN HE'LL COME TO MY DOOR--ON HIS KNEES!⟩
⟨THIS IS MY WORLD NOW.⟩
HEE HEE
YOUR WORLD?
HA HA HA HA HA

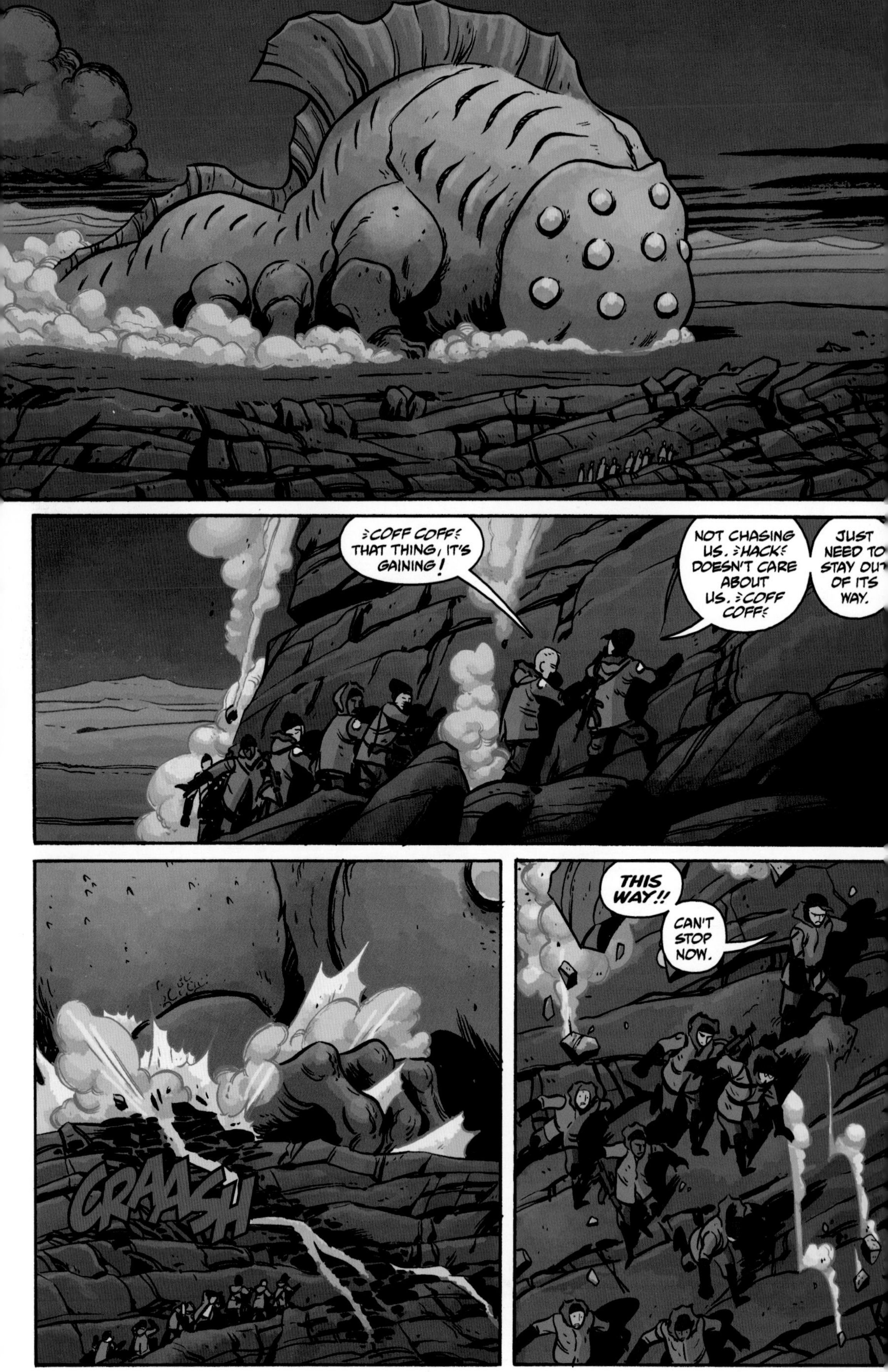

≶COFF COFF≷ THAT THING, IT'S GAINING!
NOT CHASING US. ≶HACK≷ DOESN'T CARE ABOUT US. ≶COFF COFF≷
JUST NEED TO STAY OUT OF ITS WAY.
CRAASH
THIS WAY!!
CAN'T STOP NOW.

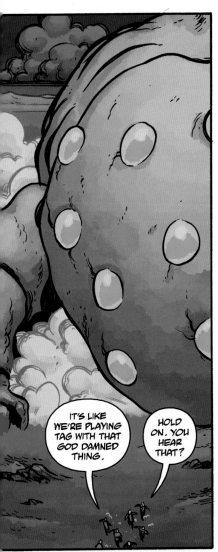

SSSHHHKOOWWW

BOOM

IT'S LIKE WE'RE PLAYING TAG WITH THAT GOD DAMNED THING.

HOLD ON. YOU HEAR THAT?

GOD DAMN CAVALRY!! ALL RIGHT!!

HEY! IS THAT CHOPPERS? TASSO SAID CHOPPERS CAN'T FLY UP HERE IN THE HIGHLANDS.

WHUPWHUPWHUP

GUESS IT DEPENDS ON THE CHOPPER...

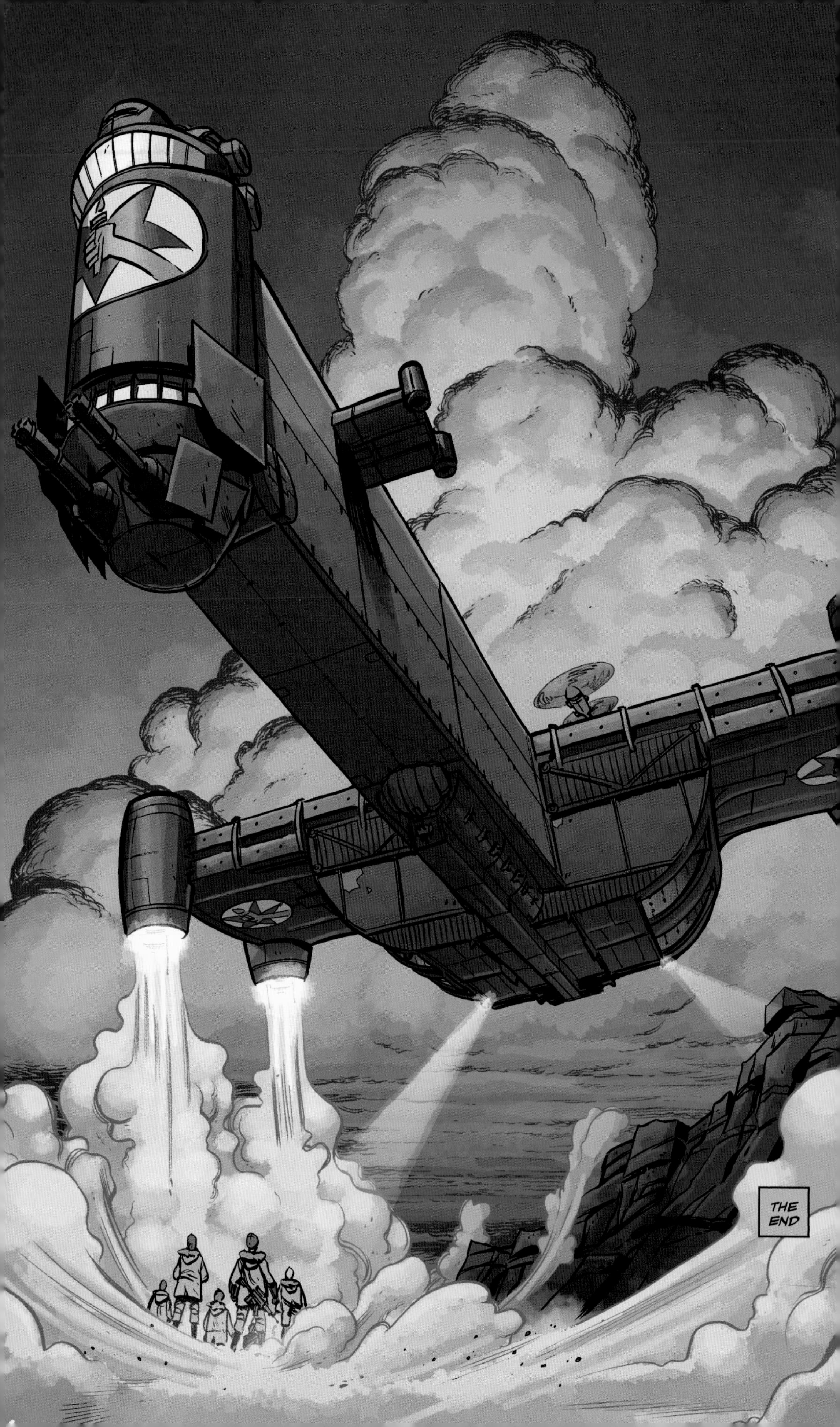
THE END

# B.P.R.D.

## SKETCHBOOK

*Notes by Tyler Crook*

The first comic book project that I ever finished was about the real, historic Rasputin, so drawing him here sometimes felt a little surreal.

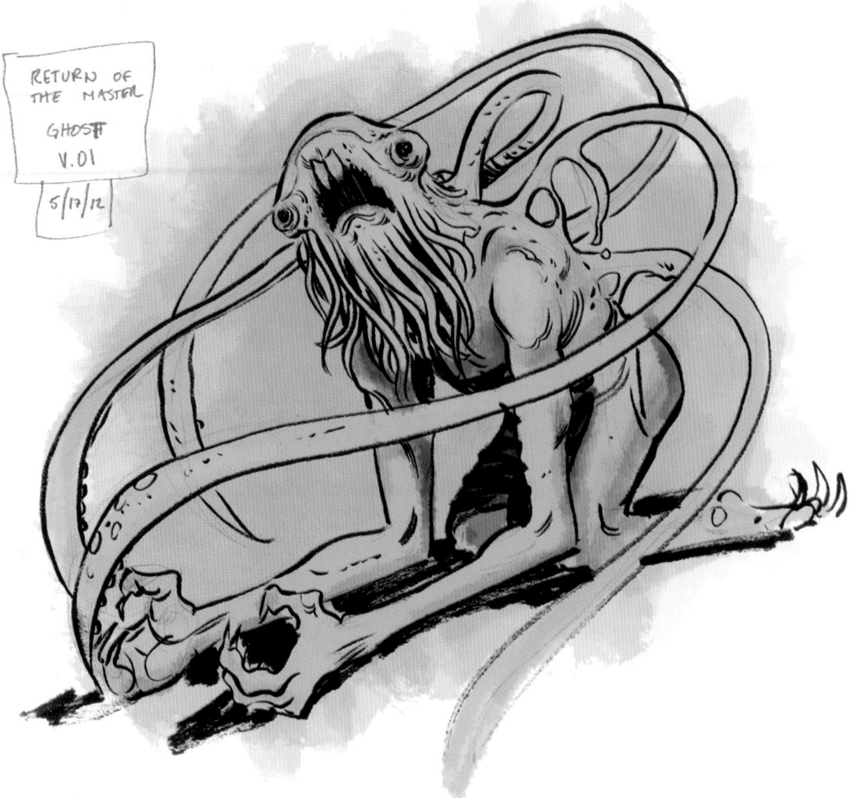
RETURN OF THE MASTER
GHOST
V.01
5/17/12

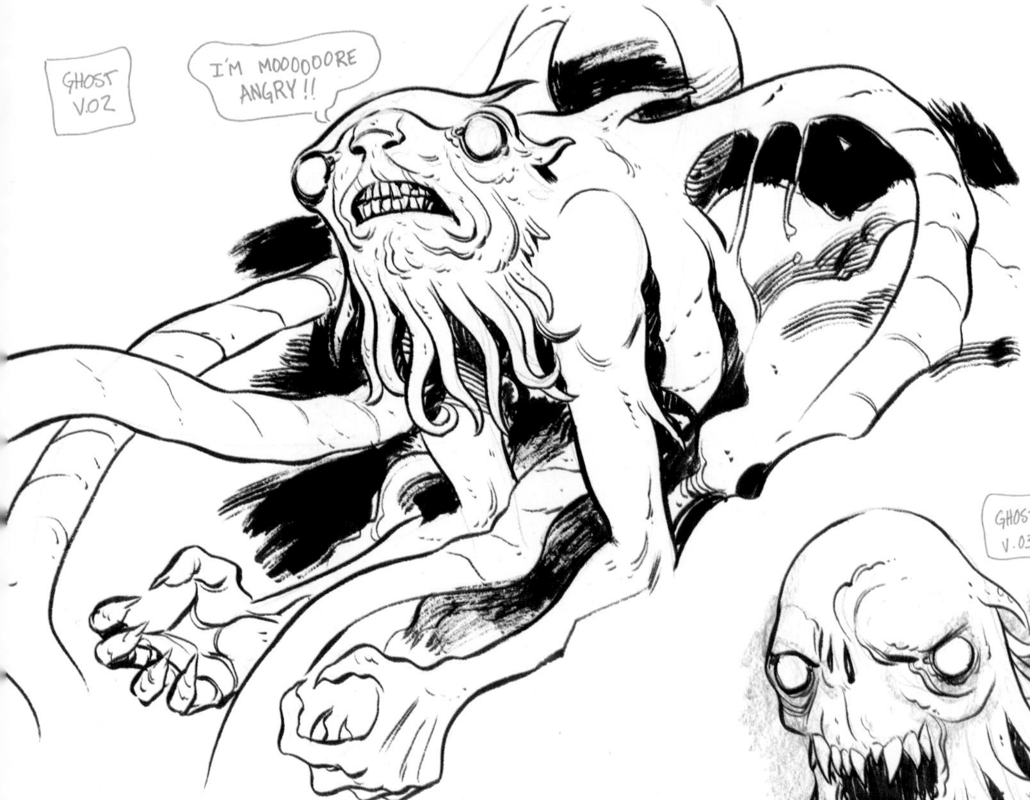
GHOST V.02
I'M MOOOOOORE ANGRY!!

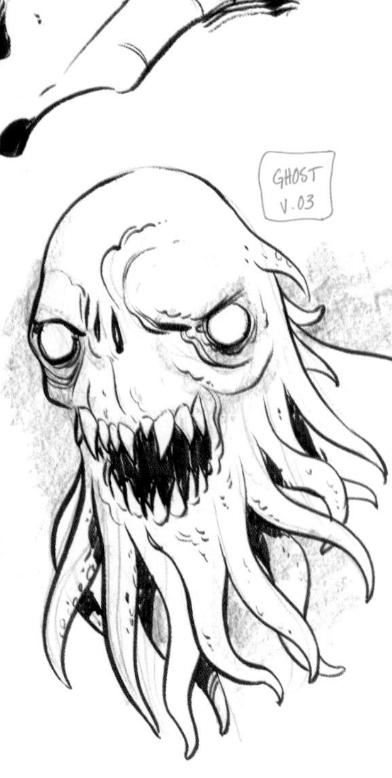
GHOST V.03

This ghost went through a few revisions.
My monsters usually start out a bit sad looking.
By the end this guy was suitably evil.

I worked on this for a little while, but every time I drew a snake with legs, it just looked like a lizard. I think Mike's design works so well because it manages to hold on to that snaky feel while still having a ton of legs.

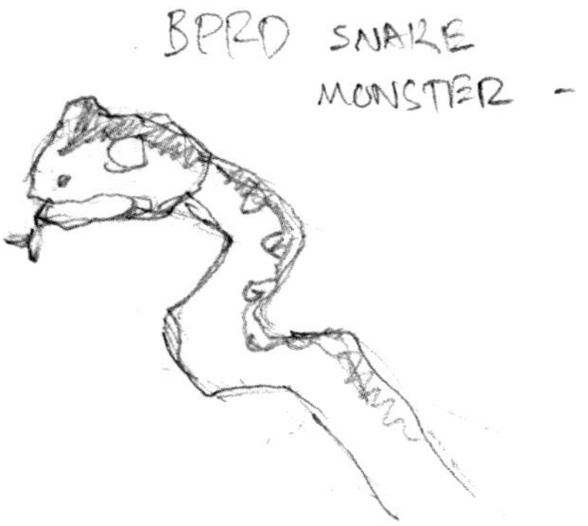
BPRD SNAKE MONSTER -

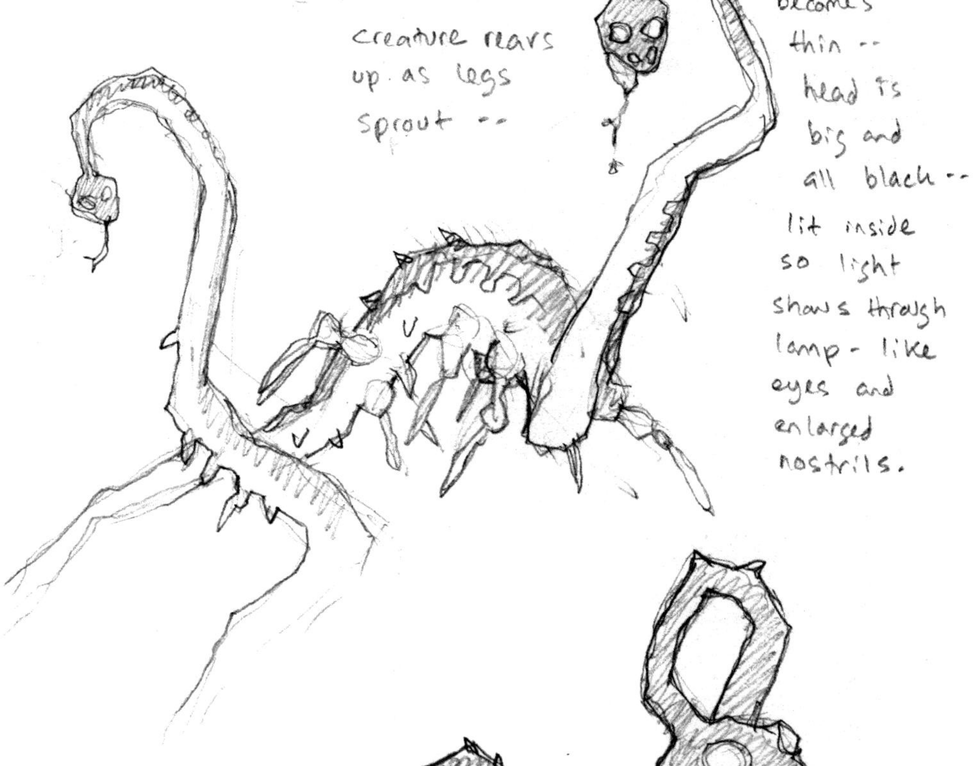
neck darkens towards head -
"neck" becomes thin -- head is big and all black -- lit inside so light shows through lamp-like eyes and enlarged nostrils.
creature rears up as legs sprout --

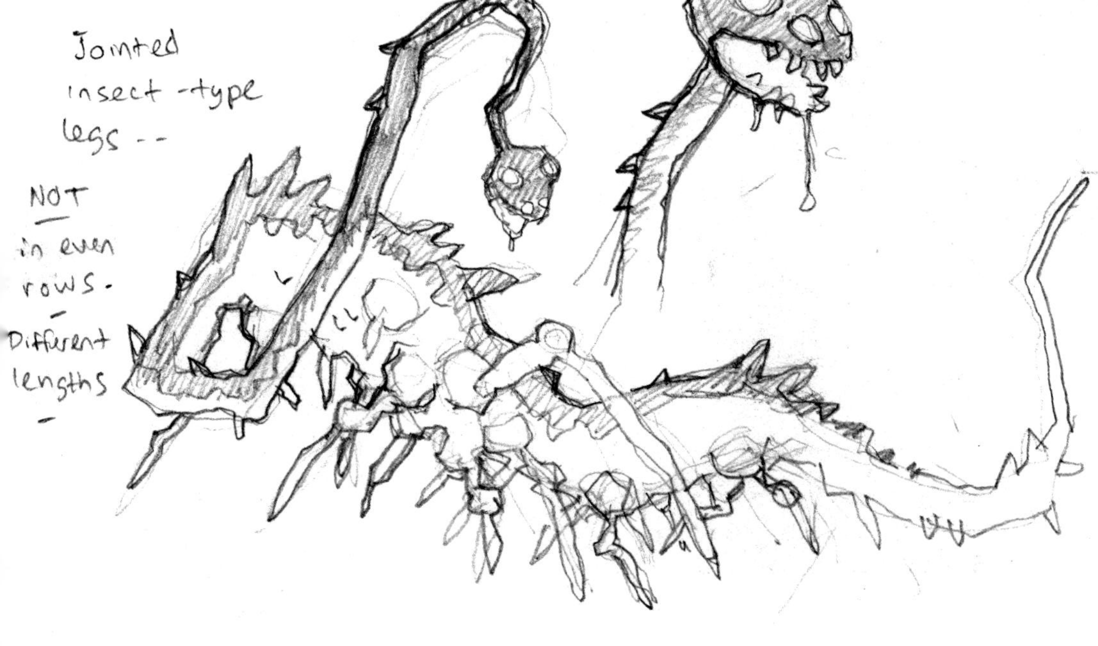
Jointed insect-type legs --
NOT in even rows -
Different lengths -

SALTON SEA EGG!

(A) KIND OF A NORMAL
EGG SHAPE
SUPER GOOEY!

(B) SLIGHTLY
SPECKLED +
SLIGHTLY
FACETED + ODD
SHAPED.

SALTON
SEA
EGG

I'M THINKING SORT OF
A TEXTURED SURFACE
LIKE SANDSTONE

SLIMY AT FIRST BUT
IT'LL DRY UP LATER, MAYBE

Sometimes it's surprising how much thought goes into something as simple as an egg. These are variations on shape, sliminess, texture, etc.

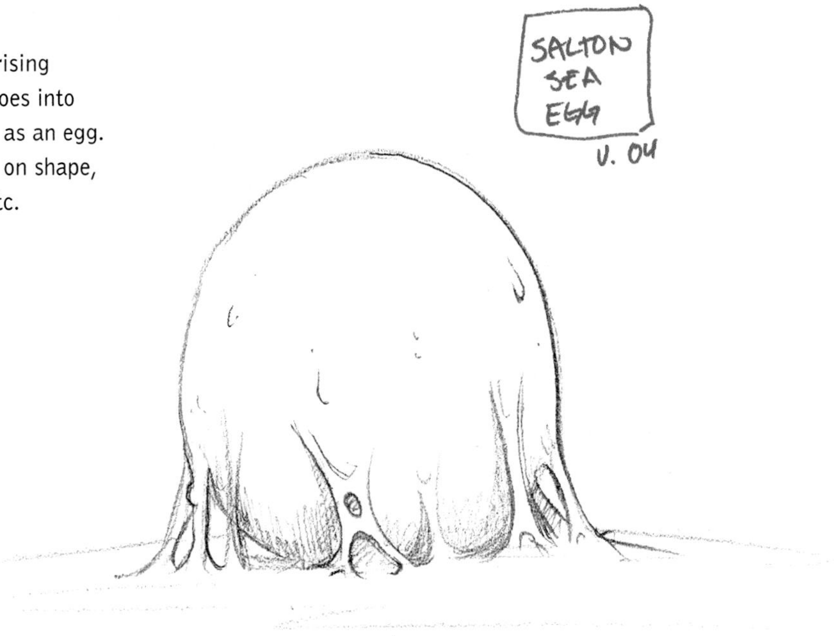
SALTON SEA EGG
V. 04

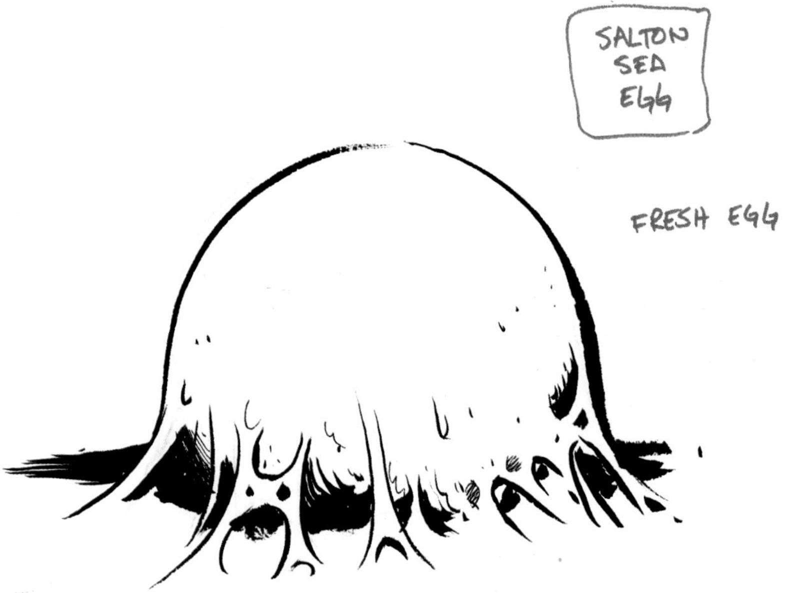
SALTON SEA EGG
FRESH EGG

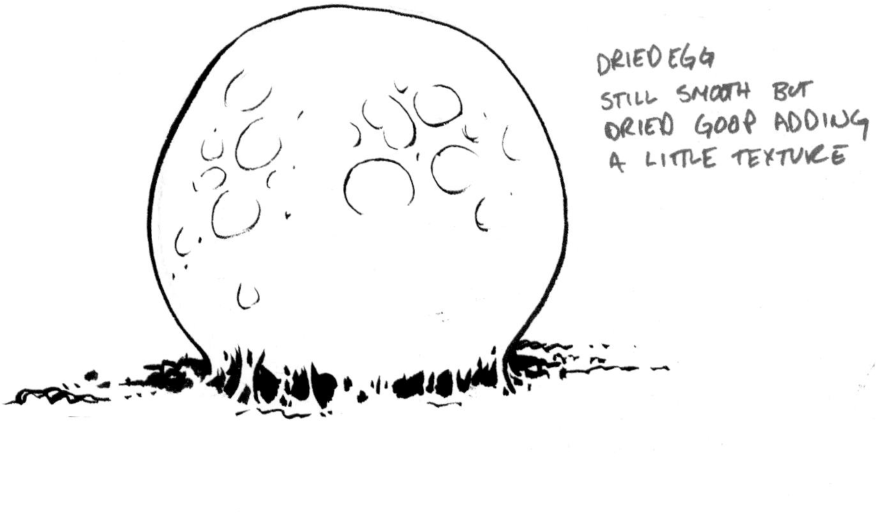
DRIED EGG
STILL SMOOTH BUT DRIED GOOP ADDING A LITTLE TEXTURE

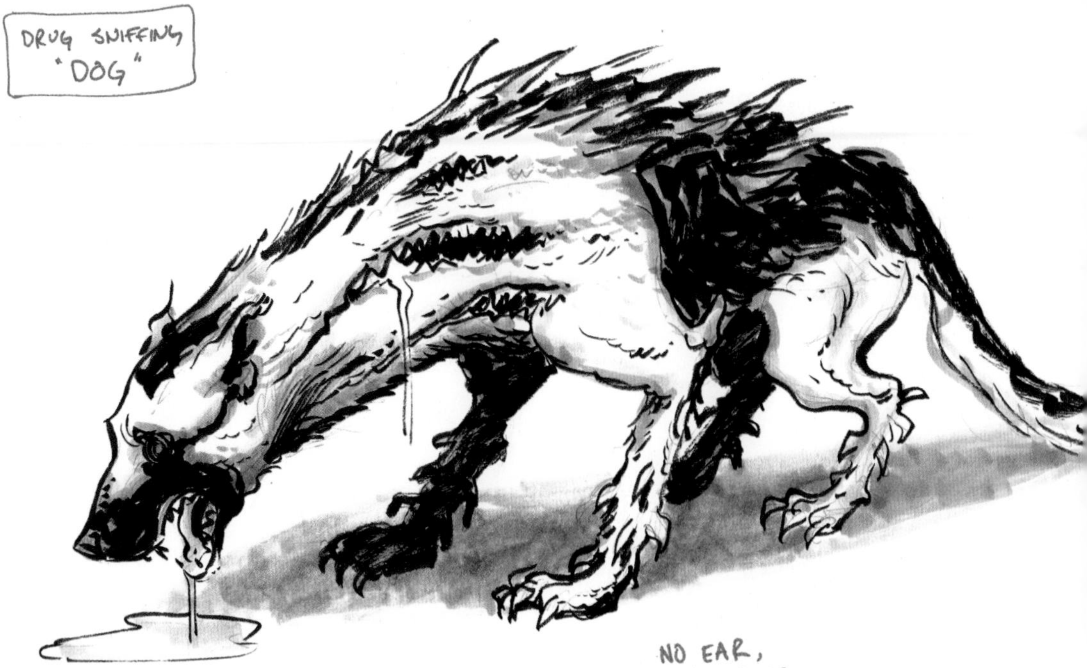
DRUG SNIFFING "DOG"

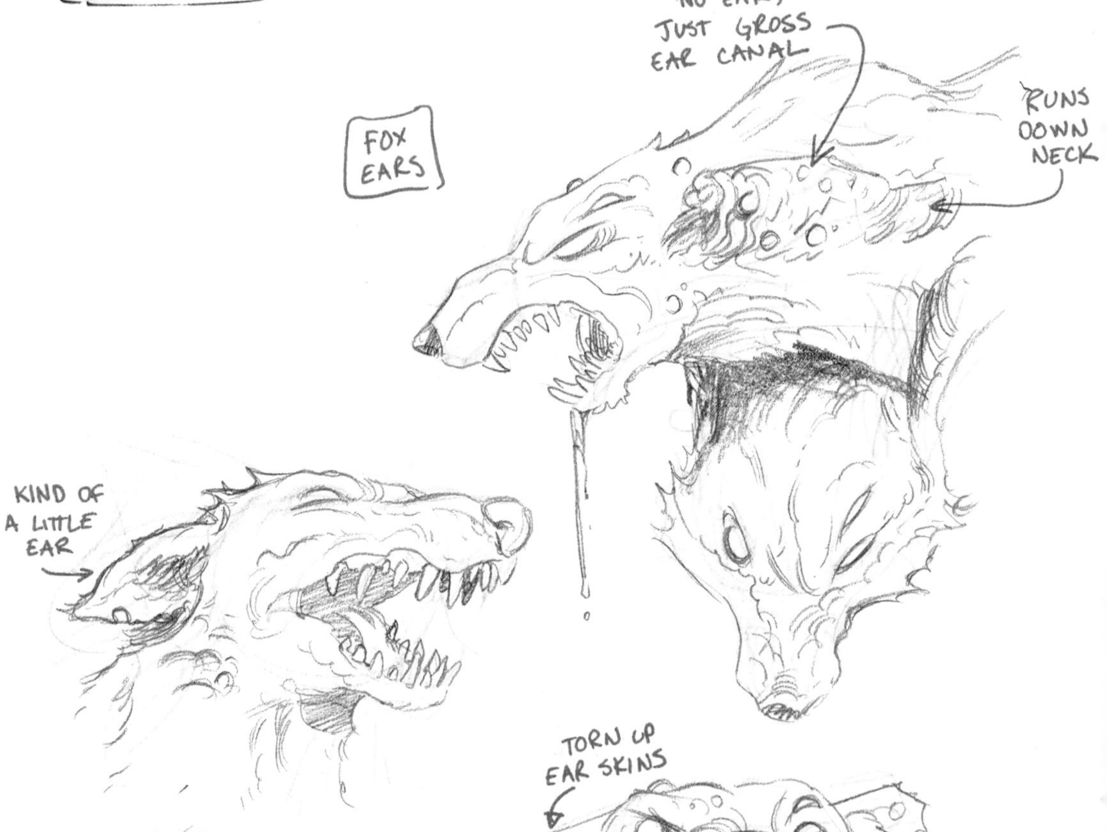
NO EAR, JUST GROSS EAR CANAL
RUNS DOWN NECK
FOX EARS
KIND OF A LITTLE EAR

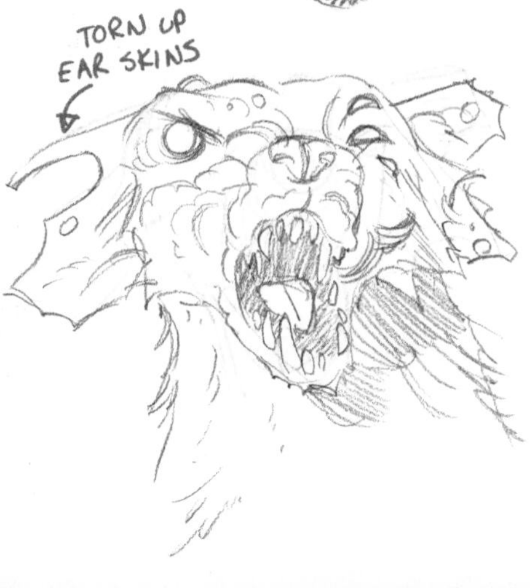
TORN UP EAR SKINS

For the mutated animals, I started with the dogs that Lazar mutates in the ferry station, then built variations off that.

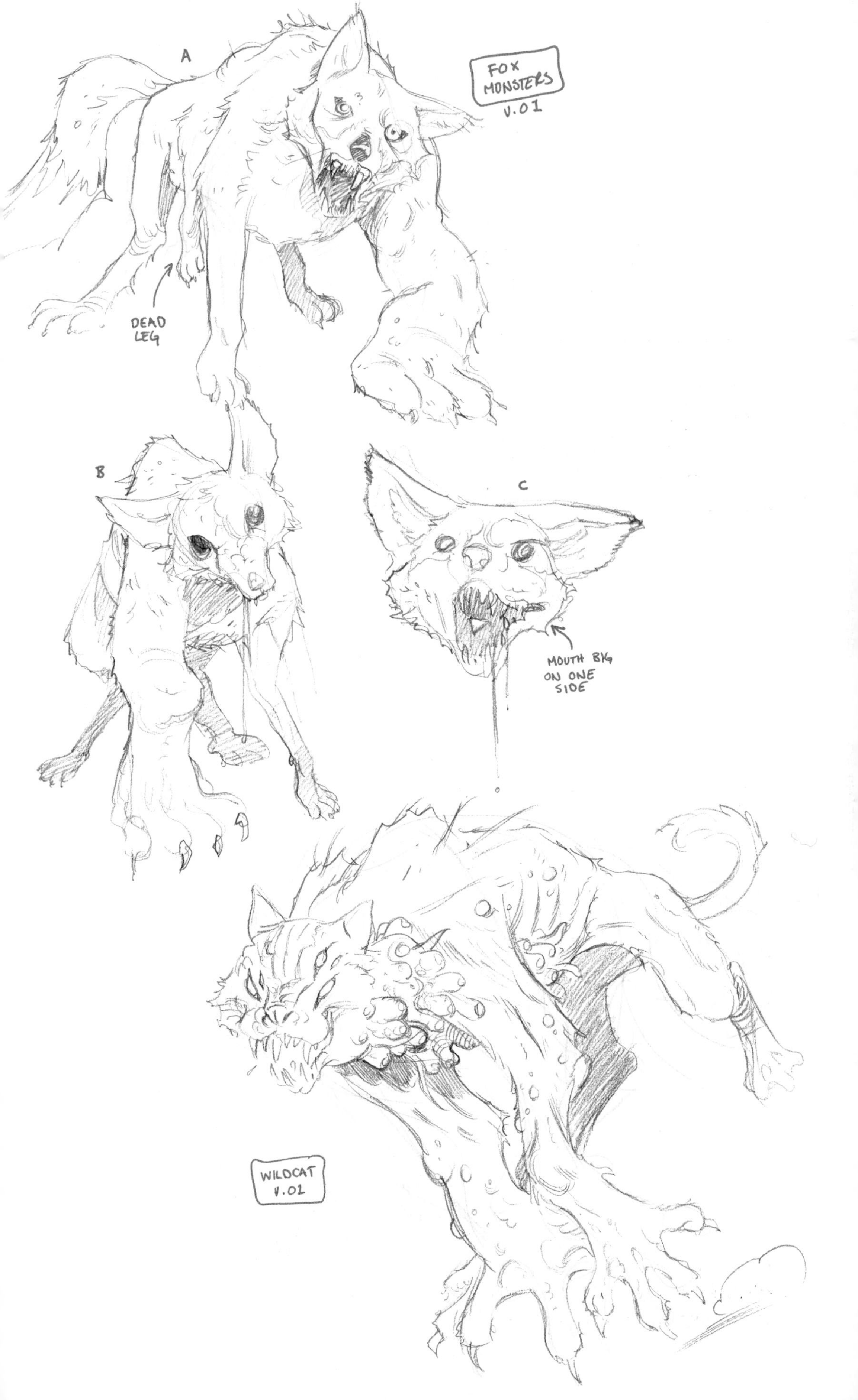

A
FOX MONSTERS
V.01
DEAD LEG
B
C
MOUTH BIG ON ONE SIDE
WILDCAT
V.01

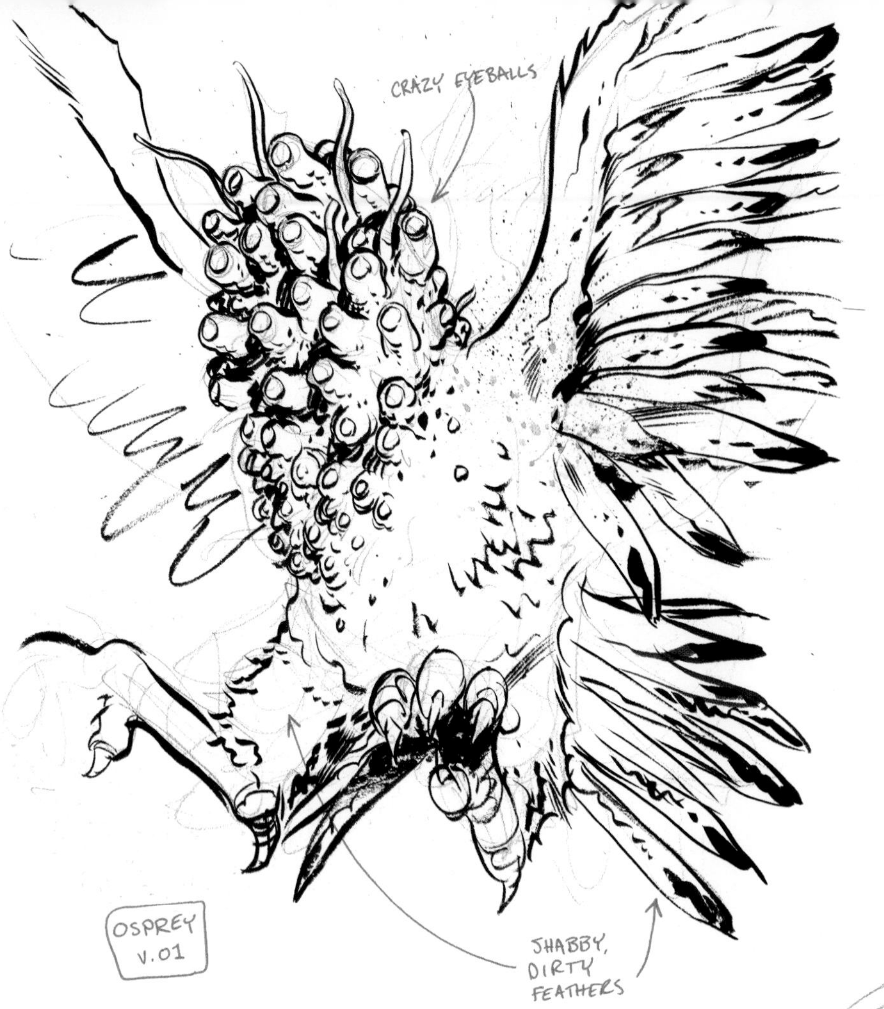
CRAZY EYEBALLS
OSPREY
V.01
SHABBY,
DIRTY
FEATHERS

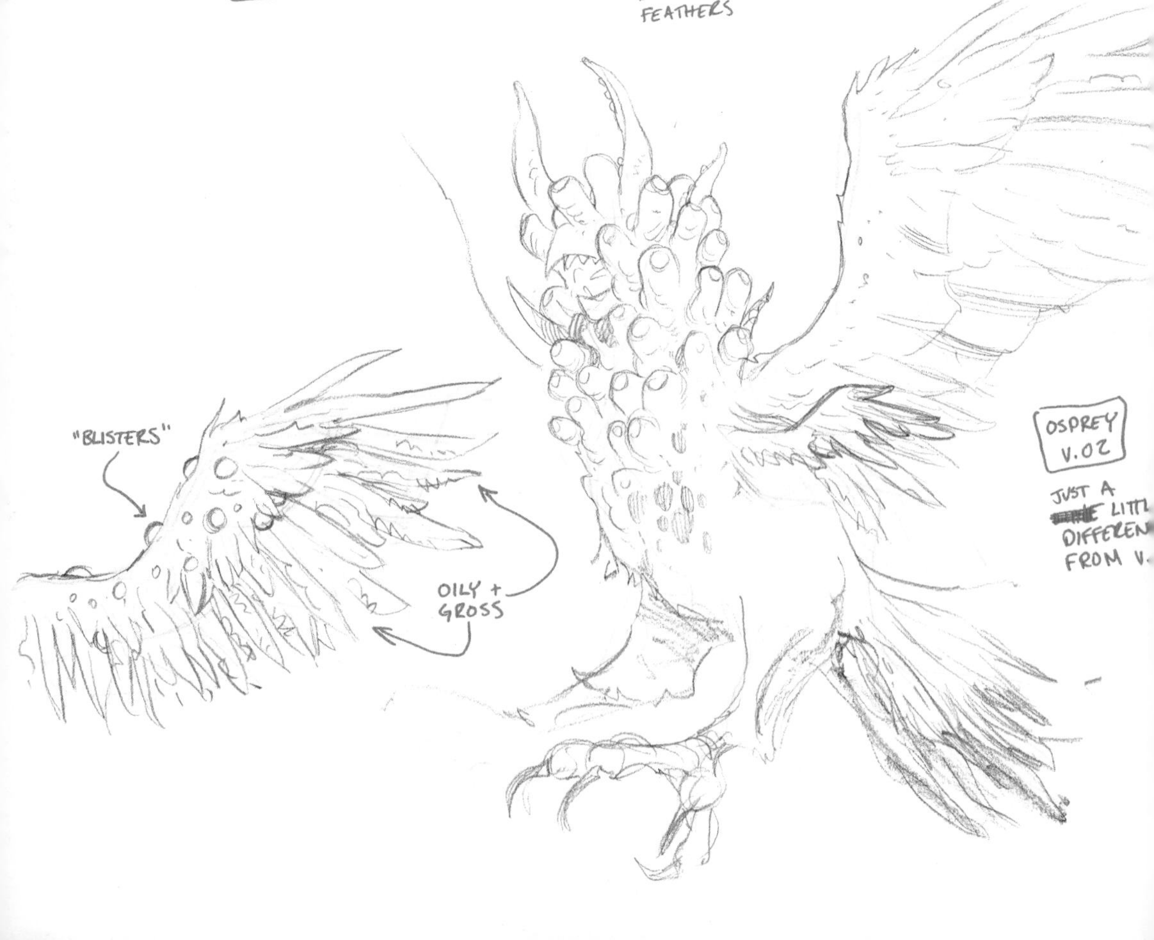
"BLISTERS"
OILY +
GROSS
OSPREY
V.02
JUST A
LITTL
DIFFEREN
FROM V.

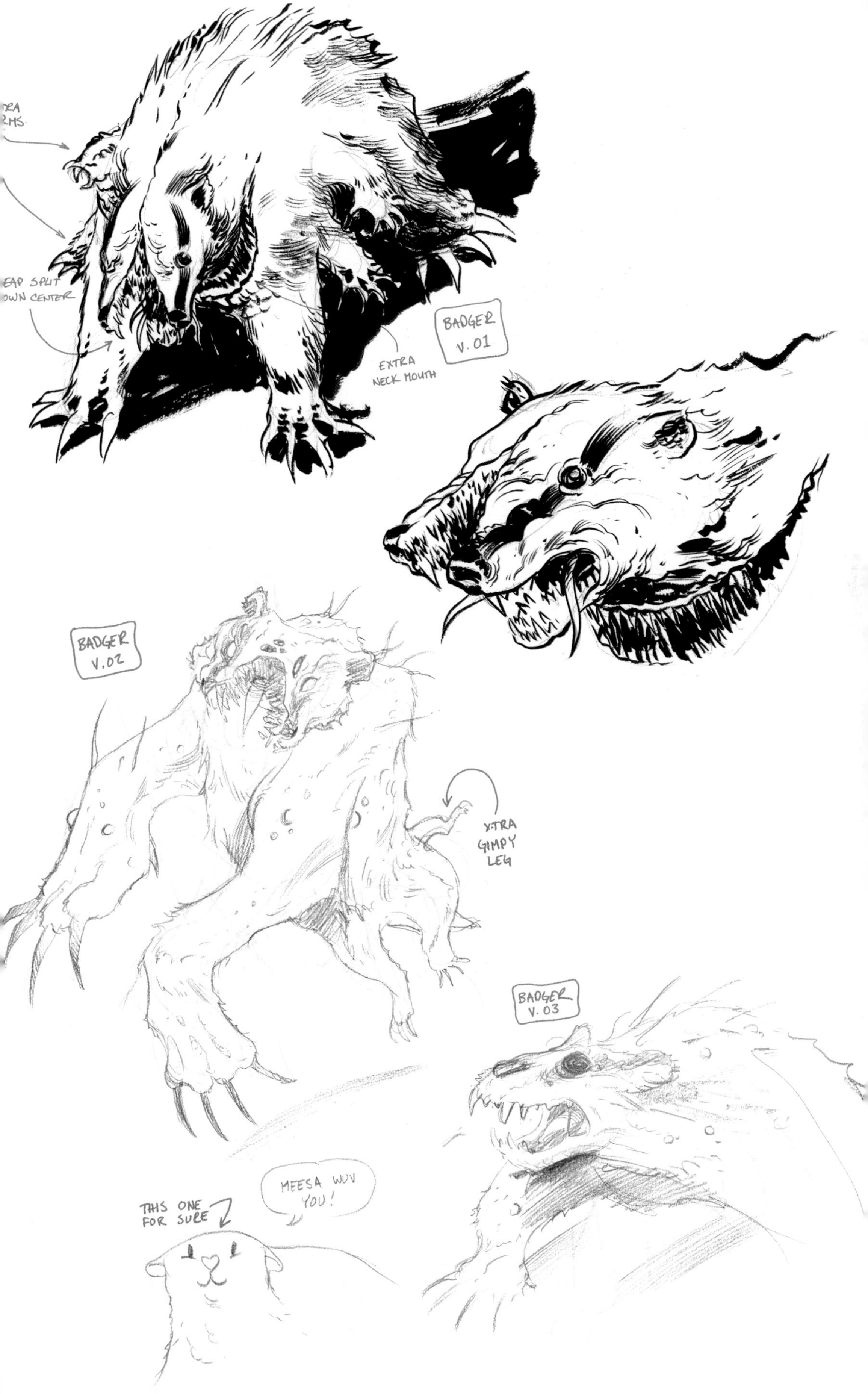

TRA
RMS.
EAP SPLIT
OWN CENTER
EXTRA
NECK MOUTH
BADGER
V. 01
BADGER
V. 02
X-TRA
GIMPY
LEG
BADGER
V. 03
THIS ONE
FOR SURE
MEESA WUV
YOU!

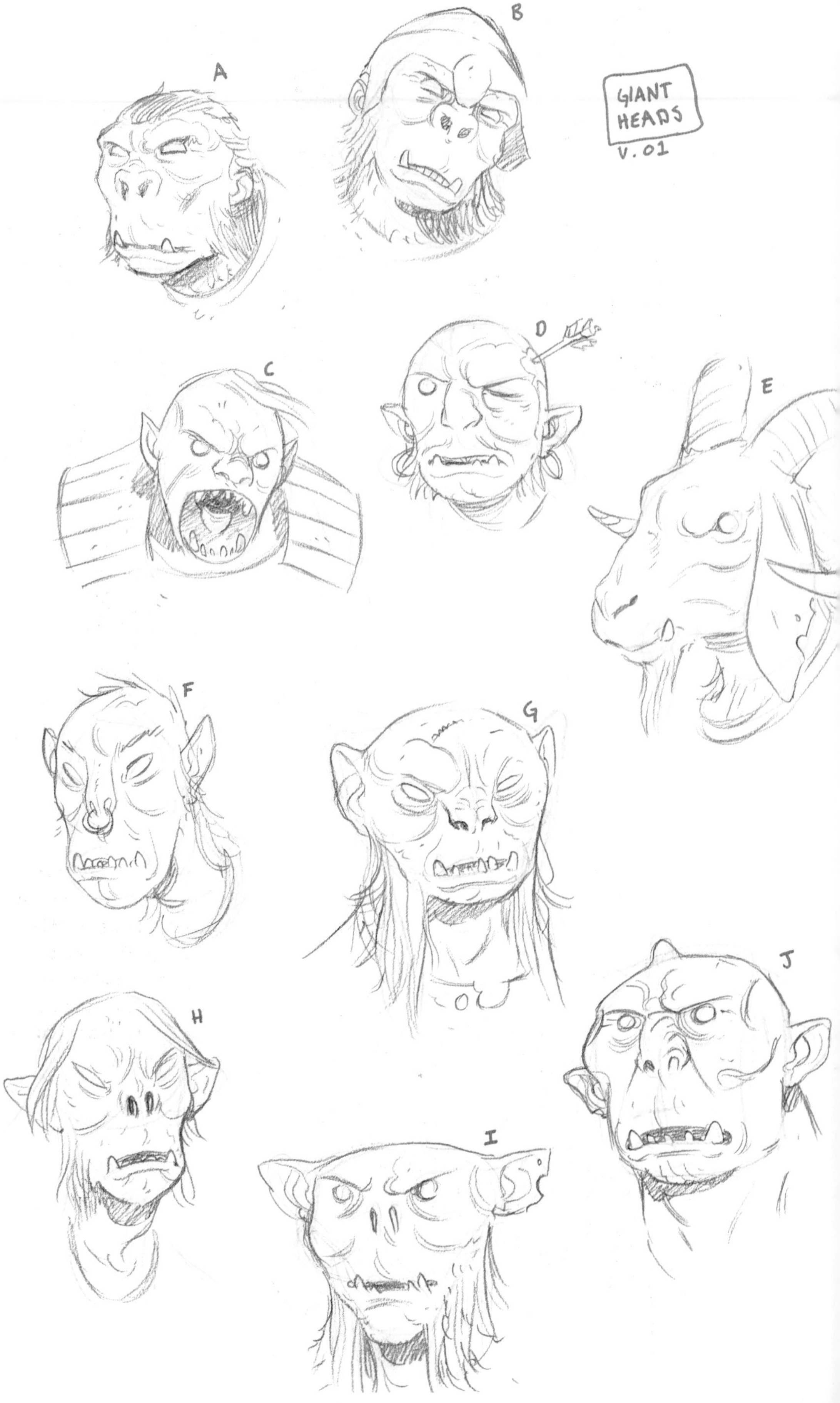
GIANT HEADS
V.01
A
B
C
D
E
F
G
H
I
J

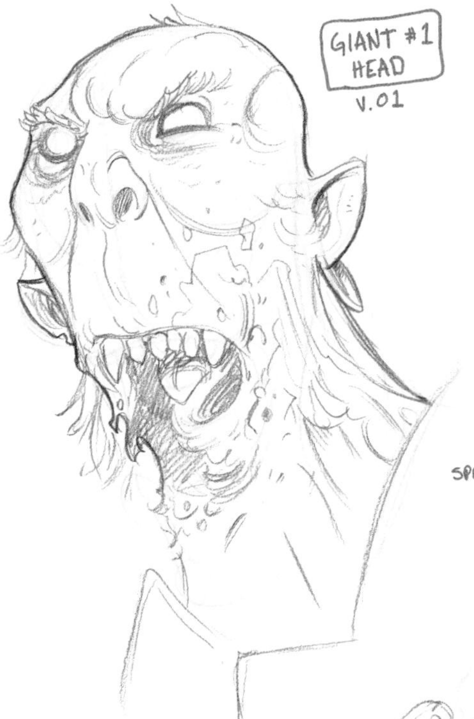
GIANT #1
HEAD
V.01

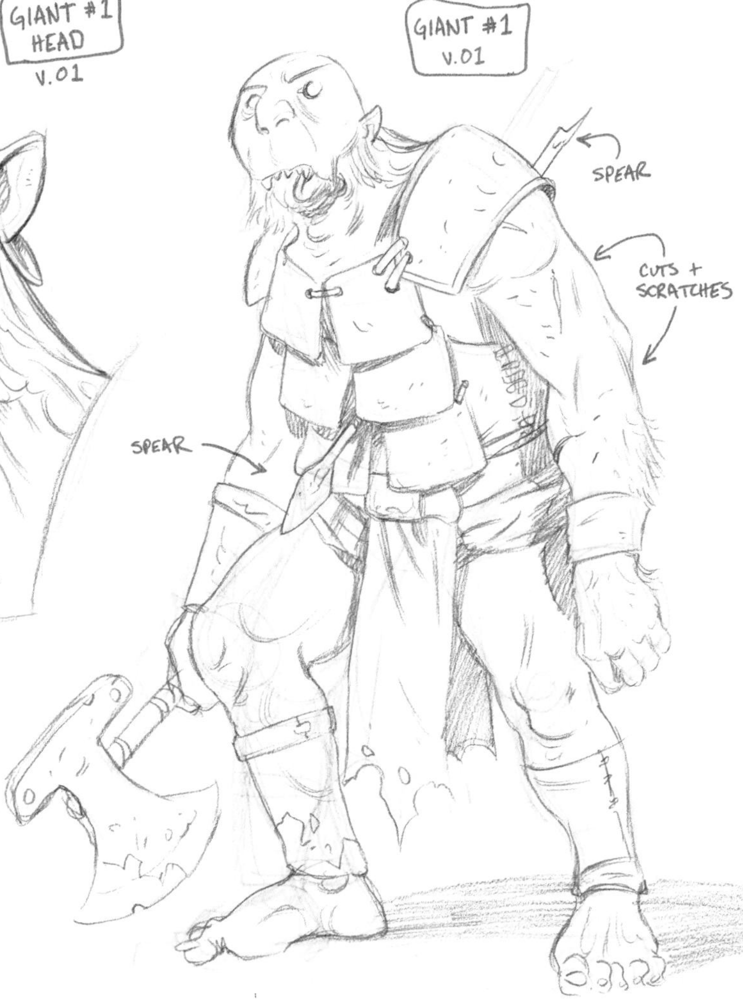
GIANT #1
V.01
SPEAR
CUTS +
SCRATCHES
SPEAR

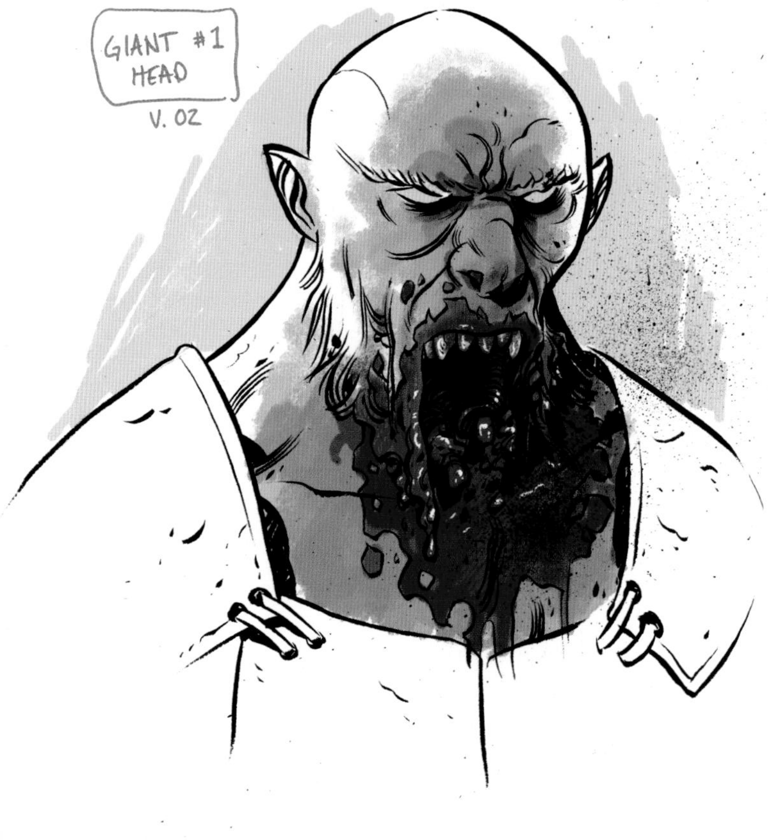
GIANT #1
HEAD
V. 02

These giants were sort of built off the work that Duncan Fegredo did in *Hellboy: The Fury*, but I got to draw them as zombies. I tried to work in some troll- and goblin-looking guys too.

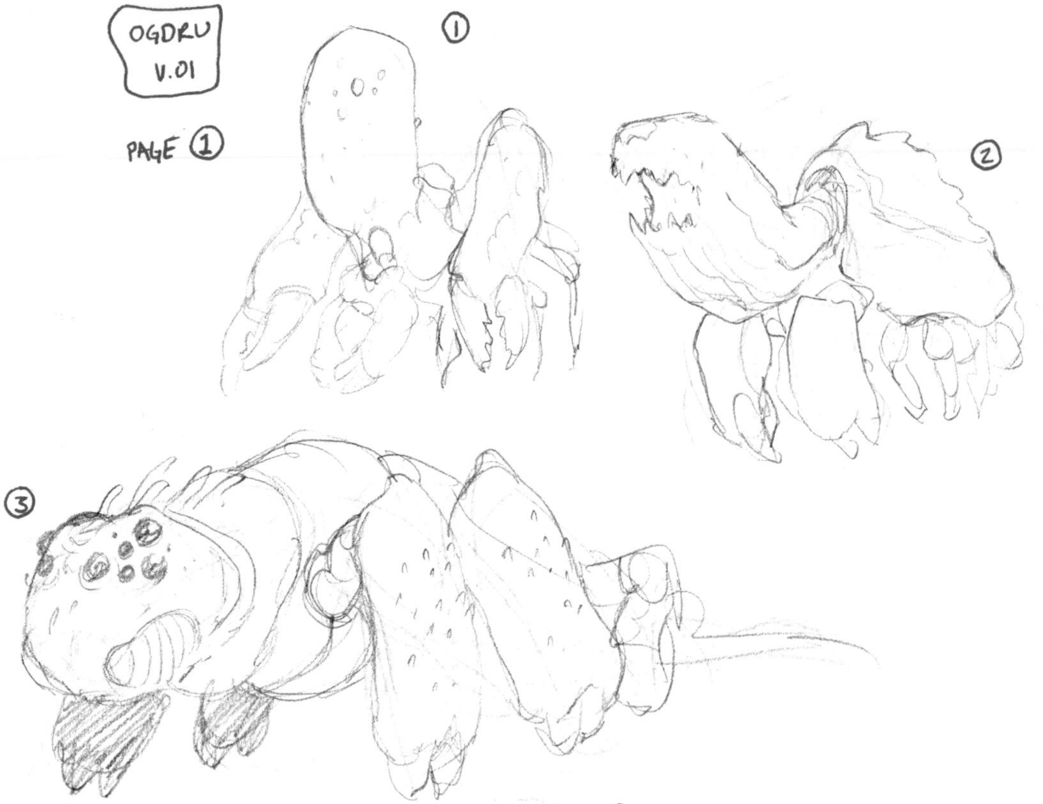
OGDRU
V.01
PAGE 1
1
2
3

We needed a ton of Ogdru Hem for the end of this series. So I tried my hand at a bunch of them . . .

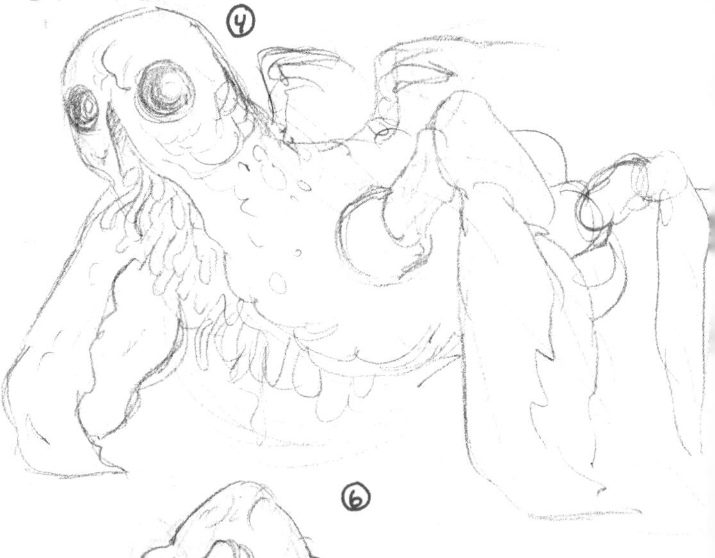
4

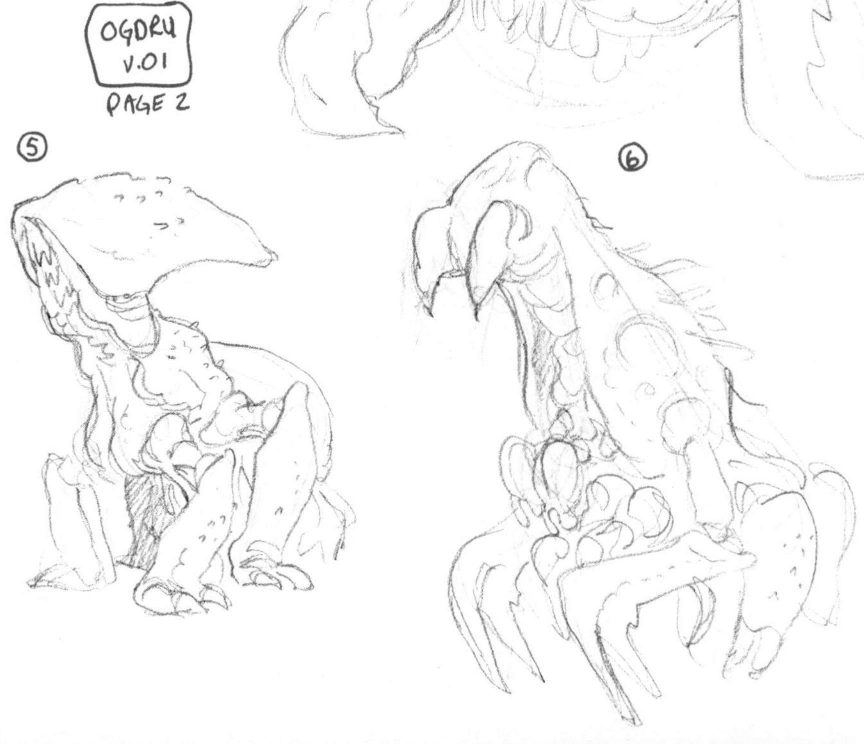
OGDRU
V.01
PAGE 2
5
6

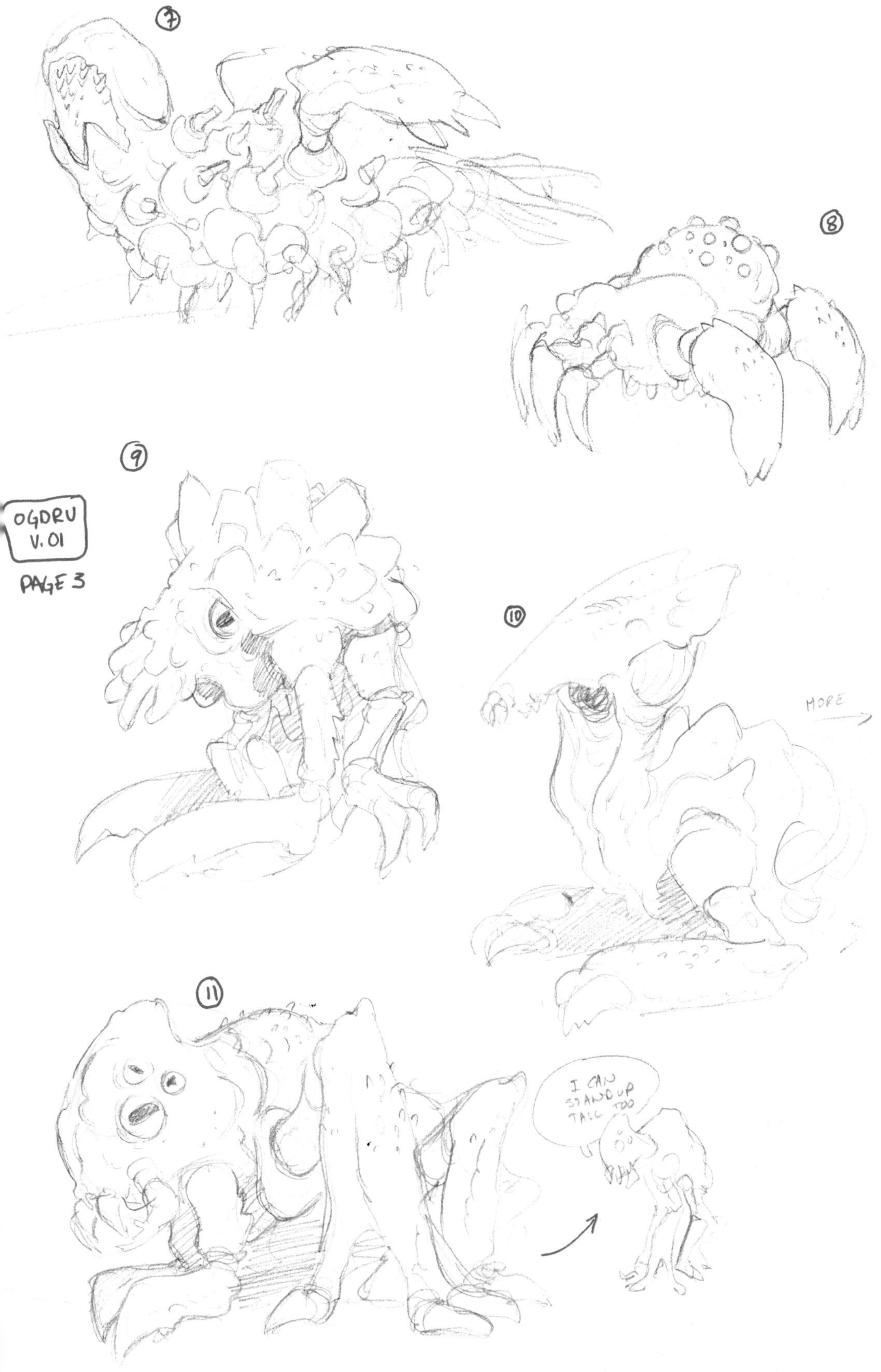

7
8
9
OGDRU V.01
PAGE 3
10
MORE
11
I CAN STAND UP TALL TOO

. . . then Mike swooped in and did it right.

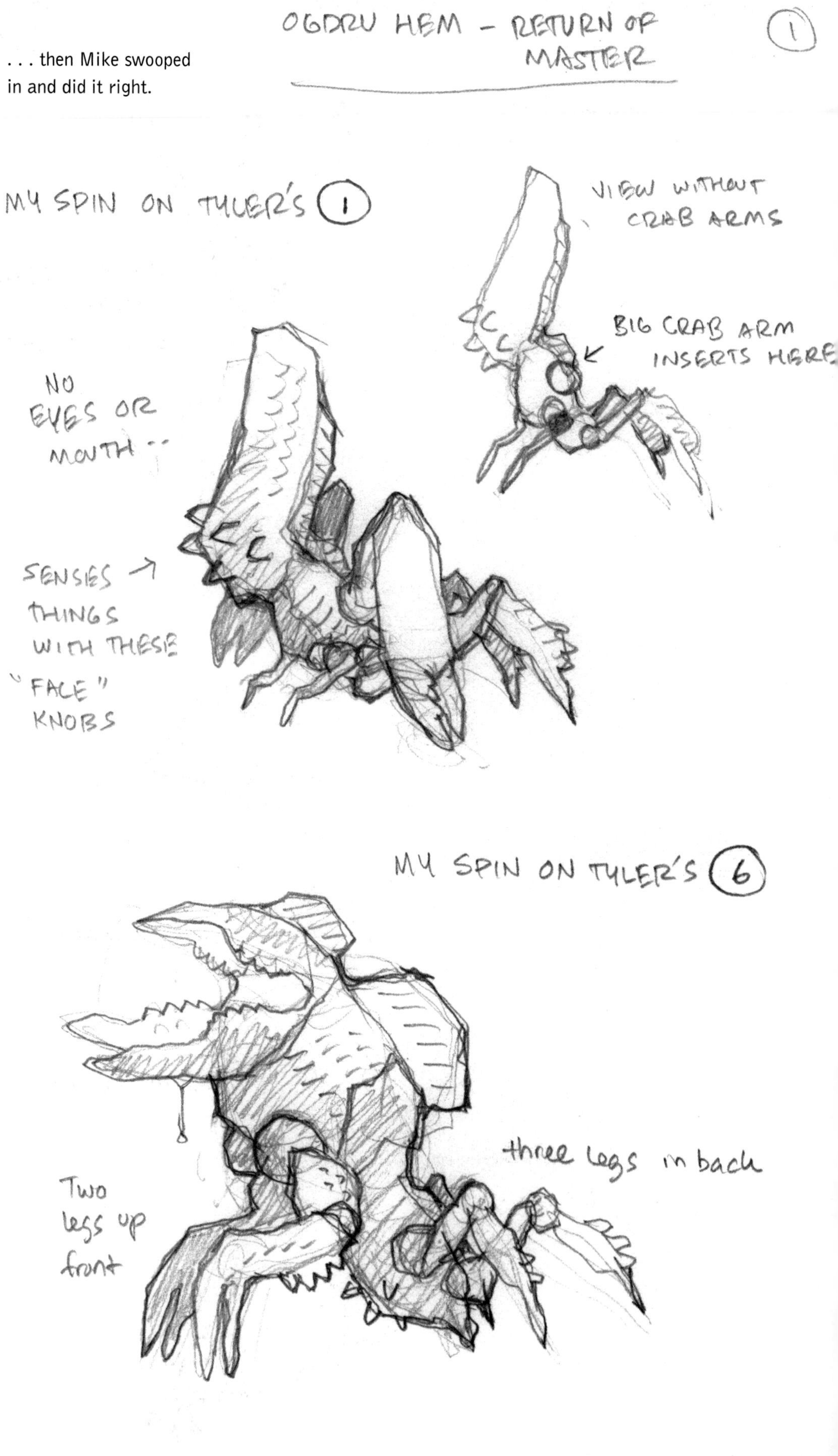
OGDRU HEM – RETURN OF MASTER
1
MY SPIN ON TYLER'S 1
VIEW WITHOUT CRAB ARMS
BIG CRAB ARM INSERTS HERE
NO EYES OR MOUTH . .
SENSES THINGS WITH THESE "FACE" KNOBS
MY SPIN ON TYLER'S 6
three legs in back
Two legs up front

OGDRU HEM - RETURN OF MASTER



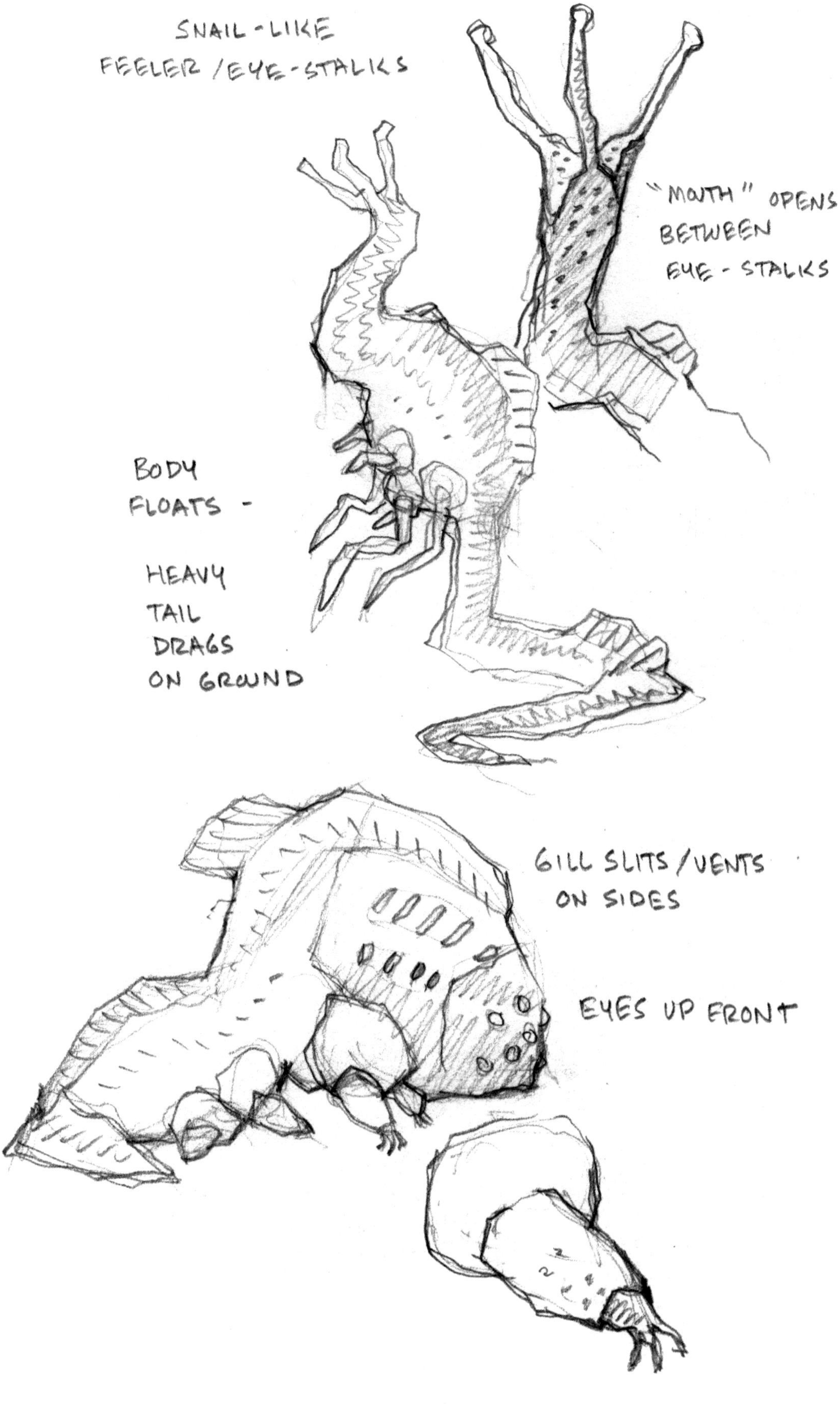
SNAIL-LIKE FEELER / EYE-STALKS
"MOUTH" OPENS BETWEEN EYE-STALKS
BODY FLOATS -
HEAVY TAIL DRAGS ON GROUND
GILL SLITS / VENTS ON SIDES
EYES UP FRONT

OGDRU HEM -
RETURN OF MASTER

4

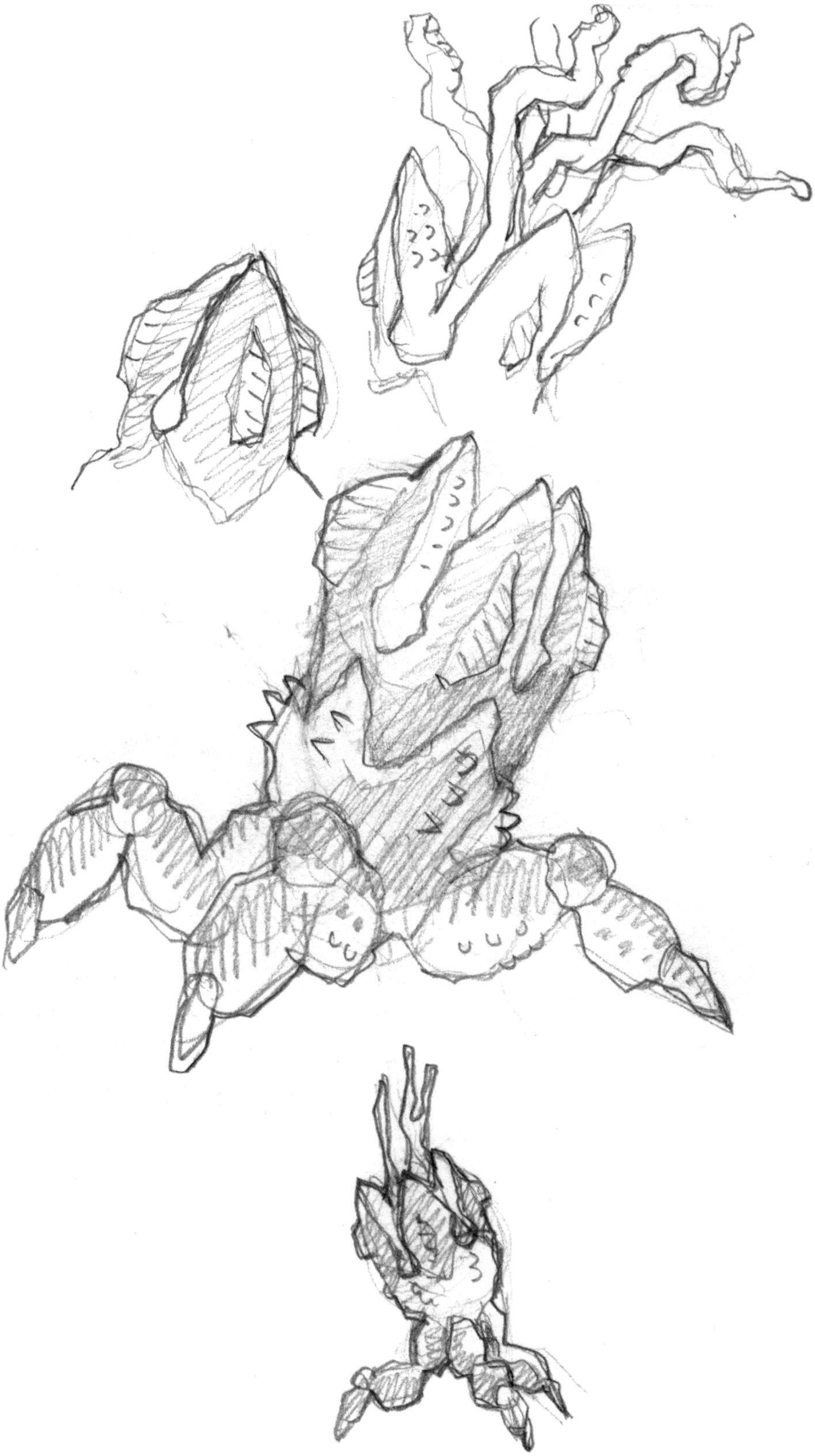

OGDRU HEM - RETURN OF MASTER

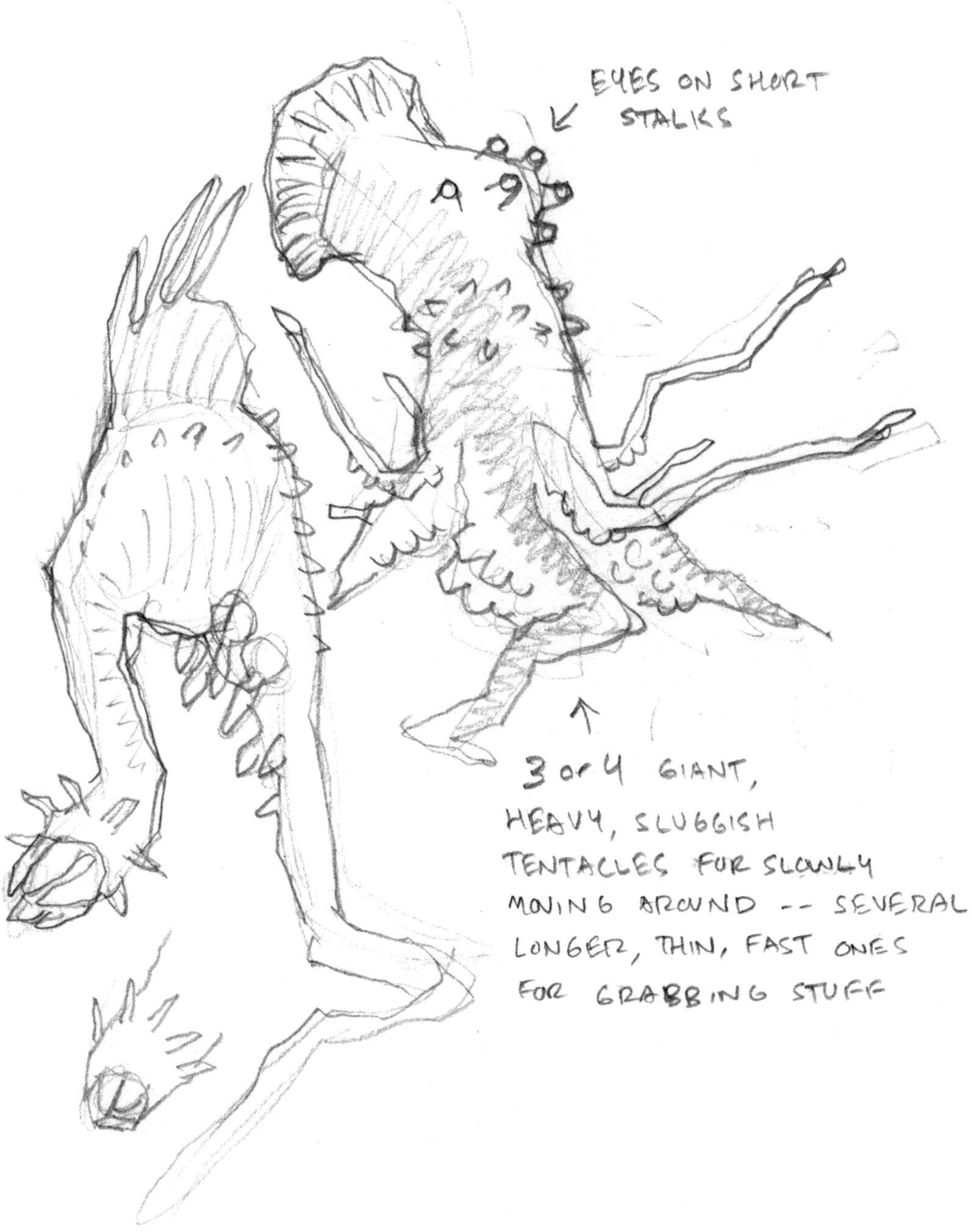

EYES ON SHORT STALKS
3 or 4 GIANT, HEAVY, SLUGGISH TENTACLES FOR SLOWLY MOVING AROUND -- SEVERAL LONGER, THIN, FAST ONES FOR GRABBING STUFF

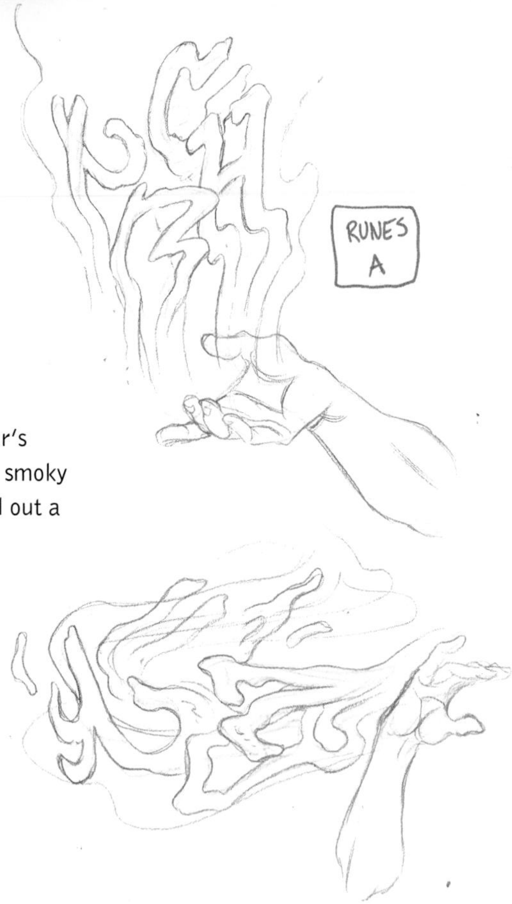
RUNES A

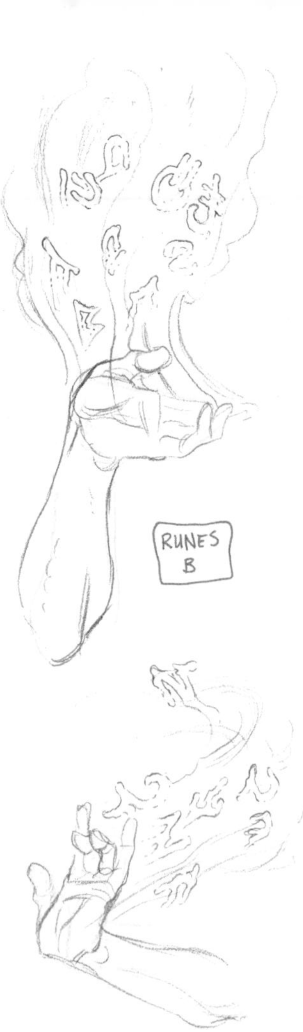
RUNES B

John wanted Lazar's magic to look like smoky runes, so I worked out a few variations.

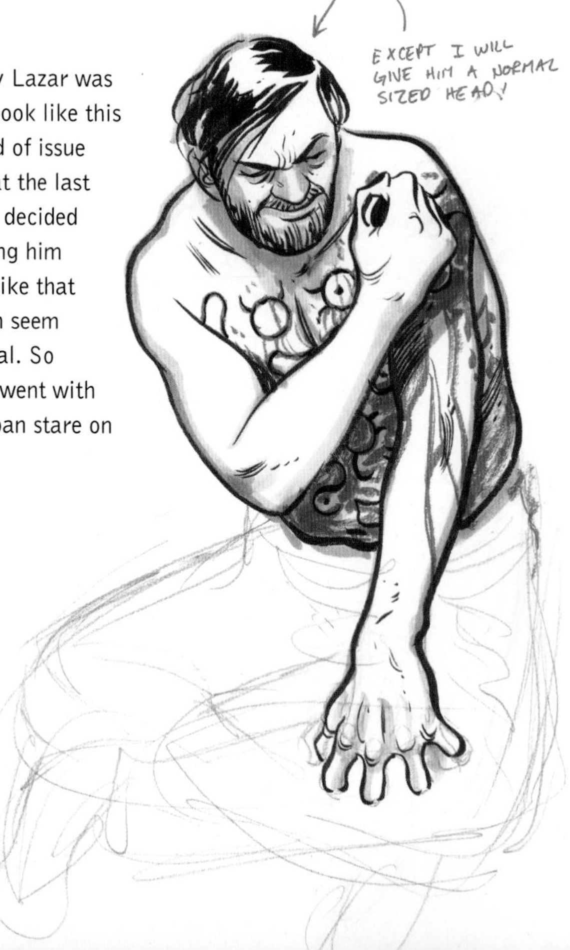
EXCEPT I WILL GIVE HIM A NORMAL SIZED HEAD!

Originally Lazar was going to look like this at the end of issue #1, but at the last minute, I decided that having him grimace like that made him seem too normal. So instead I went with the deadpan stare on page 28.

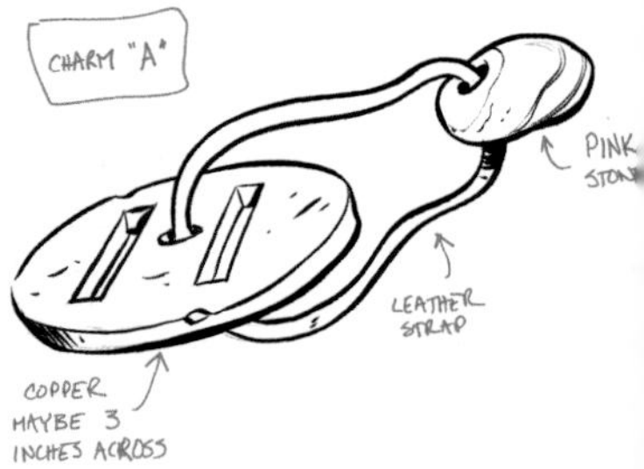
CHARM "A"
PINK
LEATHER STRAP
COPPER MAYBE 3 INCHES ACROSS

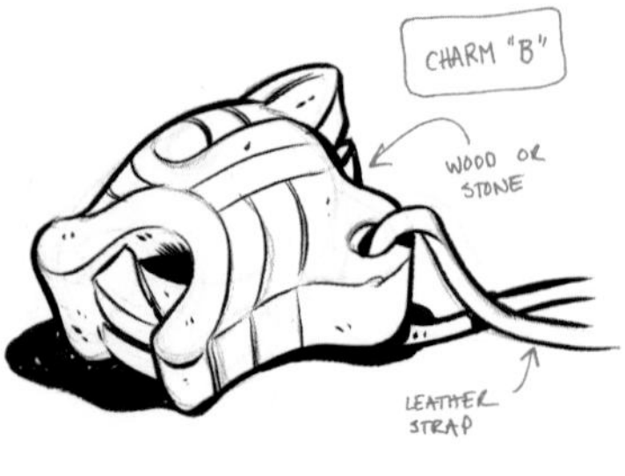
CHARM "B"
WOOD OR STONE
LEATHER STRAP

Tasso is a cool character. It's always hard to age a character and still have them be identifiable. We ended up just thinning his hair a bit and making him a little gray.

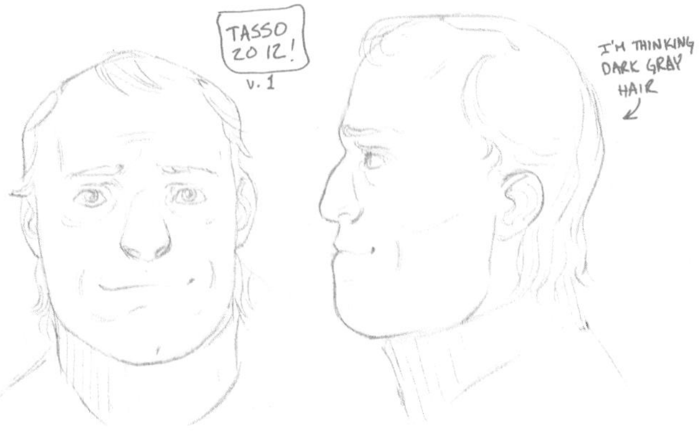

TASSO 2012!
v. 1
I'M THINKING DARK GRAY HAIR


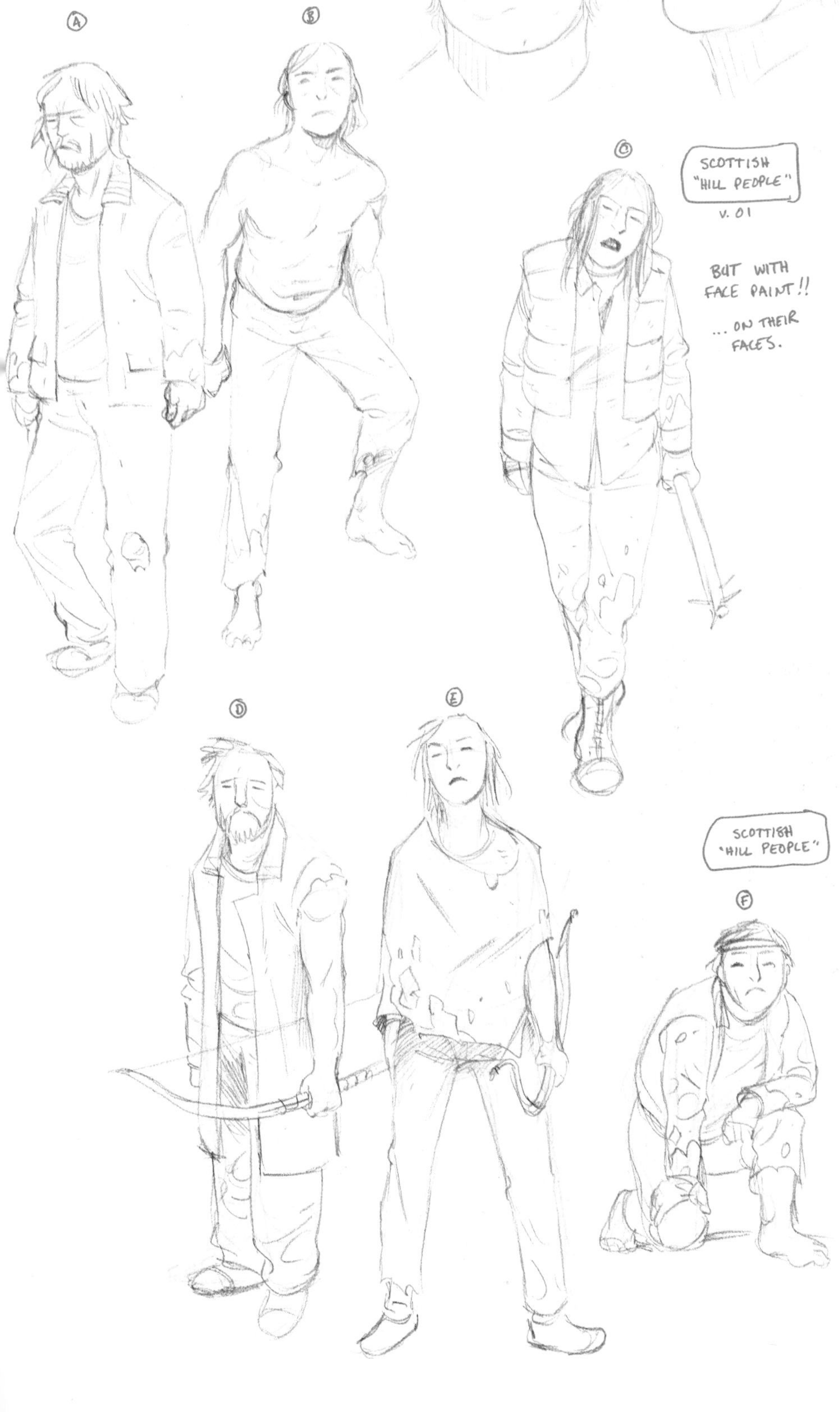

A
B
C
SCOTTISH "HILL PEOPLE"
v. 01
BUT WITH FACE PAINT!!
... ON THEIR FACES.
D
E
SCOTTISH "HILL PEOPLE"
F

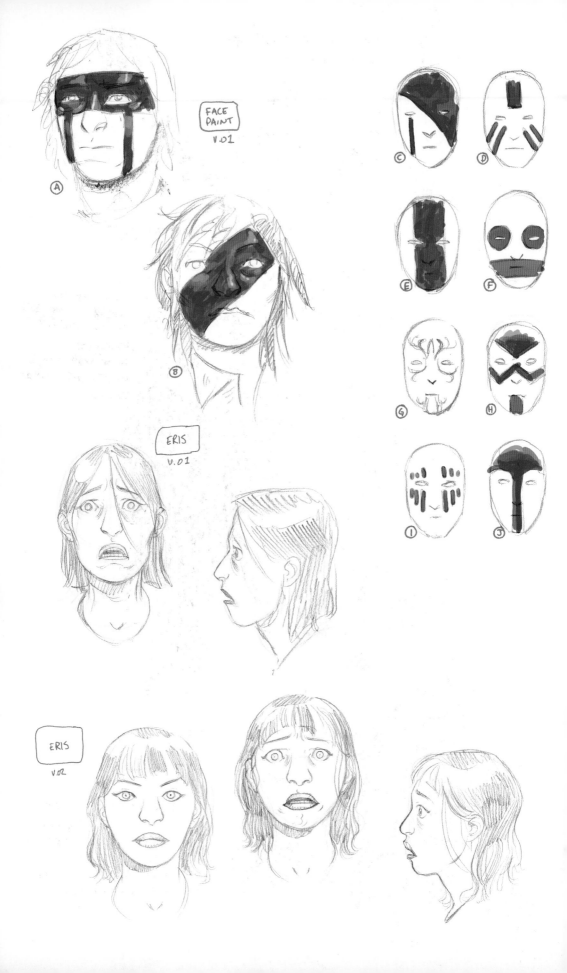

FACE
PAINT
V.01

Ⓐ

Ⓑ

Ⓒ Ⓓ

Ⓔ Ⓕ

Ⓖ Ⓗ

Ⓘ Ⓙ

ERIS
V.01

ERIS
V.02

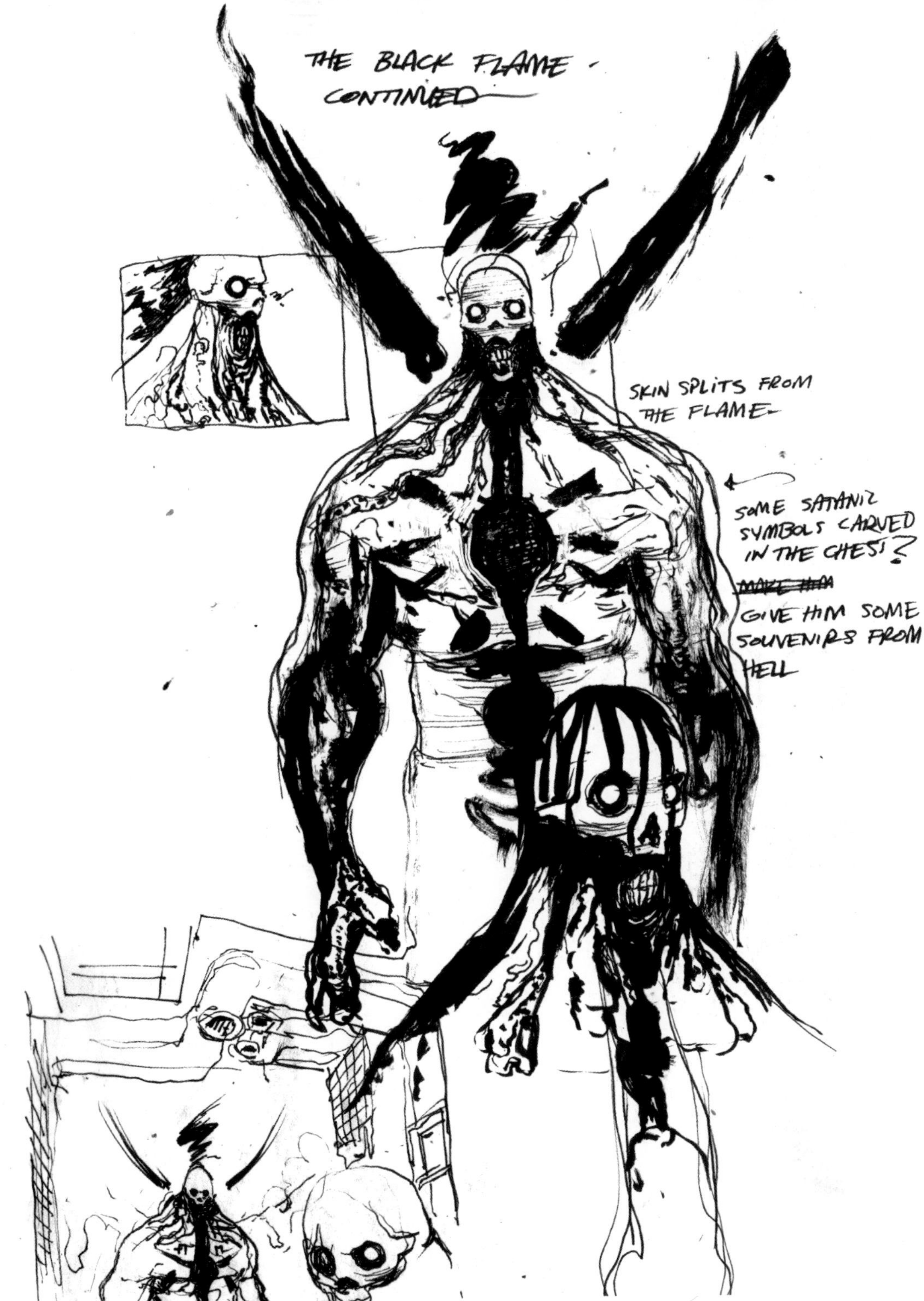
THE BLACK FLAME -
CONTINUED
SKIN SPLITS FROM
THE FLAME -
SOME SATANIC
SYMBOLS CARVED
IN THE CHEST?
GIVE HIM SOME
SOUVENIRS FROM
HELL

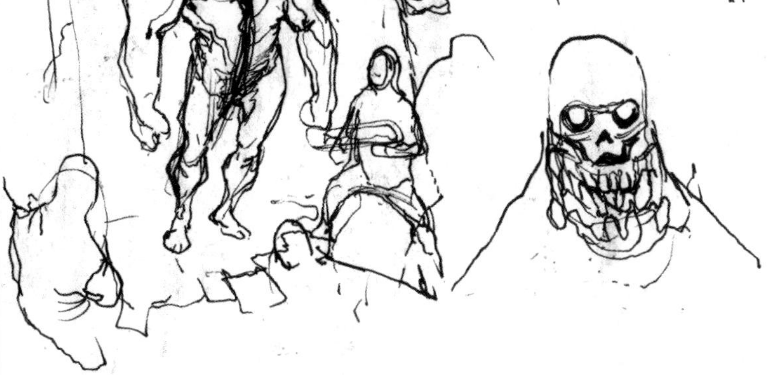

Since the new Black Flame showed up late in the book, but is central to an upcoming James Harren story, he did the new designs, on this and the following five pages.

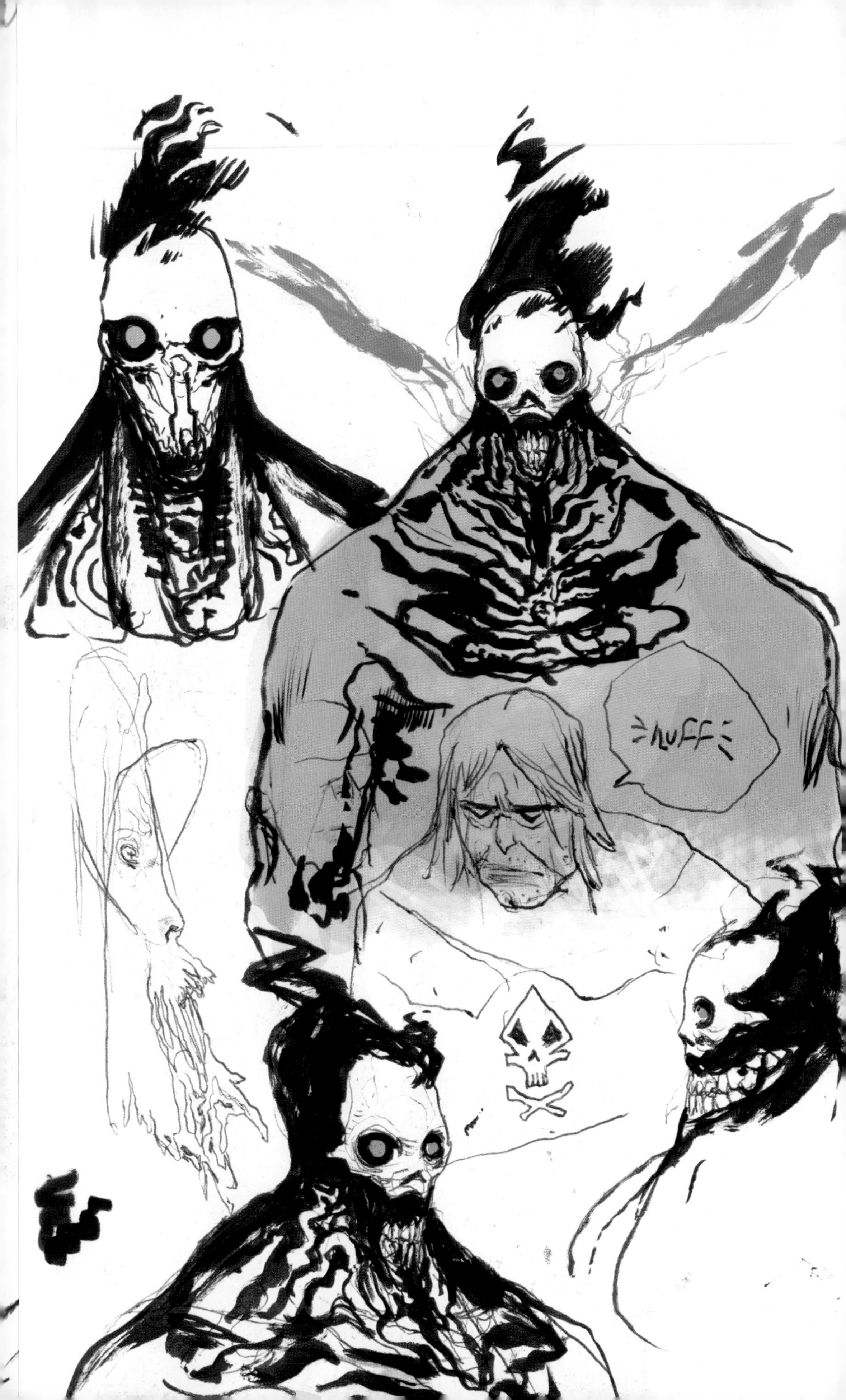
HUFF

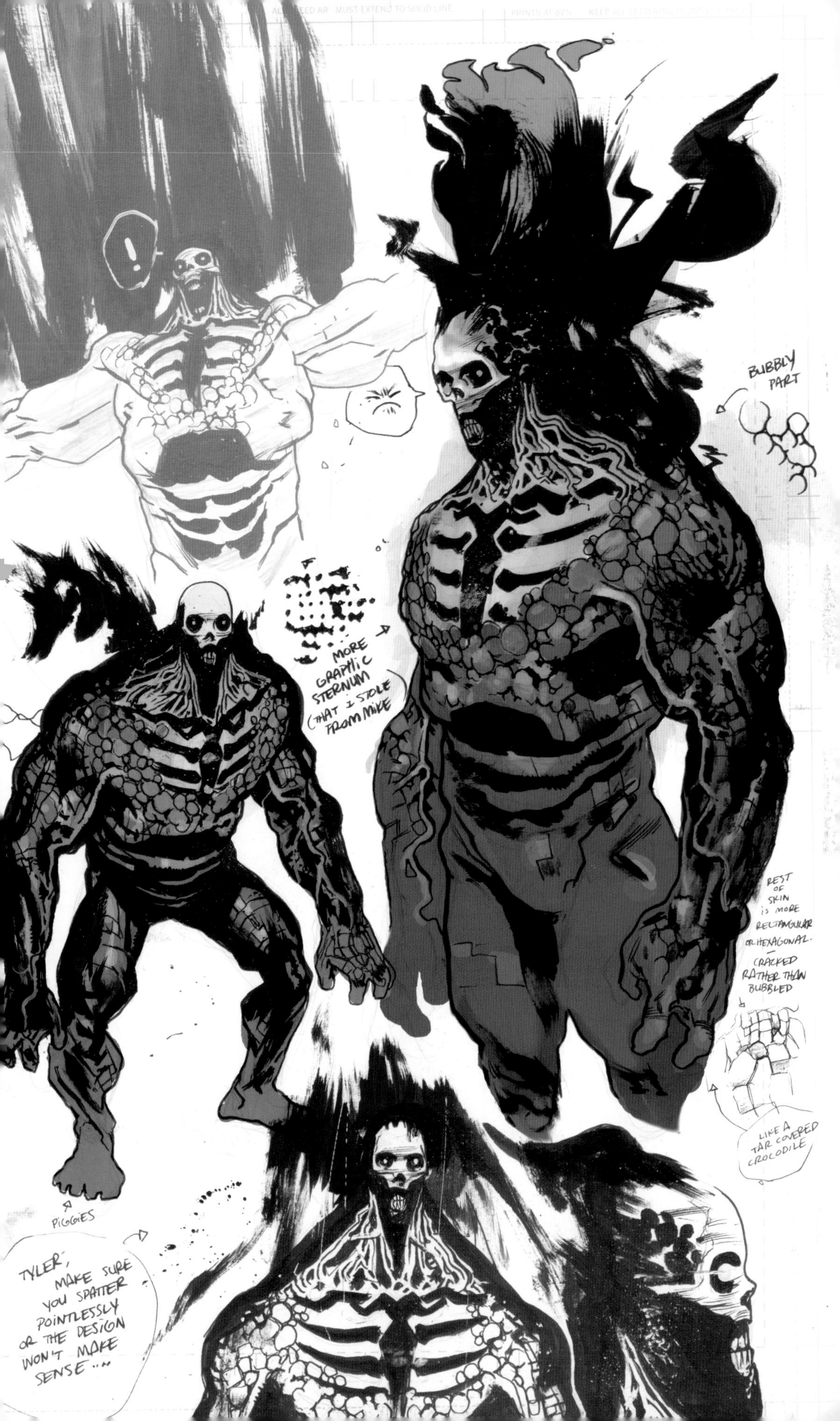
BUBBLY PART
MORE GRAPHIC STERNUM (THAT I STOLE FROM MIKE)
REST OF SKIN is MORE RECTANGULAR OR HEXAGONAL.
CRACKED RATHER THAN BUBBLED
LIKE A TAR COVERED CROCODILE
PIGGIES
TYLER, MAKE SURE YOU SPATTER POINTLESSLY OR THE DESIGN WON'T MAKE SENSE...

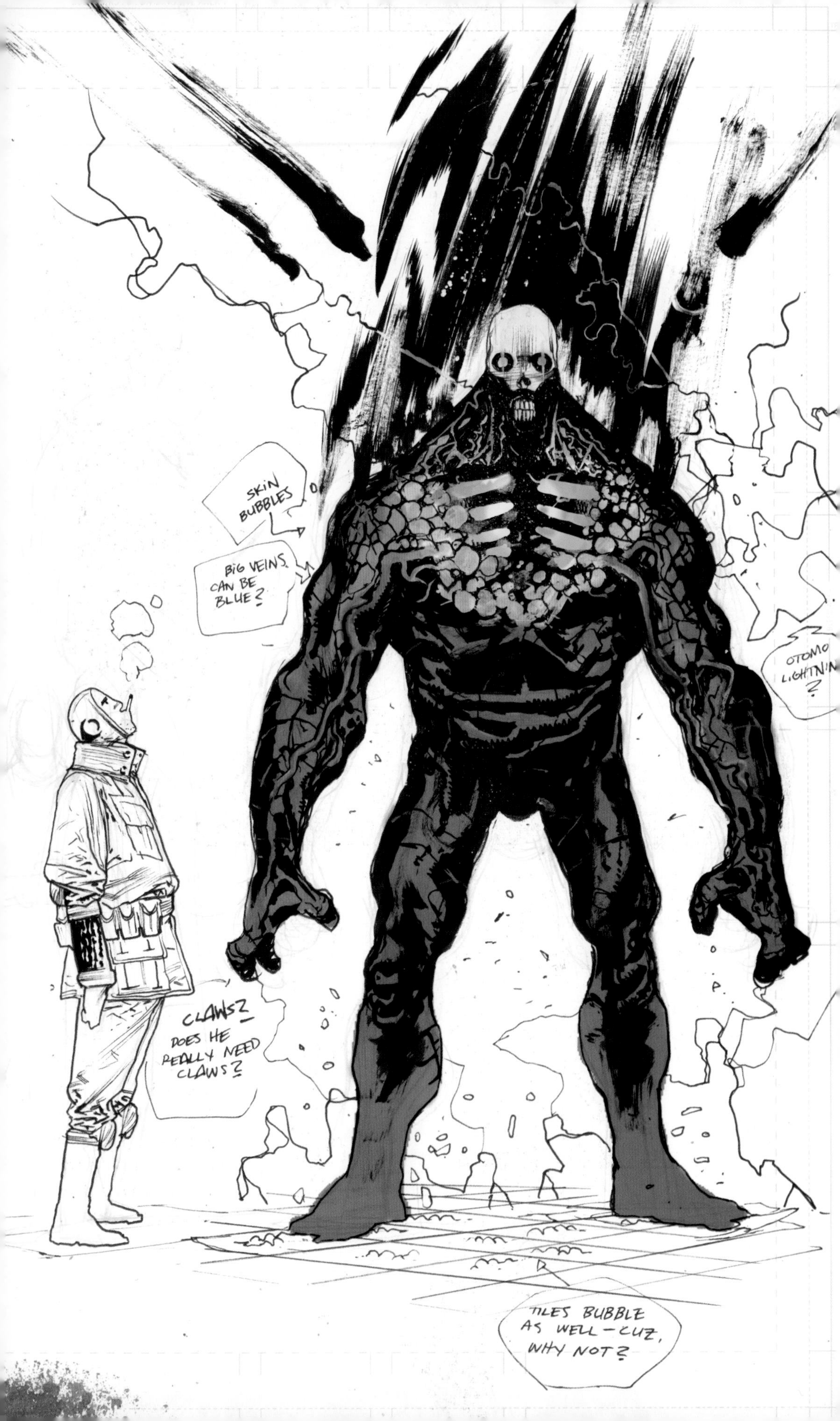
SKIN BUBBLES
BIG VEINS CAN BE BLUE?
OTOMO LIGHTNIN ?
CLAWS?
DOES HE REALLY NEED CLAWS?
TILES BUBBLE AS WELL—CUZ, WHY NOT?

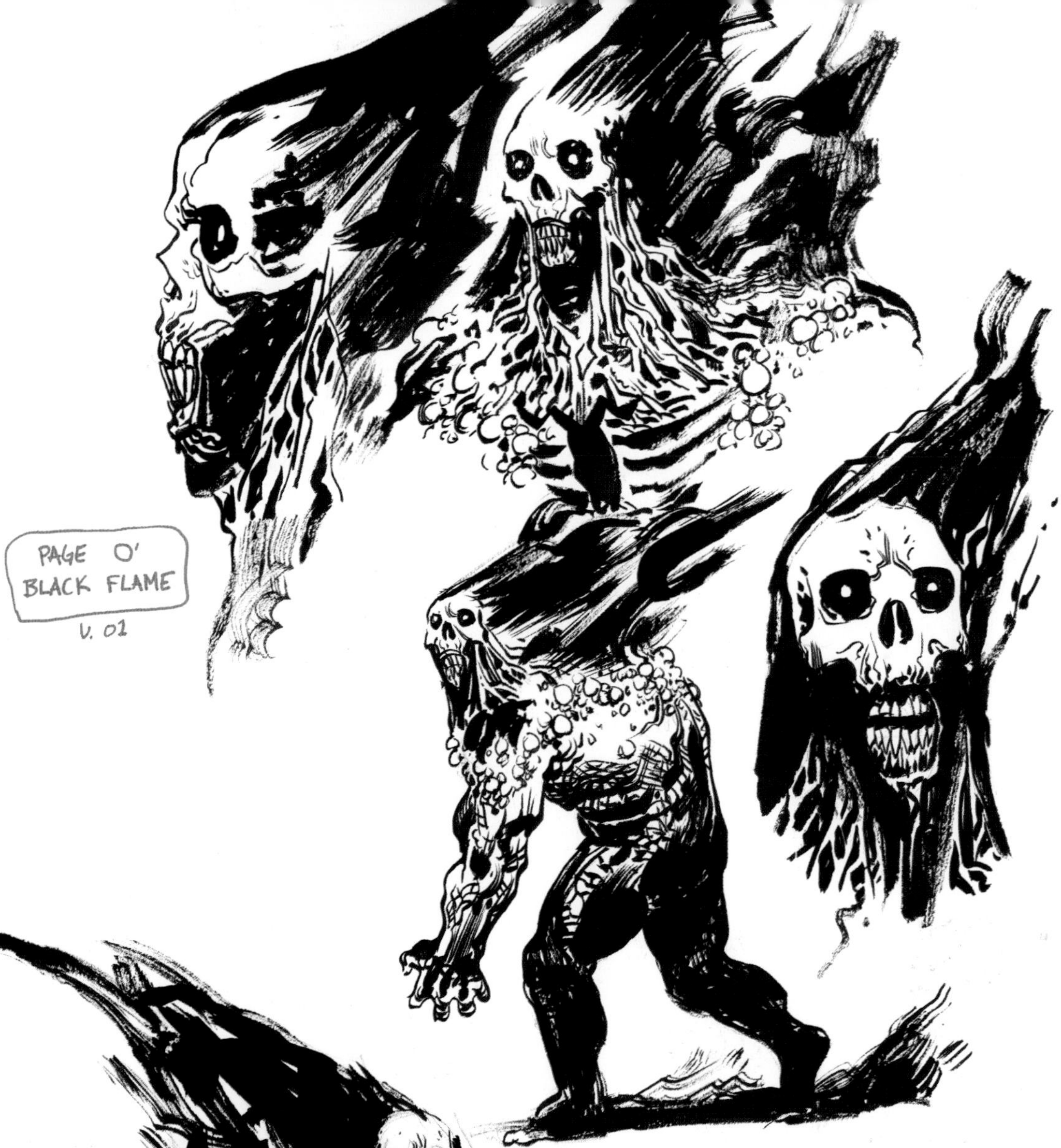
PAGE O' BLACK FLAME
V. 01

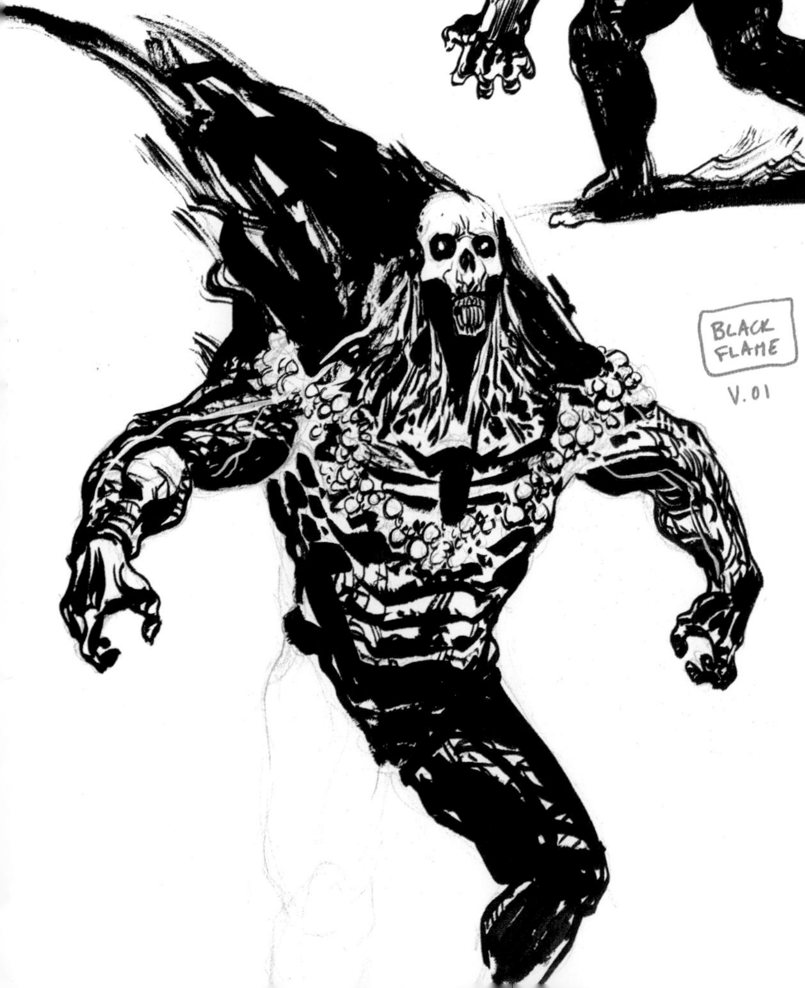
BLACK FLAME
V. 01

I don't often draw big, hulking characters like the Black Flame, so I needed a little practice. We wanted him to feel more in control than he looked here. In the end I based his poses off a bullfighter's stance.

Ryan Sook's roughs and studies for his cover to issue #4.

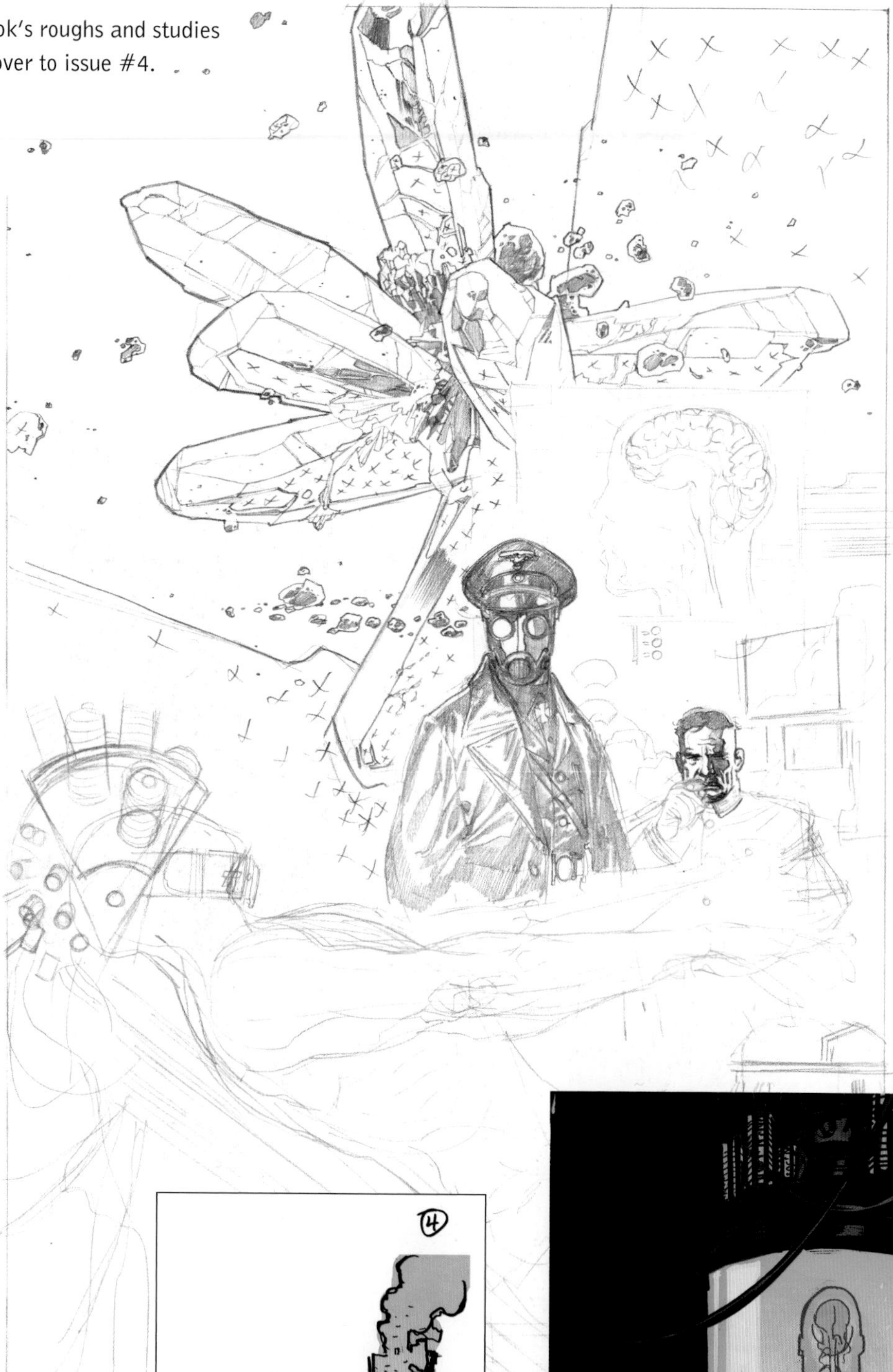

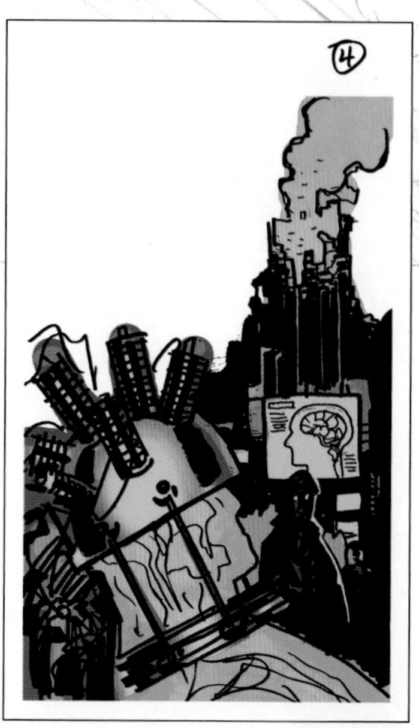
4

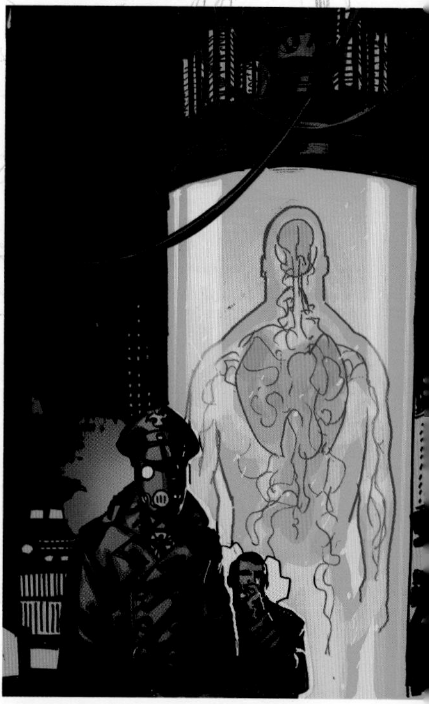

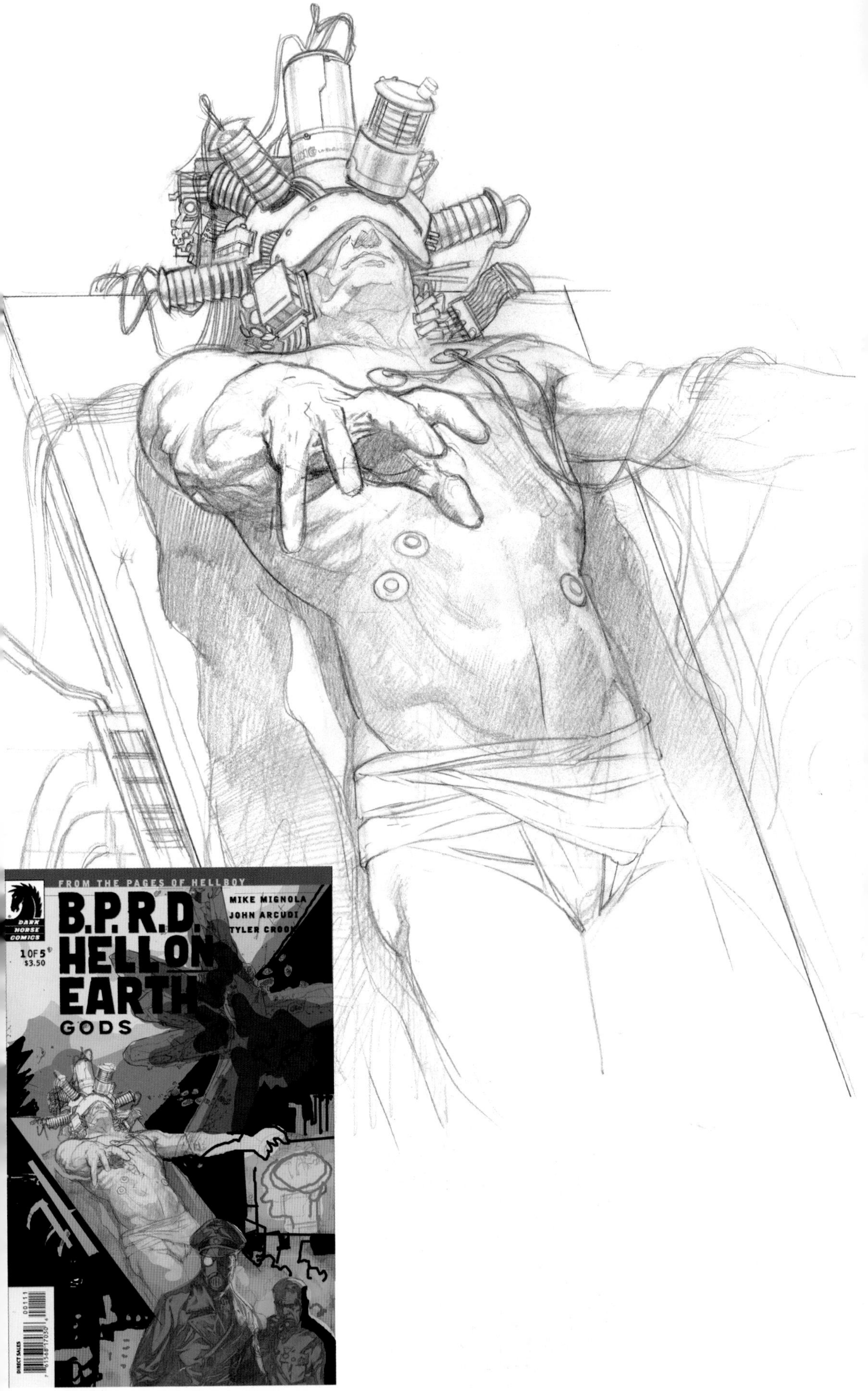
FROM THE PAGES OF HELLBOY
DARK HORSE COMICS
B.P.R.D.
HELL ON
EARTH
GODS
MIKE MIGNOLA
JOHN ARCUDI
TYLER CROO
1 OF 5
$3.50
DIRECT SALES

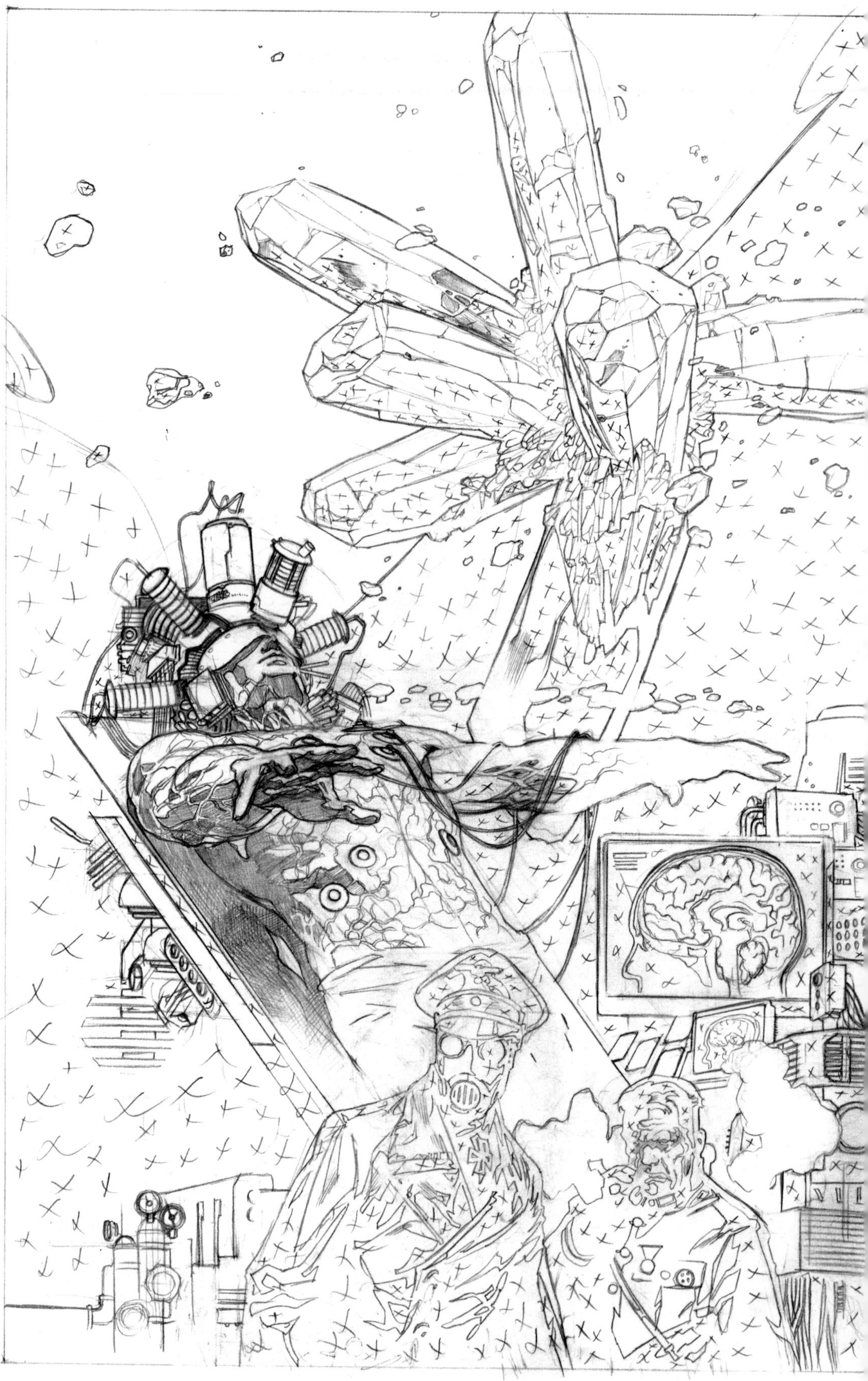

Ryan's #4 cover started with this sketch by Mike (lower left).
Mike only did cover sketches for the last two issues.

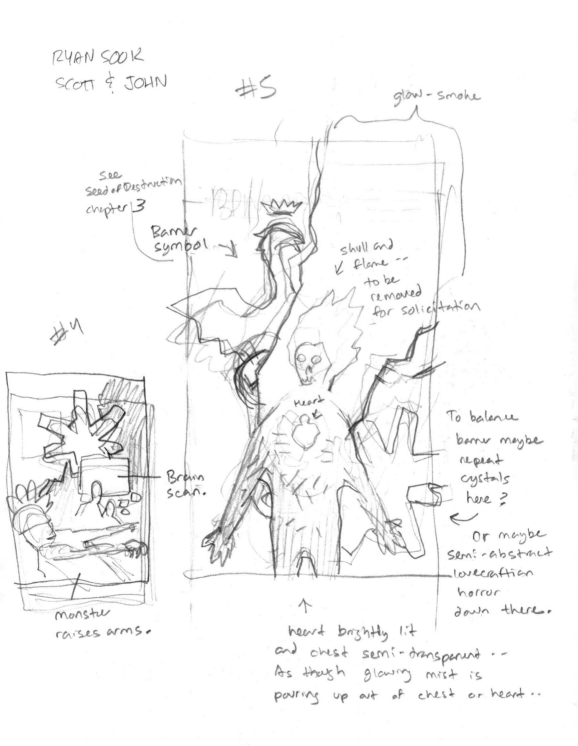

RYAN SOOK
SCOTT & JOHN

#5

glow - smoke

see
Seed of Destruction
chapter 3

Barnu
symbol

skull and
flame --
to be
removed
for solicitation

#4

Heart

Brain
scan.

To balance
barnu maybe
repeat
cystals
here ?

Or maybe
semi-abstract
lovecraftian
horror
down there.

monster
raises arms.

heart brightly lit
and chest semi-transparent --
As though glowing mist is
pouring up out of chest or heart..

For the final cover we wanted to show the Black Flame, but we didn't want anyone to see it before the big reveal in issue #4. Ryan did two versions, and we previewed the one at the top right, so readers could still think it was Rasputin coming back.

Following pages: Mike's variants for the Year of Monsters promotion.

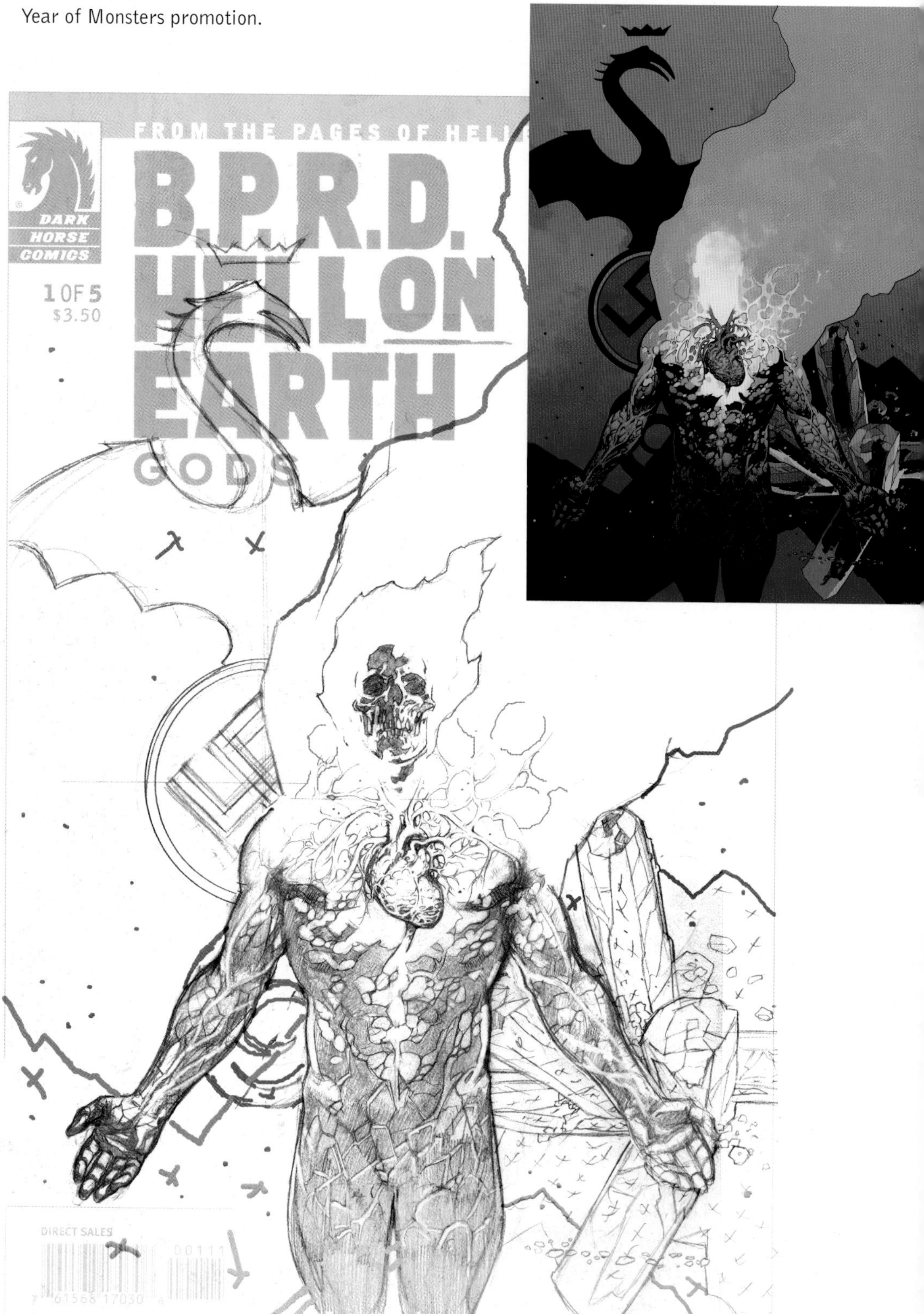
FROM THE PAGES OF
DARK HORSE COMICS
B.P.R.D.
HELL ON EARTH
GODS
1 OF 5
$3.50
DIRECT SALES

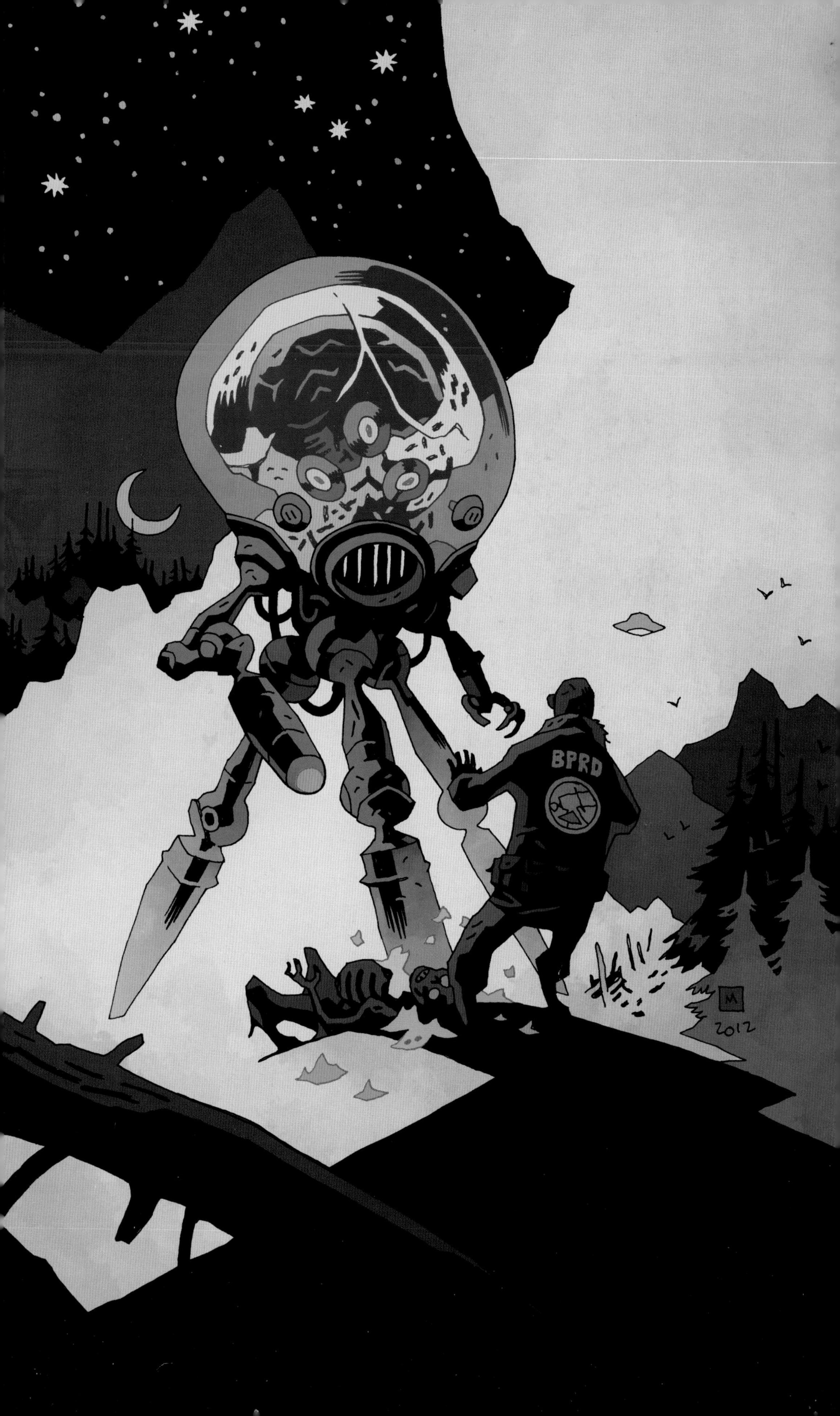
BPRD
M
2012

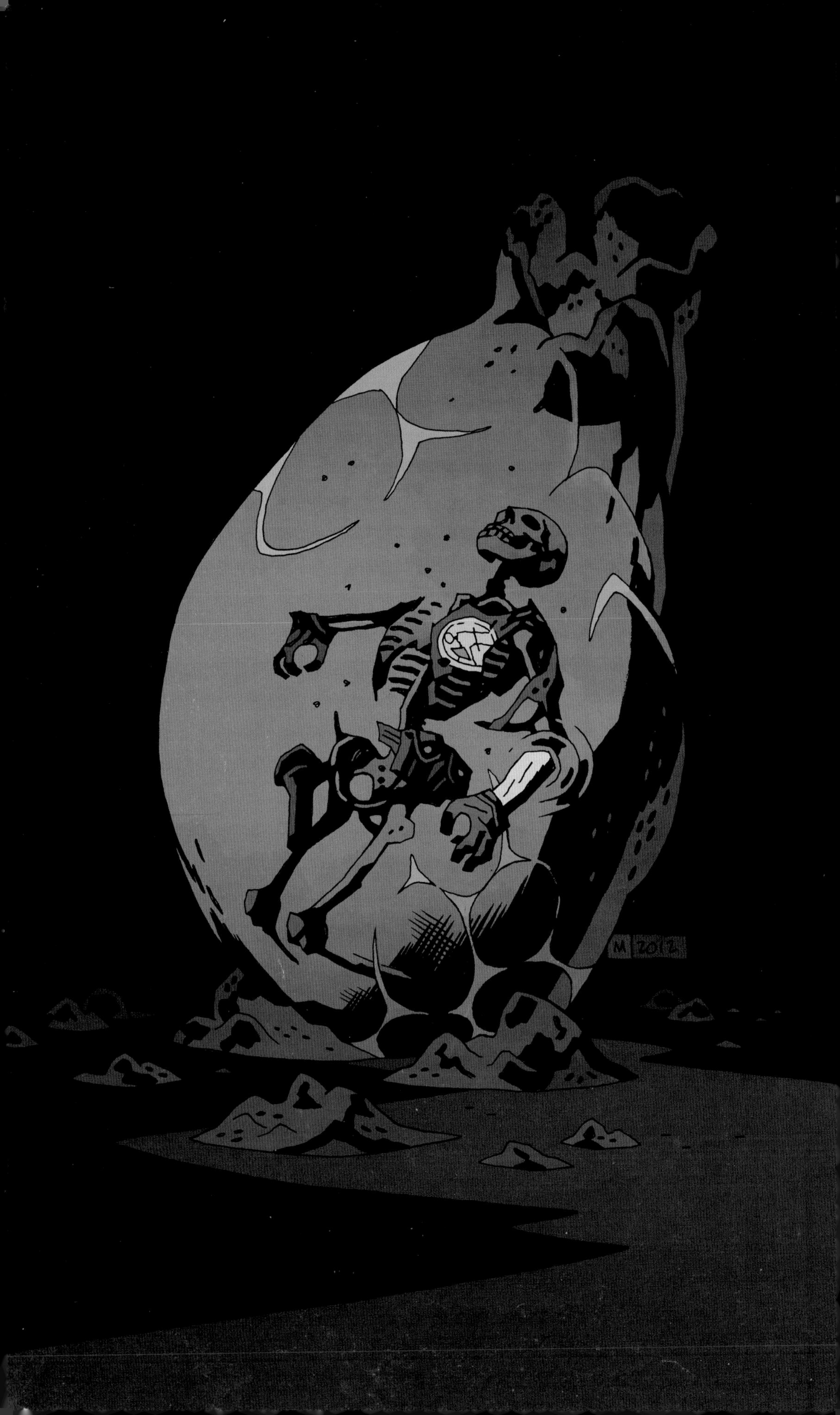
M 2012

# *Also by* MIKE MIGNOLA

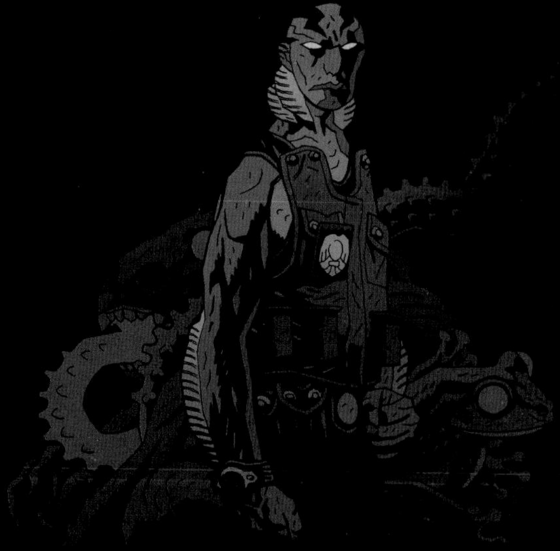

B.P.R.D.: PLAGUE OF FROGS
Hardcover Collection Volume 1
By Mike Mignola, Chris Golden, Guy Davis, and others
ISBN 978-1-59582-609-1 | $34.99

B.P.R.D.: PLAGUE OF FROGS
Hardcover Collection Volume 2
By Mignola, John Arcudi, Davis, and others
ISBN 978-1-59582-672-5 | $34.99

B.P.R.D.: PLAGUE OF FROGS
Hardcover Collection Volume 3
By Mignola, Arcudi, and Davis
ISBN 978-1-59582-860-6 | $34.99

B.P.R.D.: PLAGUE OF FROGS
Hardcover Collection Volume 4
By Mignola, Arcudi, and Davis
ISBN 978-1-59582-974-0 | $34.99

B.P.R.D.: THE WARNING
By Mignola, Arcudi, and Davis
ISBN 978-1-59582-304-5 | $17.99

B.P.R.D.: THE BLACK GODDESS
By Mignola, Arcudi, and Davis
ISBN 978-1-59582-411-0 | $17.99

B.P.R.D.: KING OF FEAR
By Mignola, Arcudi, and Davis
ISBN 978-1-59582-564-3 | $17.99

B.P.R.D.: 1946
By Mignola, Joshua Dysart, and Paul Azaceta
ISBN 978-1-59582-191-1 | $17.99

B.P.R.D.: 1947
By Mignola, Dysart, Fábio Moon, and Gabriel Bá
ISBN 978-1-59582-478-3 | $17.99

B.P.R.D.: BEING HUMAN
By Mignola, Arcudi, Davis, and others
ISBN 978-1-59582-756-2 | $17.99

B.P.R.D. HELL ON EARTH VOLUME 1: NEW WORLD
By Mignola, Arcudi, and Davis
ISBN 978-1-59582-707-4 | $19.99

B.P.R.D. HELL ON EARTH VOLUME 2: GODS AND MONSTERS
By Mignola, Arcudi, Davis, and Crook
ISBN 978-1-59582-822-4 | $19.99

B.P.R.D. HELL ON EARTH VOLUME 3: RUSSIA
By Mignola, Arcudi, Crook, and Duncan Fegredo
ISBN 978-1-59582-946-7 | $19.99

B.P.R.D. HELL ON EARTH VOLUME 4: THE DEVIL'S ENGINE AND THE LONG DEATH
By Mignola, Arcudi, Crook, and James Harren
ISBN 978-1-59582-981-8 | $19.99

B.P.R.D. HELL ON EARTH VOLUME 5: THE PICKENS COUNTY HORROR AND OTHERS
by Mignola, Scott Allie, Jason Latour, Harren, Max Fiumara, and Becky Cloonan
ISBN 978-1-61655-140-7 | $19.99

B.P.R.D. HELL ON EARTH VOLUME 6: THE RETURN OF THE MASTER
By Mignola, Arcudi, and Crook
ISBN 978-1-61655-193-3 | $19.99

LOBSTER JOHNSON VOLUME 2: THE BURNING HAND
by Mignola, Arcudi, and Tonci Zonjic
ISBN 978-1-61655-031-8 | $17.99

ABE SAPIEN VOLUME 1: THE DROWNING
By Mignola and Jason Shawn Alexander
ISBN 978-1-59582-185-0 | $17.99

ABE SAPIEN: VOLUME 2: THE DEVIL DOES NOT JEST AND OTHER STORIES
By Mignola, Arcudi, Harren, and others
ISBN 978-1-59582-925-2 | $17.99

LOBSTER JOHNSON VOLUME 1: THE IRON PROMETHEUS
By Mignola and Jason Armstrong
ISBN 978-1-59307-975-8 | $17.99

LOBSTER JOHNSON VOLUME 2: THE BURNING HAND
By Mignola, Arcudi, and Tonci Zonjic
ISBN 978-1-61655-031-8 | $17.99

WITCHFINDER VOLUME 1: IN THE SERVICE OF ANGELS
By Mignola and Ben Stenbeck
ISBN 978-1-59582-483-7 | $17.99

WITCHFINDER VOLUME 2: LOST AND GONE FOREVER
By Mignola, Arcudi, and John Severin
ISBN 978-1-59582-794-4 | $17.99

THE AMAZING SCREW-ON HEAD AND OTHER CURIOUS OBJECTS
Hardcover Collection
By Mignola
ISBN 978-1-59582-501-8 | $17.99

BALTIMORE VOLUME 1: THE PLAGUE SHIPS
By Mignola, Golden, and Stenbeck
ISBN 978-1-59582-677-0 | $24.99

BALTIMORE VOLUME 2: THE CURSE BELLS
By Mignola, Golden, and Stenbeck
ISBN 978-1-59582-674-9 | $24.99

## NOVELS

LOBSTER JOHNSON: THE SATAN FACTORY
By Thomas E. Sniegoski
ISBN 978-1-59582-203-1 | $12.95

JOE GOLEM AND THE DROWNING CITY
Deluxe Hardcover
By Mignola and Golden
ISBN 978-1-59582-971-9 | $99.99

AVAILABLE AT YOUR LOCAL COMICS SHOP OR BOOKSTORE! • To find a comics shop in your area, call 1-888-266-4226.
For more information or to order direct visit DarkHorse.com or call 1-800-862-0052 Mon.–Fri. 9 AM to 5 PM Pacific Time.
Prices and availability subject to change without notice.



DarkHorse.com

# HELLBOY™

by MIKE MIGNOLA

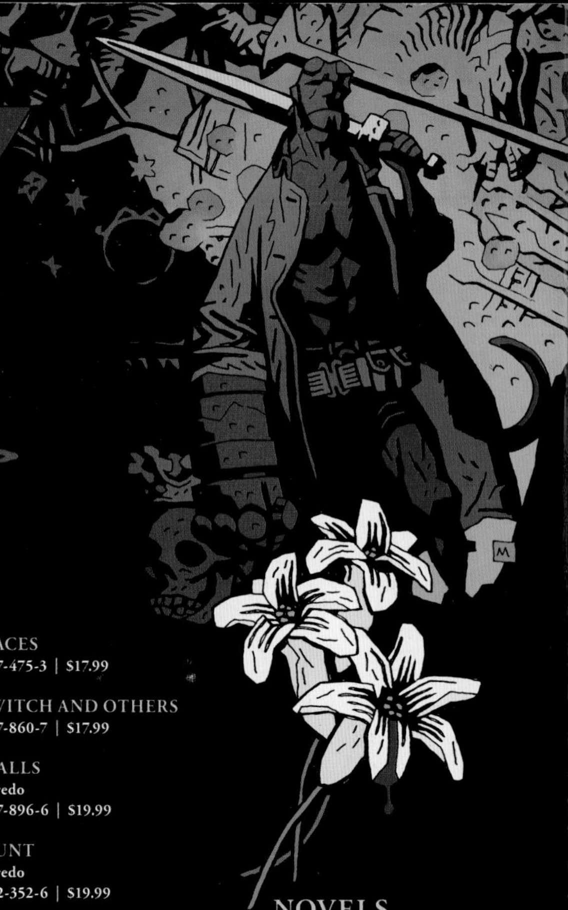

HELLBOY LIBRARY EDITION VOLUME 1:
Seed of Destruction and Wake the Devil
ISBN 978-1-59307-910-9 | $49.99

HELLBOY LIBRARY EDITION VOLUME 2:
The Chained Coffin and The Right Hand of Doom
ISBN 978-1-59307-989-5 | $49.99

HELLBOY LIBRARY EDITION VOLUME 3:
Conqueror Worm and Strange Places
ISBN 978-1-59582-352-6 | $49.99

HELLBOY LIBRARY EDITION VOLUME 4:
The Crooked Man and The Troll Witch
with Richard Corben and others
ISBN 978-1-59582-658-9 | $49.99

HELLBOY LIBRARY EDITION VOLUME 5:
Darkness Calls and the Wild Hunt
with Duncan Fegredo
ISBN 978-1-59582-886-6 | $49.99

HELLBOY LIBRARY EDITION VOLUME 6:
The Storm and the Fury and The Bride of Hell
with Duncan Fegredo, Richard Corben, Kevin Nowlan, and Scott Hampton
ISBN 978-1-61655-133-9 | $49.99

SEED OF DESTRUCTION
with John Byrne
ISBN 978-1-59307-094-6 | $17.99

WAKE THE DEVIL
ISBN 978-1-59307-095-3 | $17.99

THE CHAINED COFFIN AND OTHERS
ISBN 978-1-59307-091-5 | $17.99

THE RIGHT HAND OF DOOM
ISBN 978-1-59307-093-9 | $17.99

CONQUEROR WORM
ISBN 978-1-59307-092-2 | $17.99

STRANGE PLACES
ISBN 978-1-59307-475-3 | $17.99

THE TROLL WITCH AND OTHERS
ISBN 978-1-59307-860-7 | $17.99

DARKNESS CALLS
with Duncan Fegredo
ISBN 978-1-59307-896-6 | $19.99

THE WILD HUNT
with Duncan Fegredo
ISBN 978-1-59582-352-6 | $19.99

THE CROOKED MAN AND OTHERS
with Richard Corben
ISBN 978-1-59582-477-6 | $17.99

THE BRIDE OF HELL AND OTHERS
with Richard Corben, Kevin Nowlan, and Scott Hampton
ISBN 978-1-59582-740-1 | $19.99

THE STORM AND THE FURY
with Duncan Fegredo
ISBN 978-1-59582-827-9 | $19.99

HOUSE OF THE LIVING DEAD
with Richard Corben
ISBN 978-1-59582-757-9 | $14.99

THE ART OF HELLBOY
ISBN 978-1-59307-089-2 | $29.99

HELLBOY II: THE ART OF THE MOVIE
ISBN 978-1-59307-964-2 | $24.99

HELLBOY: THE COMPANION
ISBN 978-1-59307-655-9 | $14.99

HELLBOY: WEIRD TALES
VOLUME 1
ISBN 978-1-56971-622-9 | $17.99
VOLUME 2
ISBN 978-1-56971-953-4 | $17.99

HELLBOY: MASKS AND MONSTERS
with James Robinson and Scott Benefiel
ISBN 978-1-59582-567-4 | $17.99

## NOVELS

HELLBOY: EMERALD HELL
By Tom Piccirilli
ISBN 978-1-59582-141-6 | $12.99

HELLBOY: THE ALL-SEEING EYE
By Mark Morris
ISBN 978-1-59582-141-6 | $12.99

HELLBOY: THE FIRE WOLVES
By Tim Lebbon
ISBN 978-1-59582-204-8 | $12.99

HELLBOY: THE ICE WOLVES
By Mark Chadbourn
ISBN 978-1-59582-205-5 | $12.99

## SHORT STORIES

Illustrated by Mike Mignola

HELLBOY: ODD JOBS
By Poppy Z. Brite, Greg Rucka, and others
ISBN 978-1-56971-440-9 | $14.99

HELLBOY: ODDER JOBS
By Frank Darabont, Guillermo del Toro, and others
ISBN 978-1-59307-226-1 | $14.99

HELLBOY: ODDEST JOBS
By Joe R. Lansdale, China Miéville, and others
ISBN 978-1-59307-944-4 | $14.99

**AVAILABLE AT YOUR LOCAL COMICS SHOP OR BOOKSTORE!** • To find a comics shop in your area, call 1-888-266-4226.
For more information or to order direct visit DarkHorse.com or call 1-800-862-0052 Mon.–Fri. 9 AM to 5 PM Pacific Time.
Prices and availability subject to change without notice.

DARK HORSE BOOKS
DarkHorse.com